INTERNATIONAL POLITICAL ECONOMY SERIES

General Editor: Timothy M. Shaw, Professor of Political Science and International Development Studies, and Director of the Centre for Foreign Policy Studies, Dalhousie University, Nova Scotia, Canada

Recent titles include:

Pradeep Agrawal, Subir V. Gokarn, Veena Mishra, Kirit S. Parikh and Kunal Sen
ECONOMIC RESTRUCTURING IN EAST ASIA AND INDIA: Perspectives on Policy Reform

Solon L. Barraclough and Krishna B. Ghimire
FORESTS AND LIVELIHOODS: The Social Dynamics of Deforestation in Developing Countries

Kathleen Barry (*editor*)
VIETNAM'S WOMEN IN TRANSITION

Ruud Buitelaar and Pitou van Dijck (*editors*)
LATIN AMERICA'S NEW INSERTION IN THE WORLD ECONOMY: Towards Systemic Competitiveness in Small Economies

William D. Coleman
FINANCIAL SERVICES, GLOBALIZATION AND DOMESTIC POLICY CHANGE: A Comparison of North America and the European Union

Paul Cook and Frederick Nixson (*editors*)
THE MOVE TO THE MARKET? Trade and Industry Policy Reform in Transitional Economies

Mark E. Denham and Mark Owen Lombardi (*editors*)
PERSPECTIVES ON THIRD-WORLD SOVEREIGNTY: The Postmodern Paradox

John Healey and William Tordoff (*editors*)
VOTES AND BUDGETS: Comparative Studies in Accountable Governance in the South

Noeleen Heyzer, James V. Riker and Antonio B. Quizon (*editors*)
GOVERNMENT–NGO RELATIONS IN ASIA: Prospects and Challenges for People-Centred Development

George Kent
CHILDREN IN THE INTERNATIONAL POLITICAL ECONOMY

David Kowalewski
GLOBAL ESTABLISHMENT: The Political Economy of North/Asian Networks

Laura Macdonald
SUPPORTING CIVIL SOCIETY: The Political Role of Non-Governmental Organizations in Central America

Gary McMahon (*editor*)
LESSONS IN ECONOMIC POLICY FOR EASTERN EUROPE FROM
LATIN AMERICA

David B. Moore and Gerald J. Schmitz (*editors*)
DEBATING DEVELOPMENT DISCOURSE: Institutional and Popular
Perspectives

Juan Antonio Morales and Gary McMahon (*editors*)
ECONOMIC POLICY AND THE TRANSITION TO DEMOCRACY: The Latin
American Experience

Paul J. Nelson
THE WORLD BANK AND NON-GOVERNMENTAL ORGANIZATIONS:
The Limits of Apolitical Development

Archibald R. M. Ritter and John M. Kirk (*editors*)
CUBA IN THE INTERNATIONAL SYSTEM: Normalization and Integration

Ann Seidman and Robert B. Seidman
STATE AND LAW IN THE DEVELOPMENT PROCESS: Problem-Solving and
Institutional Change in the Third World

Tor Skålnes
THE POLITICS OF ECONOMIC REFORM IN ZIMBABWE: Continuity and
Change in Development

John Sorenson (*editor*)
DISASTER AND DEVELOPMENT IN THE HORN OF AFRICA

Howard Stein (*editor*)
ASIAN INDUSTRIALIZATION AND AFRICA: Studies in Policy Alternatives
to Structural Adjustment

Sandra Whitworth
FEMINISM AND INTERNATIONAL RELATIONS

David Wurfel and Bruce Burton (*editors*)
SOUTHEAST ASIA IN THE NEW WORLD ORDER: The Political Economy
of a Dynamic Region

Western Hemisphere Trade Integration

A Canadian–Latin American Dialogue

Edited by

Richard G. Lipsey
*Professor of Economics, Simon Fraser University, Vancouver, BC,
and Alcan Fellow, Canadian Institute for Advanced Research*

and

Patricio Meller
*Professor of Economics, University of Chile, and
Senior Researcher, CIEPLAN, Santiago*

St. Martin's Press
New York

WESTERN HEMISPHERE TRADE INTEGRATION

/1† Selection and editorial matter copyright © 1997 by Richard G. Lipsey and
Patricio Meller
Chapters 1–10 copyright ©1997 by Macmillan Press Ltd

St. Martin's Press, Scholarly and Reference Division,
175 Fifth Avenue, New York, N.Y. 10010

First published in the United States of America in 1997

This book is printed on paper suitable for recycling and
made from fully managed and sustained forest sources.

Printed in Great Britain

ISBN 0–312–16189–1

Library of Congress Cataloging-in-Publication Data
Western Hemisphere trade integration : a Canadian-Latin American
dialogue / edited by Richard G. Lipsey and Patricio Meller.
   p. cm.
Includes bibliographical references and index.
ISBN 0–312–16189–1
1. America—Commerce.   2. America—Economic integration.   3. Free
trade—America.   4. Canada—Commerce—Latin America.   5. Latin
America—Commerce—Canada.   I. Lipsey, Richard G., 1928–   .
II. Meller, Patricio.
HF3211.W474   1996
382'.09181'2—dc20   96–9135
                                                                                  CIP

Contents

List of Maps   vii

List of Tables and Figures   ix

Notes on the Contributors   xiii

List of Acronyms and Abbreviations   xvi

Introduction
Richard G. Lipsey and Patricio Meller   1

1. NAFTA in the World Economy: Lessons and Issues
    for Latin America
    Bruce W. Wilkinson   30

2. Mercosur and Preferential Trade Liberalization
    in South America: Record, Issues and
    Prospects
    Roberto Bouzas   58

3. The G3 and the Road to Continental Integration
    Juan José Echavarría   90

4. Trade Strategy Alternatives for a Small Country:
    The Chilean Case
    Raúl Labán and Patricio Meller   110

5. The Importance of Border Trade: The Case of
    Bolivia
    Jorge Aseff, Justo Espejo and Juan Antonio Morales   136

6. A Small Country Perspective on Mercosur: The
    Case of Paraguay
    Luis E. Breuer   158

7. The North American Free Trade Agreement:
    Policy- or Investment-led?
    Maureen Appel Molot   171

8. Social Issues and Labour Adjustment Policies:
    The Canada–US FTA Experience
    Ann Weston   191

v

9.   Trade Disputes and Settlement Mechanisms under
      the Canada–US Free Trade Agreement
      Richard G. Dearden   207

10.   Trade and Investment between Canada and the
      LAIA Countries
      Raúl E. Sáez   232

11.   NAFTA as a Mutually Beneficial Agreement: Com-
      mentary by Richard G. Lipsey on 'NAFTA in the
      World Economy: Lessons and Issues for Latin
      America' by Bruce W. Wilkinson   249

12.   NAFTA in the World Economy: Lessons and Issues
      for Latin America: A Reply to Richard G. Lipsey
      by Bruce W. Wilkinson   263

Notes   275

References   292

Index   304

List of Maps

North and Central America   xix

South America   xx

List of Tables and Figures

TABLES

2.1	Mercosur: Summary Information, 1994	58
2.2	Mercosur Export/Import Trade, 1990–4	62
2.3	Mercosur: Trade Intensity Indices	63
2.4	Argentine/Brazilian Total Trade Flows, 1984–93	64
2.5	Argentine/Brazilian Intra-Industry Trade, 1984–93	65
2.6	Argentine/Brazilian Inter- and Intra-Firm Initiatives	67
2.7	Mercosur: Macroeconomic Indicators, 1986–94	68
2.8	Mercosur: Exemptions to the Free Trade Area	70
2.9	Mercosur: Exemptions to the Customs Union	71
3.1	Bilateral Comparative Advantages with Respect to Mexico, Venezuela and Chile	94
3.2	Nominal and Effective Tariff Rates in Colombia, Venezuela and Mexico	97
3.3	The Liberalization Process in the G3	104
4.1	Chile's First Unilateral Liberalization Process, 1973–81	112
4.2	Second Chilean Unilateral Liberalization Process, 1982–94	112
4.3	Breakdown of Total Chilean Exports, 1970–84	113
4.4	Number of Export Firms According to Exported Volume, 1986–9	114
4.5	Sectoral Distribution of Exports According to Market Destination, 1991	116
4.6	Evolution of Processed Natural Resource Exports, 1970–90	120
4.7	Comparison of Export Growth Rates between Chile, Latin America and the World, for Specific Fruit, Fish and Forestry Products, 1970–90	121
4.8	Trend of New Types of Fruit Exports, 1970–90	121
4.9	Chilean Export Growth by Destination Markets, 1989–93	123
4.10	Importance of Destination Markets for 40 PNR Items and 24 OIP Items with an Export Level Higher than US$ 10 million, 1993	124

5.1	Bolivia's Direction of Trade, 1990–3	138
5.2	Balance of Trade with Neighbour Countries, 1993	139
5.3	Commodity Composition of Bolivia's Imports from Neighbour Countries, 1970–92	140
5.4	Trade Balance, Including Contraband, with Neighbour Countries, 1991–4	142
5.5	Bolivia's Outstanding Economic Integration Agreements with Neighbour Countries	148
5.6	Free Zones as of 31 July 1994	150
5.7	Population of Neighbour Countries in Main Towns Close to Bolivia	151
5.8	Main Entry Points to International Ground Transportation	153
6.1	Economic Indicators of Mercosur Countries	160
6.2	Paraguay: Composition of GDP	161
6.3	Paraguay: Growth Rates by Sectors	161
6.4	Paraguay: Balance of Payments	162
6.5	Paraguay: Composition of Exports and Distribution	163
6.6	Paraguay: Destination of Exports and Distribution	164
6.7	Paraguay: Composition of Imports and Distribution	164
6.8	Paraguay: Origin of Imports and Distribution	165
6.9	Paraguay: Receipts from Binational Electric EN	165
7.1	(a) Canadian Exports to and Imports from the United States	174
	(b) Mexican Exports to and Imports from the United States	174
7.2	Structure of Intra-North American Trade, 1989–93	175
10.1	Exports of Canada, 1986–93	233
10.2	Imports of Canada, 1986–93	234
10.3	Latin American Exports to Canada, 1986–93	236
10.4	Latin American Imports from Canada, 1986–93	237
10.5	Major Exports of Canada to LAIA	238
10.6	Major Imports of Canada from LAIA	242
10.7	Direct Foreign Investment Stock	245

10.8   Direct Foreign Investment Flows in the 1990s   246
10.9   Canadian Direct Investment in Chile   247

FIGURE

5.1   Bolivia's Border Towns and Main Cities   147

Notes on the Contributors

Jorge Aseff holds a research position at the Instituto de Investigaciones Socio-Económicas (IISEC). He has a degree in Economics from the Catholic University of Bolivia.

Roberto Bouzas is Senior Research Fellow at the Latin American School of Social Sciences (FLACSO) and the National Science and Technical Research Council (CONICET) in Argentina. He is also a Professor of International Economics at the University of Buenos Aires and the Foreign Service Institute. He has published extensively on international trade and financial issues. His latest edited book (with Jaime Ros) is *Economic Integration in the Western Hemisphere* (South Bend, Ind.: University of Notre Dame Press, 1994).

Luis E. Breuer is member of the Board of the Central Bank of Paraguay. He holds a PhD from the University of Illinois at Urbana-Chanpaign, where he has taught as well as at Illinois State University.

Richard G. Dearden is a senior partner with Gowling, Strathy & Henderson, one of Canada's largest law firms. Mr Dearden is an international trade law expert and acts as counsel in trade disputes and in customs, anti-dumping and countervail cases. He is a prolific writer and frequent speaker on international trade law issues and serves as a panelist in the resolution of disputes under the North American Free Trade Agreement. Mr Dearden acted as counsel for the United States Trade Representative during the Canada–US Free Trade Negotiations and for Mexico's Secretaría de Comercio y Fomento Industrial during the NAFTA negotiations.

Juan José Echavarría is Minister Plenipotentiary in the Organization of American States and adviser to the recently created Trade Unit. As Vice-Minister of Foreign Trade in Colombia he was in charge of the negotiations with Mexico and Venezuela (G3), with Chile and with Central America. Has been Vice-

Chairman of Fedesarrollo and Dean of the Faculty of Economics of the National University of Colombia. He teaches international trade and macroeconomics at the National University and at the University of Los Andes, and has published widely in the areas of industrial economics, integration and international trade. He holds a DPhil from Oxford University.

Justo Espejo is Professor of Economics at the Catholic University of Bolivia. He also holds a research position at the Instituto de Investigaciones Socio-Económicas (IISEC).

Raúl Labán is partner of the consulting firm GERENS and part-time Professor of Economics at the Catholic University of Chile. He was a senior adviser on macroeconomic issues at the Ministry of Finance of Chile (1991–3). He has advised the Ministry of Finance of Paraguay and of Nicaragua and been an adviser on international trade negotiations of Chile's Foreign Affairs Ministry. He has published extensively in academic journals both in Chile and abroad, and has made contributions to several books on economic reform and stabilization. He holds a PhD in Economics from MIT.

Richard G. Lipsey is currently Professor of Economics at Simon Fraser University in Vancouver, Canada and Alcan Fellow of the Canadian Institute for Advanced Research. He has held posts in many universities including The London School of Economics, the University of California at Berkeley, Yale and Queen's University, Kingston, Ontario. He is the author of 100 articles and a dozen books on economic theory, economic policy and free trade areas. His current research is on the determinants of long-run economic growth.

Patricio Meller is senior economist at CIEPLAN (Corporación de Investigaciones Económicas para Latinoamérica, Santiago) and Director of the Department of Industrial Engineering, University of Chile. He has taught at universities in Chile and abroad. He has published widely in international and Chilean academic and policy journals on issues related to Latin American macroeconomics and trade. He holds a PhD in Economics from the University of California, Berkeley.

Maureen Appel Molot is the Director of The Norman Paterson School of International Affairs and Professor in the Department of Political Science and School of International Affairs at Carleton University. She has published numerous articles on the political economy of North American Free Trade and the continentalization of the auto industry. She holds a PhD from the University of California at Berkeley.

Juan Antonio Morales is Professor of Economics at Catholic University of Bolivia. He is the Director of Instituto de Investigaciones Socio-Económicas (IISEC). He has published widely in international and Bolivian academic and policy publications. He holds a PhD from the Catholic University of Louvain.

Raúl E. Sáez is a Researcher at CIEPLAN. He has been an adviser on international trade issues and negotiations to Chile's Ministries of Economy, Finance and Foreign Affairs. He has also taught international economics at the University of Chile. He holds a PhD in Economics from Boston University.

Ann Weston is Vice-President and Research Coordinator at the North–South Institute, Ottawa, Canada. She worked previously in the Economic Affairs Division of the Commonwealth Secretariat, and the Overseas Development Institute, London. She has written several articles and co-authored a number of books on developing countries and the international trading system. Her most recent work focuses on regional trade agreements and women's interests in the new trade agenda.

Bruce W. Wilkinson is Professor of Economics at the University of Alberta, Edmonton, Canada. He has been Chairman of the Department of Economics and Associate Dean of Arts at the University of Alberta, and has been a consultant for various economic research organizations in Canada. His publications include many articles and a number of books on Canadian international trade, commercial policy and the balance of payments, as well as the economics of education. He holds a PhD from The Massachusetts Institute of Technology.

List of Acronyms and Abbreviations

AFTA	Americas Free Trade Area
ANDI	National Association of Industrialists (Colombia)
APEC	Asian Pacific Economic Cooperation
ASEAN	Association of South-East Asian Nations
BCNI	Business Council on National Issues
BTA	bilateral trade agreement
CACM	Central America Common Market
CANACINTRA	National Chamber of Manufacturing Industry
CARICOM	Caribbean Community
CBI	Caribbean Basin Initiative
CEPAL	Comisión Económica para America Latina y el Caribe (ECLAC)
CET	Common External Tariff
CMA	Canadian Manufacturers Association
CMC	Common Market Council
CMG	Common Market Group
COECE	Mexican Business Coordinating Council for Free Trade
COMPARMEX	Employers' Confederation of the Mexican Republic
CONCAMIN	Confederation of Chambers of Industry (Mexico)
CONCANACO	Confederation of National Chambers of Commerce
CU	customs union
DC	developed country
DSM	dispute settlement mechanism
EAITC	External Affairs and International Trade Canada
ECA	Economic Complementarity Agreement
ECC	Extraordinary Challenge Committee
ECLAC	Economic Commission for Latin America and the Caribbean (CEPAL)

EDWAA	Economic Dislocation and Worker Adjustment Assistance
EEC, EC	European (Economic) Community
EFTA	European Free Trade Area
EU	European Union
FDI	foreign direct investment
FTA	Canada–US Free Trade Agreement
G3	Group of Three
GATT	General Agreement on Tariffs and Trade
GDP	gross domestic product
GNP	gross national product
ICSID	International Convention on the Settlement of Investment Disputes
IDB	Inter-American Development Bank
IEA	International Energy Agency
ILAP	Industry and Labour Adjustment Programme
ILO	International Labour Organization
ITC	International Trade Commission
JTPA	Job Training and Placement Assistance
LA	Latin America
LAC	Latin American country
LAIA	Latin American Integration Association
LDC	less developed country
Mercosur	Southern Cone Common Market
MFN	most favoured nation
MNC	multinational corporation
MNE	multinational enterprise
MTC	Mercosur Trade Commission
NAALC	North American Agreement on Labour Cooperation
NAFTA	North American Trade Agreement
NAO	National Administrative Office
NATIR	North American Trade and Investment Regime
NIC	newly industrialized country
NR	natural resource
NTB	non-tariff barrier
OECD	Organization for Economic Cooperation and Development
OIP	other industrial product

OPEC	Organization of Petroleum Exporting Countries
PEI	Prince Edward Island
PNR	processed natural resource
PRI	Partido Revolucionario Institucional
PTA	preferential trade agreement
QR	quota restriction
R&D	research and development
SAFTA	South American Free Trade Area
SITC	Standard International Trade Classification
TAA	Trade Adjustment Assistance
TLP	Trade Liberalization Programme
UHT	ultra-high temperature
UI	unemployment insurance
UNCITRAL	United Nations Commission on International Trade Law Arbitration Rules
USITC	United States International Trade Commission
USTR	United States Trade Representative
UTL	unilateral trade liberalization
VER	voluntary export restraint
WGTA	Western Grain Transportation Act
WH	Western Hemisphere
WIR	World Investment Report
WTO	World Trade Organization

ALASKA

GREENLAND

CANADA

UNITED STATES

MEXICO

GUATEMALA
BELIZE
HONDURAS
SALVADOR
NICARAGUA
COSTA RICA
PANAMA

Introduction
Richard G. Lipsey and Patricio Meller

Canadians and Latin Americans have just acknowledged that they are in the same geographical hemisphere. A key ingredient for establishing a joint trading arrangement is mutual knowledge of eventual partners, and there is a profound mutual ignorance between Canadians and Latin Americans.

An International Conference on Western Hemisphere Trade Integration, held in Santiago, Chile on 12–13 January 1995, provided the opportunity for Canadian and Latin American economists and political scientists to exchange views about the following issues: What is the Latin America (LA) perception of NAFTA? Is NAFTA the route to Western Hemisphere (WH) integration? What should the relationship be between NAFTA and the other LA trade arrangements, more specifically, the relation between NAFTA and Mercosur? What can LA learn from Canada with respect to having a close trade partnership with the United States? Should all LA countries try to enter into NAFTA?

There was an open, frank and friendly exchange of views between Canadians and Latin Americans; there were discrepancies and coincidences among the Canadians, among the Latin Americans, and between Canadians and Latin Americans. Not only was the outcome a lively and fruitful exchange of views, but the papers presented at the conference have also been greatly improved thanks to the many useful suggestions that were made. It is hoped, therefore, that this book will help to improve mutual understanding between Canada and Latin America.

To provide an overview of the issues discussed at the conference, this Introduction is divided into two sections. The first stresses the Latin American perception of the trade issues, and the second emphasizes the Canadian view.

The Santiago International Conference and this book have both been supported by the Canadian International Development Agency (CIDA); and the CIDA programme officer, Teresa Beemans, has been instrumental in promoting the overall project. CIEPLAN acknowledges and appreciates the significant support of CIDA in promoting the exchange of views among Latin American economists as well as with our Canadian colleagues.

Due to space limitations, abbreviated versions of the original papers are included in this volume.

1 A LATIN AMERICAN VIEW OF WESTERN HEMISPHERE INTEGRATION

Latin American trade regimes and foreign investment perceptions have undergone profound changes.

With respect to trade, most LA countries have undertaken a unilateral external liberalization process in a relatively short period: (1) Maximum nominal tariffs have been reduced from a three-digit level to around 20 per cent. (2) Most LA countries had surcharges prior to 1990; these have been significantly reduced or eliminated during the 1990s. (3) A large number of LA imports were subjected to quota restrictions (QR) prior to 1990; these now play a zero or minor role in most LA countries. In short, LA is now a more open region and has become export-oriented. During the 1990s the export/GDP coefficient has significantly increased in most LA countries; however, the value of exports/capita for most LA countries is below US$700 p.a.

There has been a profound change in LA perception with respect to foreign investment. During the 1960s it was believed that the costs of foreign investment were higher than the benefits; therefore, foreign investment expropriation and nationalization were considered to be policies that would increase domestic welfare. During the 1990s, most LA countries seem to consider that foreign investment generates nothing but benefits; this view has led to a sort of LA competition in trying to attract the most foreign investment. In 1993, the whole region received almost US$20 billion of foreign direct investment.

It should be pointed out that there is a new foreign investment phenomenon in LA. Latin American firms are investing in other LA countries; furthermore, we are beginning to see joint investment ventures between LA neighbours.

Most LA countries are very interested in being admitted into NAFTA. There are several reasons: (1) to gain access to the large US market; (2) to avoid US trade barriers increasing in the future, due to domestic protectionist pressures; (3) NAFTA is a high-class club, and everyone likes to be a member of an exclusive club. In this case, NAFTA membership would provide a sort of 'seal of approval' for macroeconomic and development policies, and for 'good and reliable' government and institutions. Moreover, all of this will attract foreign investment and will generate optimistic expectations, thereby stimulating domestic investment. (4) The US government has formulated an invitation to generate a hemispheric free trade area. There has not been an equivalent invitation from either the European Union (EU) or Japan.

With the exception of Mexico, many empirical studies indicate that there will be small, static trade gains (or losses) for most LA countries if they are incorporated into NAFTA; this result is due to the fact that LA exports already face low tariffs in the United States (the Generalized System of Preferences and low tariffs for natural resources). The seal of approval argument is implicitly used to stress the fact that dynamic effects are more important than static effects in the computation of trade gains. The largest computed magnitudes of static and dynamic gains from NAFTA membership for LA fluctuate between 1 per cent and 7 per cent of GDP (Brown, 1992). Despite these figures, it is advantageous for any individual LA to be admitted into NAFTA, but it should be kept in mind that admission to NAFTA will not be an automatic solution to Latin America's economic problems.

Different perceptions exist about NAFTA. In the LA view, the reference model should be the EU, in which case there would be various implications and issues to be reassessed:

1. Membership: The EU is for Europeans only. Will NAFTA be completely open? In other words, which countries cannot be members of NAFTA? LA would prefer a Western Hemisphere geographic membership.
2. How far will NAFTA go? To date there have been two stages: free movement of goods (and services, eventually) and national treatment for foreign investment. Now a third stage is imminent: equal environmental and labour standards. Will there be further stages, e.g. (a) free movement of people across borders? (b) macroeconomic harmonization? (c) a common currency (other than the US dollar!)?
3. Per capita income differentials. In the EU there are technological cooperation mechanisms for lower per capita income countries, and there are social compensation mechanisms for poorer areas. In NAFTA, all countries are considered to be equal.

In the US and Canadian view, NAFTA seems to be – and will only be – a free trade area (FTA) not exclusive to LA. However, after the recent Mexican financial crisis, the US government played the role of lender of last resort. What will the final NAFTA model be? Is there one? Does a US and/or a Canadian vision of NAFTA exist? Or are we following the poet's approach: 'Caminante no hay camino; se hace camino al andar' ('Wayfarer, there is no road; we will make one along the way').

Another matter of great concern for LA is the absence of explicit NAFTA accession rules. The position of the present three members is more or less the following: (1) There is no need for specific rules; what is required is the agreement of all members. (2) The path to NAFTA requires a country's domestic 'house to be in order', macroeconomic issues under control, a completed process of unilateral liberalization and a domestic economy in good shape and ready to face international competition. In short, 'common-sense' principles. Mexico qualified before December 1994, yet would it have qualified today?

The LA concern is related to the need to have clear and explicit accession rules; when there are no rules, the law of the jungle prevails – the strongest rules. The key issue here is how to counterbalance the large bargaining power of the United States. Canada has taught the world that there is only one way: having a rule-based system.

Is NAFTA the way, or indeed the only way, to Western Hemisphere integration? It should be pointed out that Mercosur is 'on the move'. Mercosur's basic indicators are (1994): 195 million people, a GDP (Gross Domestic Product) of US$785 billion, total trade of US$100 billion. Intra-trade among Mercosur partners has increased from US$2.6 billion (1986) to US$9.4 billion (1994); this increase has occurred in spite of an unstable environment. Mercosur is becoming a reality because its largest members, Brazil and Argentina, have taken a political decision to push it.

The coexistence of NAFTA and Mercosur could become a source of tensions in the region.

A key question raised by US economists is related to Brazil's acceptance of NAFTA admission rules. A Brazilian would ask a symmetrical question. Would the United States accept Mercosur admission rules? The Brazilian perception is that they will be the second to last country to be admitted to NAFTA; the last will be Cuba . . . by the year 2050.

In other words, the key issue for the future is the type of relationship that will be developed between NAFTA and Mercosur: how to reduce the potential for future tension, how to reconcile the positions of the two blocs. One possibility is to have a joint NAFTA–Mercosur commission looking for convergent topics and stressing convergence. What is required is a mutually agreed convergence process, not in the short run (less than two years) but not in the long run either (more than five years), in order to avoid future rigidity and inflexibility. A joint NAFTA–Mercosur FTA would ensure the achievement of Western Hemisphere trade integration.

Until NAFTA–Mercosur convergence is obtained, there will be a two-tier LA country situation: the winners who are members of a big bloc, and the loser countries who are excluded. What, then, are the options available to an excluded LA country? There are two possibilities which are not mutually exclusive.

1. Promoting border trade. Many LA countries have signed numerous FTAs with other LA countries; most of these FTAs will be 'only paper agreements'. An undesirable outcome is that so many FTAs generate confusion within a given LA country: for example, which FTA should be given first priority? A pragmatic answer would be: the FTA between neighbouring countries, i.e. a natural geographic partnership. An increase in border trade could contribute to the establishment of a real bilateral FTA. In short, promoting border trade could have a significant economic and political effect. It is well known that each LA country has excellent diplomatic relations with all other LA countries with which it does not share a common border. Improving the movement of people, goods and investment between LA bordering countries would increase the size of domestic markets and could provide a dynamic stimulus to national and foreign investment. Furthermore, it could contribute to economic decentralization: development poles being located away from the big urban capital. Many successful border-trade arrangements could eventually help towards the Western Hemisphere FTA objective. The Inter-American Development Bank (IDB) and the World Bank should give high priority to infrastructure investment projects connecting LA neighbouring countries.

2. Opening up associate membership of the large blocs (NAFTA and Mercosur). Similar to the relationship between the EC and the members of EFTA (European Free Trade Area) which later acquired full EC membership, NAFTA and Mercosur should open associate membership.

2   CANADIAN PERCEPTION OF WH INTEGRATION

Canada's perception of Western Hemisphere trade liberalization is coloured by the importance of international trade to the Canadian economy. About 28 per cent of Canadian GDP is accounted for by foreign trade, in contrast to the US figure of about 11 per cent. Even more important, the vast majority of Canadian exports go to the United States, currently about 80 per cent. No Latin American country has a figure that high. This leaves only 20 per cent for all other countries and, as a result, only a small proportion of Canadian exports go to Latin America. However, these exports are growing rapidly, and growing at about three times the rate of growth of exports to East Asia. The importance of LA trade with the two northernmost countries of North America varies substantially from country to country, and most do only a small proportion of their total trade with Canada. None the less, this trade is also growing in importance. For example, LA countries taken as a whole currently import almost twice as much per capita from Canada as from East Asia.

Naturally, Canada's first priority for regional trade liberalization was to conclude an FTA with the United States, which went into force in 1989. Next, when the United States and Mexico decided to begin negotiations for a bilateral FTA in the early 1990s, Canada was faced with an important decision: to stand aside and let this occur, or to invite itself to the table for trilateral negotiations. Canada chose the latter course of action and, by so doing, it turned a possible US–Mexican bilateral FTA into a trilateral NAFTA, with possibilities for expansion into a Western Hemisphere FTA (an AFTA for FTA of the Americas). Notice, incidentally, that when Canadians (and Americans) talk of Latin America they almost always mean Latin America and the Caribbean. So, the idea of an AFTA includes the countries of the Caribbean basin.

The considerations that led to Canada's decision to invite itself to the US–Mexican talks will strongly influence Canada's attitude to expansion of the NAFTA to include other countries, starting with Chile. Here we mention six of the most important.

What was almost certainly the most important reason followed from considerations of political economy rather than purely economic calculations. There were two distinct models for US participation in the process of hemispheric trade liberalization. One had the key country forming bilateral agreements with a series of countries in the hemisphere. The United States already had one with Canada and it was apparent in 1990 that if Mexico were added, Chile would not be far behind. This would set hemispheric trade liberalization on the route of a 'hub-and-spoke' model in which the United States has a bilateral agreement with each other country so that the United States was the only country with unrestricted access to all the markets of the spoke countries (as well as all the other privileges conferred by a modern FTA). The spoke countries have free access to the US market only. This is a recipe for US hegemony in the hemisphere; it would make the United States even more attractive as a home for investment designed to serve the hemisphere's markets than it already is. The second model, called 'multilateral regionalism', has a single multilateral agreement which is expanded to include more and more members. Now all members have equal access to all other members' markets and all have equal rights, privileges and obligations extending multilaterally over all members. Canada's decision to enter the US–Mexican negotiations was to a great extent influenced by the desire to put hemispheric liberalization on the track of a multilateral regionalism created by a single agreement rather than a series of hub-and-spoke agreements. By succeeding in this objective, Canadian diplomacy made a major contribution to hemispheric development and equality of nations under regional trading agreements.

A second important reason for Canada's interest in creating a NAFTA was to increase the importance of its trade with Latin America. Since this trade is currently small, standard econometric measures of the gains from liberalizing it show only minor gains. Some Canadian economists have wondered aloud why, in the light of these small gains, Canada persisted in pushing to enter the negotiations. The objective, however, was not to achieve the static gains but to be inside the rapidly expanding

Latin American market in the belief that, after the lost decade of the 1980s, the whole area could take off into a period of rapid catch-up growth.

There is a new sense of expectation in Canadian–Latin American economic relations. Everywhere – in the Atlantic provinces, Quebec, Ontario, the Prairies, Alberta and British Columbia – the business community is focusing on Mexico and the rest of Latin America as future markets. For many small and medium-sized business enterprises in Canada this market appears more manageable than Japan, China or Southeast Asia (Lipsey, 1994).

A third reason was rooted in the worry that Canadian exports would suffer losses from trade diversion when the United States gained tariff-free entry to Latin American markets, which would be denied to Canada if it stayed outside the emerging FTAs.

Fourth, over the decades, Latin America has absorbed substantial amounts of Canadian foreign direct investment, particularly in resource and infrastructure industries. A stable investment regime, with freedom to make new investments and national treatment of existing investments, was a major prize that the NAFTA and its extension offered to Canadian multinationals.

Fifth, although taking part in growing trade and investment flows in the hemisphere was desirable in itself, this was also desirable as a way of reducing Canada's high dependence on the US market for its exports. Diversification of markets for exports has been an object of Canadian policy for decades, but few practical ways of achieving it have been advanced. Here was one: take part in the liberalization of the hemisphere's trade from inside and allow the resulting new trade to reduce the proportion of total trade done with the United States.

Sixth, not only would Canada's participation in a NAFTA reduce its heavy dependence on the US market, partnership with Latin American democracies was seen as a counterweight to the enormous power of the United States in economic matters. The smaller economies could make common cause against US protectionism and US unilateralism. Although most US administrations have followed liberal trade and investment policies over the last 60 years, the US Congress has not been so consistent. It has often given way to strong regional and sectional special interests that favour various forms of overt and covert trade restrictions. Over the years, Canada has been embroiled in a succession of the resulting disputes, the number increasing rather than decreasing in recent years. The United States has recently adopted a number of unilateral measures ostensibly designed to force foreign countries to reduce trade barriers, but which in effect raise barriers against these US protectionist interests (and as allies with those in the United States who held genuinely liberal views on trade). This view was reinforced by the growing strength of democratic forces in Latin America leading Canadians to look for common purposes among the smaller democratic countries in the Americas.

So much for Canada's motives for entering NAFTA. How about Canada's views on NAFTA's future evolution? Just as we saw in the last section that citizens of Latin American countries are wondering how NAFTA will evolve, so too are Canadians. In this respect, it is important to realize, particularly when comparisons are made with the EU, that NAFTA is a free trade area. Although the NAFTA does have many of the characteristics traditionally associated with a common market (proving that as times change so do institutions), it is an FTA in the key defining sense that each country has control over its own, independent, external commercial policy. Canadian policy is that NAFTA should remain an FTA and not evolve into a formal customs union. The reason is related to the overwhelming power of the United States in geopolitical matters. As a large superpower, the United States often uses trade policy as an instrument of foreign policy – as when it has restricted trade with China, Vietnam and Cuba for political reasons. As a superpower, the United States would dominate any 'joint' decisions on a common commercial policy. If NAFTA were a customs union, Canada and Mexico would, for example, now be joined with the United States in what many Canadians regard as its misguided restrictions on trade with Cuba. Canada wants to avoid becoming a US puppet in foreign policy and desires to preserve its right to do what it has done in the past: trade on terms not allowed to Americans with countries such as the former USSR, China, Vietnam and Cuba. For this reason, it is Canadian policy that the NAFTA should remain an FTA. Note that since for obvious reasons this is not an American concern, US economists and policy-makers see no objections (on these grounds at least) to the NAFTA evolving into a customs union.

On a more positive note, there is no reason why the NAFTA and its successor could not follow the computer precedent. On computers and colour TV tubes, the NAFTA countries have agreed to a common tariff and to the consequent absence of rules of origin requirements on intra-NAFTA trade in these products. This is an excellent precedent, and rules ought to be written into any further agreement for the proclamation of the removal of rules of origin on products for which the three countries achieve, and commit themselves to maintaining, a common tariff rate. This would allow the NAFTA to evolve into some of the characteristics of a customs union, including the abolition of many vexatious rules of origin, requiring a harmonization of commercial policy while maintaining each country's freedom to set its more general commercial policy against the rest of the world.

Other forms of deeper integration are possible and would most probably be welcomed by the Canadian government. Closer cooperation on standards, more investment liberalization and other similar developments are possible. Less likely are the removal of exceptions for sectors such as culture in Canada, energy in Mexico and transportation in the United States, since there are strong domestic political constituencies backing each.

Other evolutions would include measures to reinforce the rules-based system of trade and investment which is of great value to smaller countries. The existing system will be severely tested by the Americans over the next few years and it will be interesting to see how NAFTA withstands these pressures. For example, although Canada has won three separate decisions by NAFTA's dispute settlement bodies on alleged subsidies to Canadian exports of softwood lumber, US producers are preparing a fourth attack on these exports through the same dispute settlement mechanisms and are also pressuring the US Congress to introduce new legislation that would negate some of the obligations created by the NAFTA.

Canadians would like to achieve a comprehensive agreement on issues of pricing and subsidies that lead to anti-dumping and countervailing duties. First, Canada would like to see domestic predatory pricing laws replace anti-dumping duties so that goods from all NAFTA countries (imported and domestically produced) would be subject to the pricing laws ruling in the country in which they are being marketed. Second, Canada would like to reach agreement on a code of subsidies to regulate countervailing duties. Under this code, some subsidies would be exempt from countervail, some would be immediately subject to countervail and some (as few as possible) would exist under the present regime where action could be taken against them and a decision reached through the dispute settlement mechanism. All of this, however, is a very hard sell in the United States. The Congress is jealous of its abilities to influence imports and would be very reluctant to give up the present anti-dumping and countervailing regimes.

Canadian policy is favourable to an extension of the NAFTA to all the countries of Latin America and the Caribbean basin, provided only that the new members have their economies in sufficient order to be able to withstand the shocks of entering (which were not insignificant in Canada). The NAFTA includes an accession clause that contemplates allowing new members to join. Widening the agreement to include many more countries with Canadian support is a strong possibility. From Canada's point of view, although the economically stronger countries of Latin America are the main candidates for early entry, countries outside the hemisphere should not be excluded on principle. New Zealand and Australia are obvious possibilities, if they feel that entry into an expanded AFTA would not jeopardize their more important trading links with the ASEAN countries.

For several countries, particularly those in Central America, entering AFTA is the preferred option – once they have got their own houses in sufficient competitive order, which in some cases is a tall order. What happens after that will depend on how many countries see NAFTA's successor, the AFTA, as the preferred option. The amount of trade done with the United States is not the only consideration in determining the advantages and disadvantages of entering AFTA. As membership expands, countries left out will find trade and investment diversion occurring with neighbours who opt in. If enough countries join, there could be a domino effect (as there was with the EU) with the rest feeling that they cannot afford to stay outside because of the total diversion effects with all AFTA countries, not just the United States. For example, it would very probably not be viable in the long term to have all Latin American countries in the AFTA, with the only exceptions being the four now in Mercosur. Trade and investment diversion for the Mercosur countries to their neighbours would probably be too large.

In summary, Canada takes a positive attitude to NAFTA and its extension to the entire hemisphere, when and if the individual countries are economically ready. Canada, while remaining friends with its major trading partner the United States, sees other countries as natural allies against the forces in the United States which would increase protectionism and incur unilateral actions. Canada, with its long experience of dealing with the United States, provides assurance to other potential entries of an ally experienced in dealing with the United States, fostering the strong liberal forces of that country while resisting its protectionist forces.

3 OVERVIEW OF THE CHAPTERS

Bruce W. Wilkinson's chapter on 'NAFTA in the world economy: Lessons and issues for Latin America' discusses in a critical way the nature of NAFTA, and what its effects might be upon Latin America. It also outlines how Canadian interests may diverge from the Mexican and from those of the United States, and in this context considers the costs and benefits of additional Latin American nations joining NAFTA, including its social implications.

Wilkinson's main conclusions are: (1) NAFTA membership will not be an easy solution to Latin America's current economic problems. The economic gains are likely to be limited, and membership will, in fact, preclude many of the governmental policies that originally enabled all the major industrialized nations of today, as well as the newly industrialized nations of Asia, to become what they now are. (2) The future of NAFTA and its implications for the Americas and the world trading order will depend primarily on what the United States decides is in its own interests. (3) Yet NAFTA is unlikely to lead to increasingly protectionist blocs. (4) NAFTA should give us cause for concern about the international social order and the well-being of the masses.

Wilkinson provides several clues to future Latin American negotiators with the United States: (1) There is a diffusion of decision-making authority in the US political process which has several consequences. First, it gives the administration tremendous leverage in international negotiations. Officials can, in effect, appear to be willing to go along with a particular position endorsed by another nation, but then not do so on the grounds that it would not be acceptable to Congress. Second, it allows vested interests in Congress to thwart what the Executive may have agreed to in international discussions, or alternatively get special commitments from the president in return for supporting some agreement the Executive has made. (2) The United States set forth conditions which the prospective partner must fulfil as *preconditions* for entering negotiations, when in fact such items could rightly be considered items that should be part of the negotiations themselves – things which the prospective partner might be prepared to forgo in return for concessions from the United States. This approach enables the United States to get certain benefits ahead of time without giving up anything. Then they can go on with negotiations and extract *additional* concessions from partners in return for concessions from themselves.

Should Latin American nations be trying to join NAFTA? According to Wilkinson, the nations of Latin America need to see themselves as nations which together face a variety of opportunities waiting to be exploited. NAFTA in its most rigid form is only one of these. If the Latin American nations are to negotiate the best deal for themselves for membership in NAFTA, they would be well advised first to develop much closer ties with one another so that they can present a more united front. To do this it will be necessary for them to see one another not as rivals, but as partners working together in seeking a better world for their citizens. In addition, the Latin American nations should be developing detailed countervailing and anti-dumping duties, as well as safeguard laws, to parallel those in the United States, and have them in place *and be actively using them* prior to concluding any negotiations with the United States to enter NAFTA.

Roberto Bouza's chapter on 'Mercosur and preferential trade liberalization in South America: Record, issues and prospects' provides a highly informative overview of Mercosur evolution, its grade record and the problems that it is facing. Mercosur is a heterogeneous group: Brazil is a continental economy which contributes about two-thirds of regional output, with 80 per cent of the population and an extensive industrial base. Argentina, in turn, accounts for most of the remainder. Per capita GDP also differs markedly among the four partners: the relatively high per capita income of Argentina (US$8004) is almost six times that of Paraguay (US$1400). Partly reflecting differences in country size, the national foreign trade coefficients are also disparate: two-way foreign trade represents 12.8 per cent of GDP in Argentina, 14.1 per cent in Brazil and over 30 per cent in Uruguay and Paraguay (the smallest and relatively most open economies).

In the first stage of Mercosur, the main common trade policy instrument will be the Common External Tariff (CET), enforced from January 1995 onwards. The agreed CET includes eleven tariff levels with a 0 per cent minimum and a 20 per cent maximum tariff rate. About 85 per cent of total tariff lines had their CET operational from January 1995. The remainder, including capital goods, information technology and telecommunications products will keep national tariff rates vis-à-vis third countries, but will converge automatically by 2001 (capital goods) and 2006 (information technology and telecommunications products). Apart from capital goods, information technology and telecommunications products, member countries were allowed exemptions from the CET up to a maximum of 300 tariff lines until 31 December 2000.

Member countries will also develop a common regime for anti-dumping and countervailing duties applicable to imports from the rest of the world, following GATT guidelines. National anti-dumping regimes will continue in the meantime. Member countries have agreed to keep certain GATT-compatible export incentives until tax policies are harmonized. Mercosur countries also agreed on a common safeguards scheme. If rising imports cause, or threaten to cause, damage to domestic producers in one country or in the region as a whole, the Trade Commission may impose safeguard measures prior to launching an investigation. Under certain circumstances provisional safeguard measures could be applied by the national chapters of the Commission for a maximum of 200 days. Safeguards will be non-discriminatory and can take the form of higher tariffs or quotas, but they may not reduce the volume of imports below the average for the last three years. Safeguards will be applicable for four years, with an extension to a maximum of eight years.

Bouzas reviews the Colonia Protocol by which the four Mercosur countries committed themselves to provide national treatment to investors from within the region. The Colonia Protocol included a most favoured nation (MFN) obligation ensuring that regional investors are treated as favourably as any other foreign investor. As a general rule, the agreement also prohibited the use of performance requirements. However, member countries have identified a number of transitory exceptions in coverage, yet of unspecified duration. Argentina has exempted from the agreement border real estate, air transportation, shipbuilding, nuclear power generation, uranium mining, insurance and fisheries. The Brazilian list of exemptions is longer. It includes exploration and exploitation of minerals, hydroelectric power, health care, radio frequencies and telecommunications, rural property, banking and insurance services, construction and shipping. Both countries have also reserved the right temporarily to maintain performance requirements for the automobile sector. Common investment regulations outlaw expropriation, except on public interest grounds and undertaken on a non-discriminatory basis with due process and prompt payment of a fair compensation. The Colonia Protocol also forbids restrictions on capital repatriation and profit remittances in convertible currencies.

According to Bouzas, not all Mercosur countries find a preferential trade agreement with the United States or NAFTA equally desirable. For the smaller partners the main issue is subregional trade liberalization. Their main incentives vis-à-vis the United States are defensive: to make sure that preferences in the subregional market are not being unilaterally eroded. For Brazil the balance is different: exports from Brazil are likely to gain most in terms of market access from preferential trade liberalization vis-à-vis the United States, and it is also the country most seriously threatened by trade diversion in North American markets. Brazilian exports may also suffer in regional markets if NAFTA expands to other countries in Latin America. Brazil's reluctance to enter into negotiations with the United States and/or NAFTA stems from a widespread belief that adjustment and macroeconomic issues posed by trade liberalization have not received adequate attention in NAFTA, and are unlikely to do so in the future. The case of Argentina is a peculiar one. Although market access is not a key issue in US–Argentine trade relations, the Argentine government has at certain times appeared excited by the prospect of free trade negotiations with the United States and/or NAFTA. The main incentive seems to have been to consolidate (lock in) economic reforms and obtain a 'seal of approval' for domestic policies. The objective of strengthening their negotiating stance vis-à-vis Brazil may have also played a role.

Finally, Bouzas states that Mercosur countries (particularly Argentina) have insisted on seeking alternatives for incorporating

Chile into Mercosur. Yet these efforts have been counteracted by other partners' reluctance to accept a special mechanism for Chile's accession, and Chile's refusal to commit itself to the CET. It is likely that Chile will have to 'pay a price' (probably non-participation in governing bodies or a more lengthy tariff removal process) for not joining the customs union. Mercosur is an attractive market for Chilean exports, not only because of the value of trade but also because of its composition: Chile sells most of its manufactured exports to the subregion, and the share of products traded with preferences is higher for Chilean exports to Mercosur than for Mercosur exports to Chile.

Chapter 3 covers 'The G3 and the road to continental integration' by Juan José Echavarría. The G3 (Group of Three Agreement) is a free trade agreement between Colombia, Mexico and Venezuela. In Colombia and Venezuela the G3 has been seen as a bridging agreement on the road to hemispheric integration: the G3 could provide training for negotiators in government and in the private sector (in an intensive process of collaboration), which eventually could be useful for a possible future admission to NAFTA. Also, other countries interested in a similar process leading towards hemispheric integration might join.

Trade within the G3 is very limited at the present time, accounting for scarcely 2 per cent of total exports. Mexico does not even figure among the top ten trading partners of Venezuela or Colombia (and vice versa). Echavarría argues that trade flows within the G3 (first factor) may increase significantly in the coming years, considering that trade at the moment is minimal, that the pattern of exports between the three countries is radically different from the pattern of exports to the rest of the world, that transport and other services are also being freed at the same time, and that the tariff reduction will be considerable.

The structure of the G3 is similar to NAFTA. Its 23 chapters deal with the issues of national treatment and market access for goods, the automobile sector, the agriculture sector including plant and animal hygiene, rules of origin, customs procedures, safeguards, investment, intellectual property, dispute resolution, etc. Disputes are resolved through the setting up of panels, whose decisions the parties are obliged to comply with.

The G3 allows countries to keep existing export subsidies for a four-year period, after which they should gradually be eliminated between years 5 and 10. Export and production incentive measures (such as drawback schemes) are accepted, provided they have 'minimum' effects on production and are accepted by the GATT. Export taxes are not accepted, except on certain articles of basic necessity explicitly declared in the agreement. Finally, the agreement also stipulates that goods produced in duty-free zones will enjoy full benefits provided they comply with the respective rules of origin.

Echavarría says that Colombia and Venezuela accept the importance of hemispheric integration, and the G3 constitutes a key element in the process of moving towards this. But in the short and medium run, the NAFTA agreement means that Colombian and Venezuelan producers will have to complete without tariff preferences in the Mexican market with producers from the United States and Canada, especially in those sectors where Mexico frees NAFTA imports immediately: coal (100 per cent) and metallic minerals (100 per cent), agriculture (95 per cent), fishing (89 per cent) and forestry and lumber (86 per cent). In the textile, clothing and leather goods sectors where a large part of Colombia's comparative advantage lies, Mexico will free 29 per cent in NAFTA immediately, and 70 per cent in five years' time. Finally, the G3 sectors most affected by the preferences granted to the United States by Mexico will be chemicals and the publishing industry, which only become tariff-free inside the G3 in ten years' time.

In chapter 4, Raúl Labán and Patricio Meller discuss the 'Trade strategy alternatives for a small country: the Chilean case'. Two separate issues are discussed: (1) Chilean comparative advantage is mainly in natural resources. Chilean exports to industrial countries are more than 90 per cent natural resource-based: either raw materials or (first stage) processed raw materials. On the other hand, Chilean exports to Latin American countries include a significant amount of manufactures not related to its natural resource (NR) endowment. What are the problems related to specialization in natural resource production and trade for a developing country like Chile, and why should manufacturing exports be preferred to other types of exports? (2) Chile has been pursuing a unilateral trade strategy which has produced a successful expansion of exports. Why, then, should Chile change this strategy and try to become a member of preferential trade groupings?

Manufacturing exports are considered a desirable goal in the new export development strategy, but why should the export of US$100 million of blue jeans be preferred to the export of US$100 million of grapes? More generally, Labán and Meller ask, what is the disadvantage of NR exports with respect to manufacturing exports?

The discussion of Chile's second export stage focuses on bringing higher value-added to current NR exports, through processing. In other words, this second export stage is based on promoting forward NR linkages, for example by exporting apple juice, wine and canned fruit (instead of fresh grapes and apples), wood furniture and paper (instead of sawn wood), manufactured copper products, etc. The implicit assumption is that PNR (processing NR) goods will introduce and disseminate modern technology with, therefore, the highest domestic externality.

Labán and Meller argue that while the expansion of PNR exports is based on forward linkages as the mechanism for introducing modern technology, the growth of fruit exports shows that the exploitation of backward linkages can also have an important effect on the application of modern technology. Exporting fresh fruit is a highly complex process, which requires careful coordination and supervision of the whole chain of production, distribution, wholesale and retail trade. The preservation of fresh quality requires a cooling system to keep temperatures constant through the different stages of the period between production and wholesale trade. Chilean ports have had to upgrade their systems of operation, install special, isolated, temperature-controlled storage places and speed up the ship-loading system. To avoid rotting and pest infestation in the many different stages, fumigation has to be incorporated into the cooling system, and special modern packaging is required. Modern technology is used to produce a standard-sized, high quality fruit product catering to the tastes of developed country consumers.

In brief, backward linkages induced by fruit exports have required the introduction of technological innovations. It would be very difficult to specify which type of technology has had the largest external effect on the economy: the technology used in the forward processing of NR exports or the technology used in the backward linkages related to fruit exports. In other words, the production of NR could be a way to introduce modern technology in a developing country which is in some cases as good as the production of industrial goods.

The main features of Chilean trade strategy up to 1993 have been the following: (1) A far-reaching unilateral trade liberalization process. (2) An export market diversification strategy, which implies the absence of any 'natural trade-partner' relationship. (3) The small country assumption, or the importance of being irrelevant: Chile would always find a niche in foreign markets. Then, Labán and Meller state that this strategy, in which Chile has taken its own decisions autonomously, has been very successful in expanding exports. So, if something has had positive results, why should it be changed? Why is Chile interested in entering trade agreements with different commercial partners?

Despite the significant gains obtained in the last two decades in terms of diversifying and expanding the volume of exports (in particular since the mid-1980s), if Chile wishes to sustain a strong and stable output growth path in the future, it will have to maintain the dynamism of the export sector and diversify it more into manufacturing.

Improved access conditions for such exports to foreign markets, among others things, are necessary to increase manufacturing exports. Both developed and developing countries impose greater restrictions on products with a higher value-added; there is a significant escalation in the tariff structure according to a product's value-added content. It will certainly not be possible to obtain improved access conditions for these products by a simple unilateral tariff reduction. The formation of a trade bloc represents a threat for a non-member country, since the latter's ability to compete is severely curtailed by the granting of preferential access (e.g. preferential tariff treatment) to potential competitors in its export markets.

Jorge Aseff, Justo Espejo and Juan Antonio Morales, in 'The importance of border trade: the case of Bolivia', discuss the state of Bolivian economic relations with its close neighbours, in the light of the regional trend towards economic integration. Bolivia has a peculiar geographical position in South America, flanked by five countries, Argentina, Brazil, Peru, Chile and Paraguay. This feature should give Bolivia's trade distinct advantages, but this has not been the case, partly because of Bolivia's landlocked situation, rugged terrain and generally poor transport infrastructure.

Bolivia's traditional exports have been mainly of high-value raw materials, such as tin and silver, and natural gas. These exports are directed, to a significant extent, towards its neighbours. Equally important, neighbouring countries are the most important source of Bolivia's imports; a significant share of this trade is deemed to be border trade, although figures are hard to come by.

A recurrent theme in chapter 5 is the extent to which some features of border trade can be spread to increasingly larger zones. There is also the related question of whether the economically integrated zones should be no more than extensions of border trade, or whether they should have their own distinct characteristics, many of them resulting from bilateral negotiations.

The Bolivian government has been trying to attract investment in maquila[1] industries in towns close to the borders. Due to the absence of a border development policy, almost all duty-free zones are located close to the country's largest cities. As is well known, maquila industries are most advantageous when producing finished products, using a well-known technological process, and for large markets that can be easily reached. This is not so in the Bolivian border towns, where the country can only offer cheap, unskilled labour. Even so, the number of workers in the border towns has not yet reached the critical mass required to make the towns attractive to maquila industries. While border towns cannot yet host maquilas, the city of La Paz, with its supply of services and abundant labour, has been doing so with some success, especially in the clothing and jewelry industries.

The border economy is still weakly integrated into the rest of the economy, but greater integration can be anticipated mainly through the services that border towns can offer to facilitate trade. These services can be especially relevant for bulky products, such as semi-processed industrial inputs, which are a high proportion of Bolivian imports. Also special border services are needed for most of Bolivia's non-traditional exports, which are also bulky. The border zones do not, and in the next few years are not expected to, generate much income for the economy from goods-producing activities. Only when a fully integrated economic region is constituted will this occur.

The conclusions of chapter 5 stress that the importance of border trade cannot be underestimated, even if on the surface it seems remote from the main concerns of trade policy. Locally, border trade has the potential to increase production and consumption in regions that often are far from the main cities. It means economic activity in areas that otherwise would have very little, and it is a source of stable incomes. Moreover, border trade in many ways, has been a precursor of current attempts at regional integration. Goods and factors have circulated freely for years within limited areas across national boundaries. As the costs of trading spatially decrease and the policy-generated barriers to international trade disappear, many (but not all) characteristics of border trade will naturally spread to the rest of the economy. Yet, geography will continue to have policy relevance: increasingly, economic policy should strive to extract the maximum benefit from location. One avenue for this is the formation of economically integrated 'regions', with the term 'region' used in a somewhat narrow sense.

In chapter 6 Luis Breuer provides 'A small country perspective on Mercosur: the case of Paraguay'. Paraguay entered Mercosur as its most junior partner. Its economy is small and open, and as such quite vulnerable to the external economic environment, including changes in terms of trade, international interest rates and investment flows. Its exports are undiversified by destination and especially by commodity breakdown, and prices are determined internationally. Mercosur involves both opportunities and risks for Paraguay. It is a unique opportunity because it addresses one of the main structural impediments to Paraguayan growth – the size of domestic markets which are too small to allow economies of scale. However, there are also considerable risks for the country which cannot be ignored, including the propensity towards macroeconomic instability of the other member countries, the accelerated nature of the integration process and the lack of definition on a number of critical issues which are still being negotiated.

Yet, Paraguay's access to Mercosur was not only desirable on economic grounds, it was unavoidable. Locking in market access to Argentina and Brazil was simply essential. Moreover, moving into a rules-based trading arrangement with its larger neighbours was clearly to Paraguay's benefit, as were the opportunities in terms of attracting foreign investment. Most business and intellectual groups in Paraguaya approved of entry into Mercosur, as it was seen as an insurance to the democratic process, as well as an opportunity to expand domestic markets and redress the informalization of the economy. Initial misgivings, however, were expressed by the commercial sectors of Ciudad del Este, since the adoption of the common external tariff would greatly reduce their possibilities for engaging in commercial arbitrage. Similarly, peasant (*campesino*) and labour organizations have consistently opposed the country's participation in Mercosur.

According to Breuer the main risk faced by Paraguay is that of integration with larger and more sophisticated economies. Moreover, the transition periods for both the free trade area and the customs union are brief, and there are no redistributive mechanisms similar to those of the European Union to allow for the levelling of the playing field.

Thus, it is quite possible that market penetration by products from Argentina and Brazil could lead to a sharp rise in structural unemployment. Paraguay, however, cannot afford a social safety net like Europe's. In the absence of agreements on free movement of labour, this situation may lead to social problems which could call into question the political sustainability of the integration process. Moreover, the lack of progress in the areas of economic convergence and macroeconomic policy coordination creates additional uncertainty, as it exposes Paraguay to sharp changes in its terms of trade.

In spite of all this, Breuer concludes that the opportunities that arise from integration into Mercosur might well be the driving force for the modernization of the Paraguayan economy in the next decade, despite the considerable risks involved.

In chapter 7 Maureen Appel Molot examines the question: 'The North American free trade agreement: policy- or investment-led?' The *demand* for a regional trade arrangement must be seen as both a reflection of the structure of a domestic economy and as an evolving phenomenon. What the North American experience demonstrates is that states can be ahead of Multinational Enterprises (MNEs) in their assessment of the importance of regional trading arrangements. States may determine that participation in a free trade agreement is the best guarantor of economic growth, regardless of whether there is much domestic demand. What then unfolds, whether economic ties move in the direction of deep integration, is the result of corporate decisions about the attractiveness of the new strategies of production.

The link between trade and investment within North America is evident. Moreover, intra-firm or inter-affiliate trade is increasing as a proportion of total trade within North America and will increase further, as investment restrictions in Mexico are removed and more US (and a few Canadian) multinationals locate in Mexico. According to Molot, the deep economic ties that have evolved within North America are largely the result of firms' decisions regarding the most efficient organization of production, while state policies have facilitated the rationalization of production across the three countries.

Reviewing the evolution of the North American trade and investment regime, Molot perceives a change in attitude on the part of all three countries in North America towards negotiated free trade agreements. This change in perspective has been the result of new assessments of the global economy on the part of important domestic actors in Canada and Mexico. In both countries firms were becoming more export-dependent and intra-firm trade was growing in importance.

According to Molot, Canadian economic agents were less enthusiastic about NAFTA than about the FTA. Canada's economic ties with Mexico were, and remain, limited. For Canadian firms adjusting to the FTA, particularly those that were labour-intensive, the prospect of another free trade agreement, particularly one with a low-wage partner, was of great concern. There was also concern about competition with Mexican producers for the US market. None the less the business associations which supported the FTA all argued that Canada had to participate in the NAFTA talks because it could not allow others to define the North American trade and investment regime. Most of the provincial governments that had supported the FTA took a similar stance on NAFTA.

US MNEs that had rationalized at least some of their production supported NAFTA as a means to opening the Mexican economy further. These firms, which had already committed the resources necessary to alter the character of their operations in Mexico from market- to efficiency-seeking lobbied hard for strong investment provisions in the NAFTA agreement. Some industries (for example, autos) pressed the US administration to negotiate NAFTA clauses to protect their interests. Smaller US corporations that supply inputs to the MNEs and those that would face domestic competition from Mexican goods were more uncertain about NAFTA; many of these corporations also demanded special treatment under the agreement. US glass- and steelmakers expressed concern about their ability to compete with Mexican products. Fresh goods producers, already facing competition from Mexico, opposed NAFTA because they anticipated an additional deterioration in their position. US labour was vehemently opposed to NAFTA, as were a variety of environmental and religious groups.

Although the state's free trade perspective was shared by Mexican MNEs, the state none the less undertook to organize corporate support for its initiative. Its vehicle was a state-sponsored forum or 'peak association' on free trade, COECE (the Mexican Business Coordinating Council for Free Trade), whose role was to bring together various business associations to develop a common strategy for the negotiations. Groups wanting input into the formulation of a Mexican position on NAFTA had to belong to COECE. There was no other association with any legitimacy. Through their associations and COECE, major Mexican firms enjoyed a close working relationship with the state during the NAFTA talks, and had the capacity to anticipate the impact of NAFTA on their sectors.

Molot concludes that the Canadian, US and Mexican experiences demonstrate the difficulty of separating policy-led from investment-led integration. There is a continuing interaction between the two, one that has been enhanced by the globalization of production and the increasing importance of intra-firm trade. The North American experience also illustrates the importance of ideology and of changes in ideology; in both Canada and Mexico political leaders radically altered their views on the appropriate national relationship with the United States. Both states led their corporate sectors into support for free trade. In terms of wider hemispheric integration, the FTA and NAFTA negotiations demonstrate that whether regional trading arrangements evolve and deepen depends on the investment decisions of firms.

In chapter 8 Ann Weston covers 'Social issues and labour adjustment policies: the Canada–US FTA experience'. Increasing international economic linkages, resulting from a surge in trade and especially investment flows, have brought with them concern about social standards. Even though it is well known that increased trade should bring welfare gains through a reallocation of resources, greater specialization and increased output, there has been mounting concern about short-term adjustment problems.

The question in the Canadian discussion is what the appropriate response should be. Weston points out that two types of approach are advocated to varying degrees. The first stresses increased adjustment assistance in the form of training and, given the lag before this translates into increased employment, income support. The second, while agreeing that changes are needed in the social programmes, feels that the emphasis should not be on the 'right' to adjustment support so much as the 'responsibility' to adjust (the criticism being that past programmes have created disincentives to retrain and seek employment in other industries). In this case, there is more optimism about the capacity of the Canadian economy to adjust without intervention. Others have called for mechanisms going beyond the present safeguard clauses or trade remedy laws of the GATT/WTO – for example, to include social standards, allowing the use of duties of offset social dumping, etc. Even well-known advocates of trade liberalization within the Canadian government have argued that as economies become more integrated discussion is needed on positive norms for behaviour, in the area of social policy as well as competition policy and environmental standards.

Chapter 8 focuses primarily on Canadian experiences – and experiments – with social policies in the context of trade liberalization, as well as fiscal reform, new technologies and changing demand. The ongoing debate about the future of Canadian social policies is being driven by three concerns: the fiscal deficit, unemployment and poverty. All three are closely interconnected. They appear to have been exacerbated by the restructuring of the Canadian economy. The discussion has focused on what types of social programme Canada both needs and can afford given its increasingly open economy. Would the mobility of investment and trade following the FTA put pressure on Canada to reduce its social programme costs? Could Canadian producers argue that the lower fiscal costs of US social programmes give US producers an unfair advantage? On the other hand, could US firms complain about the cross-regional and industrial subsidies implicit in the Canadian Unemployment Insurance (UI) system? These are some of the issues explored in chapter 8.

UI is the major labour market support policy in the United States, though it covers less than 40 per cent of unemployed workers. Compared to the Canadian scheme, its wage replacement rate is lower (35–40 per cent of the previous year's wages) and of shorter duration (6–9 months). As in Canada, however, the United States has tended to place greater emphasis on income maintenance (over 70 per cent of all labour market spending) than on employment promotion. In addition to UI, the United States has operated a special trade adjustment assistance (TAA) programme for workers and firms displaced by trade. Since 1962 TAA has been attached to most key Trade Bills in order to win political support for trade liberalization. The terms of access (less rigid eligibility and speedier delivery) and level of benefits have been expanded over the years. Even so many requests for assitance have been rejected, partly because of the difficulty in establishing whether trade was in fact the major cause of labour displacement.

As part of its NAFTA implementing legislation, the United States introduced a special NAFTA–TAA programme. This goes further than the traditional TAA in that it offers assistance to workers displaced by production shifting offshore to Mexico (or Canada), as well as workers displaced either directly or indirectly by imports. In addition, farm workers or family farmers not covered by UI are eligible.

Weston points that there is no financial mechanism in the NAFTA for addressing labour adjustment or social policy issues in the three countries. With an expanded hemispheric membership, it would be appropriate for the Inter-American Development Bank (IDB) to fund social programmes to help countries adjust to economic integration and to strengthen labour standards covered by the agreement.

In chapter 9 Richard G. Dearden provides an overview of the 'Trade disputes and settlement mechanisms under the Canada–US Free Trade Agreement'. The Canada–US FTA's dispute resolution mechanisms have been responsive and workable, providing a way to enforce the FTA's structure of rules and obligations which has imposed a positive discipline on the enormous trading relationship between Canada and the United States. This chapter highlights the operation of the FTA's dispute resolution mechanisms, discusses some of the panel decisions rendered under the FTA and concludes with an analysis of the effectiveness of the FTA's dispute settlement system in the resolution of trade disputes between Canada and the United States over the past five years.

Anti-dumping and countervailing duty disputes were affected in two significant ways by Chapter 19 of the Canada–US Free Trade Agreement: (1) no amendments could be made to existing anti-dumping and countervailing duty laws without notification and consultation with the other party; and (2) binational panels were created to review final anti-dumping and countervailing duty determinations rendered by the various governmental agencies relating to international trade. However, the FTA and NAFTA did not alter the substance of existing anti-dumping and countervailing duty laws. In this way, each country reserved the right to apply its anti-dumping law and countervailing duty law to goods imported from the territory of the other party. The parties also reserved the right to change or modify their anti-dumping law and countervailing duty law. However, if a party proposed to amend an anti-dumping or countervailing duty 'statute', notification and consultation requirements arise and a binational panel review could be invoked.

Dearden examines the effectiveness of the binational panels that were established under the Canada–US Free Trade Agreement in resolving trade disputes. If effectiveness is measured against the goal of ensuring a predictable commercial environment for business planning and investment, then, the FTA's dispute resolution mechanisms improved predictability, but in no way guaranteed security of access for Canadian exporters to the US marketplace. The experience reviewed by Dearden reveals that domestic interests in both countries were very aggressive in using trade remedies and in defending the use of non-tariff barriers to restrict access of foreign goods and services.

In regard to the effectiveness of the binational panels that were established during the operation of the Canada–US Free Trade Agreement, Dearden argues that Canadian exporters should be quite pleased with the outcome of panel results under Chapters 18 and 19; his assessment is not based upon a win–loss record. In the case of general disputes, Canada could rely upon rules with time-limits to seek to resolve disputes with the United States.

According to Dearden the lack of use of Chapter 18 panels may be due in part to the fact that the parties wanted certainty in the outcome of the resolution of a dispute, something which may occur when you negotiate the solution, but not when the decision is left in the hands of a panel of five experts. In the first Chapter 18 panel decision (*Pacific Salmon & Herring*) the panel provided the parties with its solution to the problem although its terms of reference did not ask for this advice. This proposed solution reportedly surprised the parties. They subsequently negotiated a solution that was close to the one the panel recommended.

Dearden concludes that Chapter 18 FTA panels' reasons, and effectiveness in general, suffered as a result of a lack of resources. The panels should be given technical support such as that provided to GATT panels by its Secretariat.

In chapter 10 Raúl E. Sáez provides data on 'Trade and investment between Canada and the LAIA countries' in order to offer a quantitative overview of the economic relations between Canada and Latin America; his analysis is restricted to the relatively larger countries of the Western Hemisphere.

Canadian exports to the Western Hemisphere have grown from just under US$2 billion in 1986 to US$2.5 billion in 1993, with exports to the LAIA countries rising from US$1.5 billion to US$2.1 billion. The most dynamic export market for Canadian products in the region has been Mexico, which has replaced Brazil as Canada's largest market, with exports doubling between 1986 and 1993. Canadian imports from the Western Hemisphere grew from US$2.6 billion in 1986 to US$5.1 billion in 1993, while those from the LAIA countries rose from US$2.1 to US$4.5 billion. Imports from Mexico are by far the largest from the region, rising from US$849 million in 1986 to US$1.6 billion in 1990, then jumping to US$2.9 billion in 1993.

In short, the Western Hemisphere, including LAIA, is not yet a significant trade partner for Canada. About 2 per cent of Canadian exports go to countries in the Western Hemisphere other than the United States, and about 3 per cent of imports come from these same countries. From the perspective of Latin American countries, Canada is still a relatively small trade partner. In spite of the increase in both exports to and imports from Canada, the share of Canada as a market for exports and as a source of imports is not rising. Both from a Canadian and a Latin American perspective, trade with the rest of the world is, in general, growing faster than between the two. Reversing this trend should be the goal of economic relations between Canada and the Americas in the future.

With respect to foreign direct investment (FDI), Canada has been an important foreign investor in Bolivia, Brazil and Peru. In each of these countries Canada's share in the foreign capital stock among developed countries is above 5 per cent. In Argentina, Venezuela and Colombia the figure is between 2 per cent and 3 per cent. However, in some countries Canadian investment has recently become more significant than in the past. In countries such as Bolivia, Brazil and Chile, Canadian foreign investment has accounted in recent years for 20 per cent or more of the flows of FDI from developed countries. The result is that Canada has become the second or third most important source of FDI in these countries in the 1990s.

1 NAFTA in the World Economy: Lessons and Issues for Latin America

Bruce W. Wilkinson

1 INTRODUCTION

This chapter discusses the nature of NAFTA, how it might evolve both institutionally and geographically, and what its effects might be. It also outlines how Canadian interests may diverge from those of the United States, and in this context considers the costs and benefits of additional Latin American nations joining NAFTA, including the social implications. The chapter is organized as follows: section 2 discusses what NAFTA is and what it is not; section 3 examines potential expansion of NAFTA (with a particular emphasis upon the role and characteristics of US policy); and section 4 considers NAFTA in the world economy. My main conclusions are:

1. NAFTA membership will not be an easy solution to Latin America's current economic problems. The economic gains are likely to be limited, and membership will, in fact, preclude many of the governmental policies that originally enabled all today's major industrialized nations, as well as the newly industrialized nations of Asia, to become what they now are.
2. The future of NAFTA and its implications for the Americans and the world trading order will depend primarily on what the United States decides is in its own interests.
3. Yet NAFTA is unlikely to lead to increasingly protectionist blocs.
4. NAFTA should give us cause for concern about the international social order and the well-being of the masses.

2 NAFTA: WHAT IT IS AND WHAT IT IS NOT

What It Is

NAFTA is much more than a simple free trade agreement, even though many in Canada still see it as no more than a classic free trade deal (e.g. McDonald, 1993), unrealistically relying on the absence of any formal, general external tariff.

Americans are not so naive, and are much more willing to admit that NAFTA is an economic integration arrangement in the process of being completed rather than a free trade area, for even without formal agreement on a common external tariff, competition will force member countries to reduce their tariffs on capital goods and intermediate components in products to the lowest level of any of them (Morici, 1994: 11–12). Pressure thus exists for a common external tariff to evolve. In NAFTA, the resulting tariff is unlikely to be a compromise between the highest and lowest tariffs of the member nations. Rather, it will probably be what the United States already has, or desires.

Also, detailed rules of origin requiring high North American content have been established for a wide range of consumer goods, providing much the same protection against non-member countries as a common external tariff (Morici, 1993; 1994: 12). Finally, NAFTA's other wide-ranging provisions also establish it as an economic community in the making.[1]

In addition to these many integrative features, the fact that already about two-thirds of Canadian–US trade and 50 per cent of US exports to Mexico are simply shipments from transnational firms to their affiliates (Vernon, 1994: 31) points to the formation of a closely-knit economic community with a great spectrum of national rules and regulations in Canada and Mexico gradually being harmonized to conform with US regulations and the US view of how the community ought to evolve.[2]

It is important to emphasize that the US vision goes beyond harmonization. Morici (1994), for example, argues that a considerably stronger institutional framework is needed for NAFTA to develop and administer dispute settlement issues, relations with non-members, and the wide variety of industrial policies relating to research and development and state-provincial procurement, regional subsidies and disciplines on governments attempting to develop new policies to circumvent current NAFTA-imposed constraints on their traditional policy tools.

What It Is Not

While NAFTA is, in so many ways, a comprehensive economic integration arrangement rather than a traditional free trade deal, *it lacks a number of the beneficial characteristics of a common market-economic integration agreement.*

First of all, it is not an example of 'plurilateral regionalism' or 'a model of equals' as it has sometimes been understood in Canada (Lipsey, 1992: 108; Lipsey, Courant and Purvis, 1994: 509). One can hardly call an agreement where one partner, the United States, is eleven times larger than the next biggest partner, with a GDP comprising over 85 per cent of the area total, and which absorbs 75 per cent and 82 per cent of the exports of the other two countries, thereby making them extremely dependent upon it for their export and domestic prosperity, an example of a model of equals.

Morici does suggest a need for sensitivity to the sovereignty concerns of the national governments involved, but he fails to address the overwhelming US dominance which gives it the muscle and bargaining power to impose its own perspective on many issues. Nor does he give any attention to the leverage power of special interest groups within the US political system.

Second, NAFTA does not provide a set of harmonized rules and regulations on how dumping and subsidies should be defined and dealt with among the members. The United States continues to be able to use, without restraint and for protective purposes, its detailed laws and precedents, which are by far the most comprehensive in the world. That this is so is also further evidence of the assertion in the previous paragraph that NAFTA is certainly not a model of equals. Canada entered the NAFTA negotiations 'on the explicit understanding' that these issues, left unsettled in the Canada–US economic integration agreement, would be determined in NAFTA (MacLaren, 1994: 4–5). But even as supporters of NAFTA agree, these hindrances to market integration were left unresolved (Lipsey, Schwanen and Wonnacott, 1994: 127). In fact, under NAFTA there is now even less commitment to do anything about them than there was under the Canada–US deal.

Third, NAFTA does not provide for any inter-country cooperation on technological progress. NAFTA has nothing comparable to the variety of European Union (EU) programmes to encourage research consortia. In fact, Canadian-based firms are generally prevented from joining US government-supported consortia by means of US 'patent, national competitiveness and national defence legislation' (Caldwell, 1993: 2).

Fourth, NAFTA does not provide for any transborder assistance from the prosperous countries or regions to the disadvantaged ones, such as the section of the Single European Act of 1986 entitled Economic and Social Cohesion, which commits the member countries to 'reducing disparities between the various regions' (article 130A) and to coordinating their economic policies to achieve these objectives (article 130B).

Fifth, and closely related to the preceding point, unlike the EU, NAFTA makes no provision for a *common approach* to enhancing management–labour relations, or to improving working conditions such as the health and safety of workers (article 118A–1), or for promoting the interests of small and medium-sized firms (article 130F–2). Nor is there anything comparable to the EU's Charter of Fundamental Social Rights, adopted in 1989.[3]

Finally, the EU provides for the mobility of workers across national borders which NAFTA does not – except for select groups of service, professional or business personnel.

Generally then, although the European system is far from perfect, it does have much greater provision for backward regions as well as for people disadvantaged by the greater integration of trade and investment than does the NAFTA, which virtually ignores these issues, or simply provides that each nation can retain its own standards.[4] This omission may perhaps be in part because the United States at this time has no interest in, or sense of responsibility to, any disadvantaged groups outside its own borders. Or it may be a function of the belief that *everyone* benefits from a liberalization agreement of this type, and so there is no need to provide assistance to losers. Whatever the rationale, the difference between NAFTA and the EU in this area is marked, even though in many other ways NAFTA bears all the characteristics of a supranational integration arrangement.

3 THE POTENTIAL EXPANSION OF NAFTA

NAFTA enlargement will depend on the attitudes and strategies of both existing membes and potential new members.

Canada

Canada is now an enthusiastic advocate of an expanded NAFTA. This was not always so. When the United States and Mexico announced their intention to pursue a trade and investment liberalization arrangement, Canada was not entirely pleased. It had seen its 1987 deal (effective 1 January 1989) with the United States only as giving it a degree of access to the US market which no other nation had (except tiny Israel).

When a quantitative assessment was done of the costs and benefits of Canadian participation, it was clear that net benefits would probably not be large. With only 0.5 per cent of Canadian exports going to Mexico and about 1.9 per cent of imports coming from there (at an average duty of 2.4 per cent, with over one-third of all *items* and 80 per cent of the *value* of imports already duty-free) (Government of Canada, 1993: 9) the estimated net gains of 0.1 per cent of GDP seemed reasonable.

The models used allowed for the increased competition for Canadian firms in the US market from the 2500 products both countries sell in common in the United States, expansion of Canadian imports from Mexico, some enlargement of Canadian exports to Mexico and a possible increase in investment in Canada if productivity and profits expanded (e.g. Harris and Cox, 1992; Brown, 1992; Roland-Holst et al., 1992; reviewed in Watson, 1993; Stanford, 1993). *On the cost side*, the models did *not* make adequate provision for such things as the ability of US buyers to play Mexican and Canadian suppliers against one another, the locational advantage of US firms in supplying Mexico, the implications of nearly two-thirds of Canadian industry (measured by sales) being foreign – often US – owned or controlled and the tendency to supply Mexico from parent locations in the United States rather than Canada, and the possible shift of manufacturing from Canadian to Mexican locations because of lower labour costs there. *On the benefit side*, the models did not fully account for the gains which may come as Canadian financial and resource-development firms invested in

Mexico, or for some modest increases in access to US government procurement programmes. But on balance, the estimates of minuscule gains for Canada were probably about right.

The decision to participate, therefore, was made for two other reasons: (1) to rectify weaknesses in the Canada–US Free Trade Agreement (FTA), such as a lack of agreement on the definition and handling of subsidies and dumping (MacLaren, 1994) – a goal which, as mentioned in the previous section, was not achieved; and (2) to forestall the advantages the United States might gain from a deal with Mexico to which Canada was *not* a party. Having a separate agreement with Mexico would give US producers privileged access to the Mexican market, duty-free access to lower-cost, labour-intensive Mexican inputs, and make the United States a favoured location for new investment designed to serve all of North America. At the same time, without these advantages, Canada would still face increased competition in the US market from Mexican goods, and not have a say in any agreement reached, to which it might later want to become a party (Lipsey, Schwanen and Wonnacott, 1994: 22–4).

The popularity of this 'hub-and-spoke' argument is fascinating, if not amazing, for it ignores (1) that Canada might have negotiated a separate deal with Mexico to offset the possible disadvantages of not being a party to the US–Mexico deal,[5] and (2) that even a tripartite deal does not eliminate the hub-and-spoke dominance of the United States, but only disguises it (Grinspun, 1993: 17–20). It may well be that Canada would not have negotiated as favourable a deal as it did by tagging along on the US coat tails. But on the other hand, it may not have had to give up some of the things it did either.

In any event, Canada went ahead, and today it is advocating negotiations for Chile to accede to NAFTA under the accession clause, and is also open to considering membership by other nations not only from Latin America but also such countries as Australia, New Zealand, Singapore and Korea. The government sees the expansion of NAFTA as contributing to greater global openness and increased multilateralism (MacLaren, 1994: 5–6). It also recognizes that the world economy is rapidly evolving. It sees it as important on the one hand, to encourage Canadian industry to adapt to these enormous changes, and on the other, to have

Canadian viewpoints and priorities reflected, if possible, in the new institutions being devised (Hart, 1993: 3–7). It would also undoubtedly like to see its enormous dependence on US markets reduced – an issue which has *become more pressing* as dependence has increased.

Since Canada has already taken the step of embracing Mexico in NAFTA, the possibility of an agreement with additional low-wage countries is not seen as adding significantly to the pressure from low-wage lands. Apparently the opportunities for, and stimulus to, Canadian firms to invest in and sell to these other nations are believed to outweigh any new competition from these countries in Canadian markets or in Canadian sales to the United States, and the potential for US buyers to play off Latin American suppliers against Canadian suppliers and vice versa.

However, given that 60–5 per cent of Canadian manufacturing and natural resource production (measured by sales) is foreign-owned, with decisions being made primarily in the interest of the parent companies situated in other countries, it may well be that the net benefits to Canada will not be as large as those who tend to ignore the massive foreign ownership of Canadian industry want to believe. But the hope seems to be that by bringing in additional partners, the current tremendous economic and political dominance of the United States in the NAFTA would be reduced.

In order for any new trade arrangements encompassing more nations in Latin America to have any really significant effects upon Canadian trade with this region, a major shift in priorities will have to occur in Canadian business initiatives and in the allocation of trade development resources of External Affairs and International Trade Canada (EAITC). Only 2 per cent of Canadian merchandise exports go to this entire region (with only about $200 million to Chile, although some Canadian resources firms have major investments in Chile). And although increased EAITC trade development resources have been assigned to Mexico, absolute decreases to the rest of Latin America and the Caribbean actually occurred between 1990 and 1993 (Cameron and Tomlin, 1994: 6–7).

It is reasonable to suggest, however, that whether NAFTA *per se* is enlarged to include other nations will not be determined by Canadian initiatives alone.

Mexico

There is one major reason why Mexico might not want to see NAFTA augmented by the addition of other Latin American nations. It would no longer enjoy the privileged position it now has of being the sole low labour-cost production location with tariff-free access to the US and Canadian markets. It would also face competition from new Latin American members in attracting foreign investment to production destined for sale in the United States and Canada.

Second, Mexico could well be better off negotiating bilateral trade and investment liberalization agreements with individual Latin American countries. This would give it improved access to these economies for its own products and enable it to capitalize on its head start in domestic market reform and liberalization, without necessarily sharing its greater access to the US market with them.

Of course, this policy would not preclude the United States or Canada from negotiating bilateral agreements with these other nations too.

This latter possibility suggests two reasons (not strong ones) why Mexico may favour other Latin American countries joining NAFTA. It would give Mexico some limited say in the negotiations which might otherwise go ahead on a bilateral basis. Also, additional members would increase the number of countries which might, on occasion, be able to side with it and Canada to influence US policy. But only if Brazil were included (which at this time seems unlikely), and perhaps not even then, would the combined weight and influence of Latin American nations plus Canada be much of a counterbalance to US economic power and influence.

On balance, then, it would not appear to be in Mexico's best interests to include other Latin American countries in NAFTA at this time.

Latin America Excluding Mexico

Net Gains: A Brief Assessment
By any measure, the trade gains from accession to NAFTA will be diminutive.[6] Total sales by all the Latin American nations *together* to the United States are less than Mexico's shipments to

that country. On average, only 25 per cent of these nations' exports now go to the United States. Their trade ties with one another, and/or with overseas nations such as Japan and the European Union (EU), are often considerably greater, such as Chile's with Japan. Entering NAFTA could thus result in trade diversion rather than net trade creation.

Second, many of the products they export to the United States are already entering relatively free of obstruction.[7] Chile in general faces lower tariffs vis-à-vis the United States than it does vis-à-vis a variety of other nations in South America, so in this respect it would be more valuable to Chile to have these other tariffs reduced than to enter a deal with the United States (Clark, 1994). What membership in NAFTA might do is simply lock these nations into a resource-sharing commitment, as Canada now has as a consequence of the FTA, so that in times of shortage, or even on other occasions, they would have less freedom in the sale and pricing of those resources internationally.[8] We should also note in this context that much of the current foreign direct investment into the mineral sector in countries like Chile, and the consequent job creation and prosperity, should not be attributed to the possibility of Chile entering NAFTA. Rather it is that (1) Chile now has a stable, democratic government which is attempting to follow sound macroeconomic policies, and (2) Chile has extremely rich and accessible ore resources, global demand for which will ensure their continued exploitation regardless of whether Chile is in NAFTA.

Third, a number of these countries' exports to the United States which are currently facing restrictions are not likely to gain much, if any, relief should they join NAFTA. Iron and steel from Argentina, textiles and clothing from Brazil and some Central American economies, cut flowers from Columbia, and apparel from Uruguay fall into this category. These products tend to have restricted access to the United States because of voluntary restraint agreements or the repeated application of US countervailing and anti-dumping duties, which are unlikely to be removed.

Fourth, it needs to be recalled that many countries are already successfully exporting manufactured products of all types to the United States without the benefit of a free trade agreement. Producers from these countries have been able, by employing contemporary technology to find market niches in the United States for their products, without the benefits of free trade.

Fifth, even for those countries and products that do benefit from greater access to the US market, the gains will be diluted the more Latin American nations join NAFTA and thereby end up competing with one another in the US market.

Sixth, the dilution of benefits applies to *investment* as well. One of the gains envisaged from membership is that the nations involved will be seen by the international community as more attractive places in which to invest. But the more nations join, the less will be the absolute amount of foreign investment going to any one of them.

The Mexican experience is instructive here. Studies in 1993 and early 1994 noted that much of the foreign investment was portfolio investment rather than direct investment. Where direct investment occurred, it was often in the service sector – fast food franchises, retail distribution, banking, cellular telephones, and the like. The motive seems to have been to increase control of the domestic market and/or provide new markets for the products and services of the international firms investing. Consequently, the import content of Mexican production and consumption rose substantially and the former Mexican trade surplus with the United States turned into a deficit.[9] The multinational firms in Mexico, and even domestically owned ones, generally seem to be more interested in short-term opportunities in distribution, finance and assembly operations than in development of longer-term technological capabilities in manufacturing (Unger, 1994; also Ruis-Napoles, 1994).

This result is consistent with the US view of itself as the main repository for the Americas of research and development and sophisticated technological production (Morici, 1994), and with the observed tendency for multinational firms to locate much of their advanced production in the largest market, in this case the United States (Niosi, 1994; see also Eaton et al., 1994: 64–5). It is also consistent with what has been observed in the EU where the large firms prefer to locate their sophisticated research and production in the central core areas rather than in peripheral areas such as Greece (Petrokos and Zichos, 1991; 1994). Even within the relatively small Canadian market this phenomenon has been observed as over the decades manufacturing firms have eschewed the maritimes as a place for investment in favour of central Canada, even though maritime locations would provide cheap sea transport to United States and other world markets.

To repeat, then, the trade and investment gains for individual Latin American nations from joining NAFTA may well be fairly minimal. This will be more so the greater the number of nations choosing to join and thereby diluting the benefits to any one of them.

Another set of considerations concerns the macroeconomic policies and market-oriented reforms which the United States is demanding as preconditions for membership. These transformations, which Mexico and to a large extent Chile have already instituted, imply considerable adjustment in the way economic policies are formulated in Latin America. Membership in NAFTA would mean, to a large degree, the locking in of these changes, so that even with a different government the nation would have little freedom to amend them, short of withdrawing from the NAFTA completely and suffering the dislocation to trade, industry and finance that this would mean.

To the extent that Latin American nations see these required policies as bringing long-term benefits, they may swing the pendulum in favour of NAFTA membership. On the other hand, if they do join, they should not expect to duplicate the outstanding success stories of the Asian Tigers, which relied on a wide variety of government interventions and policies, most of which would be precluded by either the preconditions or the NAFTA articles.[10]

The United States

US Objectives
The United States' position is quite different from Canada's. First, it appears to have little interest in extensions of NAFTA beyond the American hemisphere. George Bush's Enterprise for the Americas Initiative of 1990 remains the focus for US trade and investment intentions (Morici, 1994).·

Second, unlike Canada, which envisages a wider NAFTA as a move towards improved multilateralism *per se*, the major US concern seems to be to build a larger group of countries, closely knit by trade and investment concessions to one another, and under its leadership/domination, which will give it more bargaining chips and economic clout in discussions with the European Union and Japan in order to promote US exports to these areas

(Morici, 1994: 16). This US objective undoubtedly takes on greater significance in the context of current and projected EU expansion, and as Japan looks increasingly towards the Russian Far East, China and Mongolia for natural resources and for new markets for its high-technology production, and strives to increase its trade with areas around the Japan Sea and the rest of Asia, while simultaneously developing the cities on its west coast (Koyama, 1994).

Third, the United States sees its comparative advantage to be in technology-intensive products and related services. Accordingly, expanded Latin American markets for these products are a means of spreading R&D costs and keeping the sophisticated jobs in the United States, something Japan has been able to do through its expansion of markets in Asia (Morici, 1994: 7).

Fourth, an enlarged NAFTA will provide US buyers of raw materials and raw materials-based products greater scope for playing off the supplying countries, including Mexico and Canada, against one another so as to maximize the benefits to them.

Fifth, a formal agreement with Latin American nations will enable the United States to ensure that economic and political reforms will be locked in, so that future governments will not easily be able to reverse them (Morici, 1994).

One American view is that NAFTA need not be enlarged simply by other nations adhering to *all* the existing terms of NAFTA. Rather, there could be 'associate membership' for those countries prepared to instigate the market reform preconditions for membership and to adhere to many of the main provisions of NAFTA, without going the full distance towards a single united market. Alternatively, members of Mercosur, the Andean Pact, Caricom and CACM could be offered greater access to the US market in return for agreeing to certain things the United States was primarily interested in. These arrangements could be different in content and timing for different Latin American countries or groups of countries (Morici, 1994: 27–9; Whalley, 1993).

Once again, it is likely that the United States would be calling most of the shots. Other nations in the world clearly understand this. Japan certainly does. As Westney (1994: 57) observes:

Japanese policy makers and businessmen apparently believe that the United States will set the NAFTA terms relevant to Japanese investment, and therefore their strong focus on understanding and influencing US policy need not be modified significantly to take account of regional rather than national politics.

Although the net gains for South and Central American nations from accession to NAFTA may well not be large, and the new constraints on their policy-making fairly severe, substantial enthusiasm for accession exists. As a way of emphasizing the need for caution and in the hope that Latin America can learn from others' experiences, I shall highlight three characteristics of US institutions, attitudes and strategies.

US Characteristics

1. There is a diffusion of decision-making authority in the US political process which 'is unmatched among the industrialized countries' (Vernon, 1994: 39).

This has several consequences. First, it gives the administration tremendous leverage in international negotiations. Officials can, in effect, appear to be willing to go along with a particular position endorsed by another nation, but then not do so on the grounds that it would not be acceptable to Congress. Other nations, including Canada, cannot do this, for their negotiators are acting for the government which also controls the House of Commons.

Second, it allows vested interests in Congress to thwart what the Executive may have agreed in international discussions, or alternatively get special commitments from the president in return for supporting some agreement the Executive has made. For example, in return for supporting NAFTA some senators from wheat-producing states won an Executive commitment to launch a review of expanded Canadian durum wheat exports to the United States, even though the matter had effectively been resolved (in Canada's favour) using procedures set forth in FTA.[11]

Third, this complex system results in inconsistent laws vis-à-vis other nations. Canada, for example, has an arrangement with the US Department of Agriculture whereby it inspects and certifies potato exports to the United States in order to satisfy US grading standards. Yet, in spite of this agreement, the US Farm Bill requires random spot checks of Canadian potatoes entering the

US northeast, thereby hindering their flow and making them a less reliable source of supply (Government of Canada, 1994).

2. The United States sees itself as able to do things that it objects to other nations doing. The basic underlying criterion is whether the US interest is served, not whether policies are consistent or morally right.

Canada has certainly had numerous experiences of this. For example:

(a) The United States alleged Canadian firms were dumping potash in its market, at the same time as US firms were dumping potash abroad (Wilkinson, 1989).
(b) The United States says it is wrong for Canada to restrict the export of raw logs to them and that such action is countervailable, yet simultaneously the United States has restrictions on the export of raw logs.
(c) The United States accuses Canada of subsidizing durum wheat exports to them (which repeated FTA reviews say it has not been), while simultaneously the United States directly subsidizes durum wheat exports to third countries. They also subsidize exports by providing cheap water for irrigation (Wilkinson, 1986), and government-maintained inland waterways with no user tolls (Government of Canada, 1994: 1);
(d) At the same time that the United States was pressing Canada to remove restrictions on foreign direct investment, it passed the Exon-Florio Amendment to the 1988 Omnibus Trade and Competitiveness Act (section 5021) which 'empowered the President to suspend or prohibit any acquisition, merger or takeover by a foreign person on national security grounds' (ibid.: 17).

This attitude is also reflected in the lip-service the United States pays to the concepts of 'the level playing field' and 'letting the market work', which many Canadian economists have repeatedly swallowed and regurgitated (see Wilkinson, 1993). The level playing field argument is frequently used by the United States to justify the imposition of its patent and copyright laws, or national treatment laws for financial, manufacturing or other institutions in other nations, particularly less advanced nations. But it fails to recognize the great difference in technological expertise and economic strength between the United States and the foreign firms of these nations. It is also completely at odds with everything the United States itself stood for, and did, during its earlier history when it lagged far behind Britain and continental Europe in its technological and economic capability. Then, it saw protection and privileged support for its own industry as quite acceptable (even as it often does now) – and it certainly had little, if any, respect for other nations' patent or copyright laws.[12]

As for 'letting the market work', the same inconsistency arises. From the US perspective, the market should only be allowed to work if it works in what is perceived to be in the US interest. Government procurement restrictions are a good example, where the United States hides behind the veil of 'national security', never fully defined, to limit Canadian and other foreign bidding on US contracts. Or if foreign products like Canadian durum wheat seem to be having too much success in US markets, then the market must be controlled by US government intervention. Yet the United States wants to get rid of institutions like the Canadian Wheat Board on the grounds that it involves government interference in world wheat markets.

A related US tactic, when the market seems to be working too well and foreign exporters are gaining ground in the US market, is to launch an investigation of that particular foreign industry under one or another of the US contingency laws. This requires that the foreign industry provide, at its own expense, full cost and operating details of the different aspects of its production. The result is that US industry gets, free of charge, full information on a competitor's operation – which it could probably get by no other means – thus enabling it to see where and how it needs to improve its own performance to be more competitive. A neat trick! (Benoit, 1994).

3. The United States has a particular view of its manifest destiny in the Americas and the world, which has important implications for the future of Canada, and Mexico, and probably for all the Americas.

The United States has long seen itself as somehow divinely commissioned to be in charge of the Western Hemisphere. This attitude, or vision, sometimes very actively pursued, sometimes dormant, has persisted for over two centuries and shows no sign of disappearing. It is the cornerstone of the US view of itself in the world.[13] In so far as Canada has been concerned, it was there even prior to the American Declaration of Independence when American troops invaded Montreal and then Quebec City in an attempt to seize Canada and make it the fourteenth American colony. It was present when the United States invaded Canada in 1812, and again when John L. Sullivan, editor of the New York *Morning News*, declared on 27 December 1845 that international law was irrelevant and that it was the United States' 'manifest destiny to overspread and to possess the whole of the continent which Providence has given us' (Weinberg, 1935: 145). It was also apparent in 1867 when the US House of Representatives unanimously condemned the formation of Canada as an independent nation, and when the United States attempted to use the Manitoba Red River Rebellion of the 1880s to annex all the land from Manitoba to Vancouver. It was clear when Mr Armour, the US Ambassador to Canada during the negotiation of the 1935 trade agreement between Canada and the United States under the authority of the US Reciprocal Trade Agreements Act, wrote to US Under Secretary of State William Phillips that the agreement was a means of 'bringing Canada not only within our economic but our political orbit' and of shifting Canada more towards being a resource exporter and away from manufacturing which competes with US production. And it was present when Clayton Yeutter, the US Trade Representative, said on 3 October 1987 shortly after the CUFTA was signed: 'We've signed a stunning new trade pact with Canada. The Canadians don't understand what they've signed. In twenty years, they will be sucked into the US economy' (*Toronto Star*, 6 October 1987).

More recently we see this perspective expressed in relation to Mexico as well, when former President Jimmy Carter, in defending the incipient NAFTA, said, on 14 September 1993, that one reason why the United States should make the deal with Mexico was that without it, 'The Japanese and others will move in and take over *the markets that are basically and rightly ours*' (emphasis added). Why are Mexican markets 'basically and rightly' theirs? Does the United States accept that the markets of the nations adjacent to the EU rightly belong to the EU, and that those of nations in close proximity to Japan are rightly for the Japanese only? One can only make sense of this attitude by harkening back to the US view of its own supposed destiny.

Many Canadian economists, politicians and businessmen have never heard of, or choose to ignore, or make light of, this US manifest destiny perspective and its possible implications for the future of Canada. I am suggesting that Canada – and indeed Latin America too, in view of the Enterprise for the Americas Initiative – should treat it seriously and factor it into their thinking and negotiations.

US Negotiating Ploys
Latin America would do well to take note of a number of negotiating techniques employed by the United States to protect its own interests and to ensure US interests are protected:

1. Openly express an interest in negotiating an agreement with a prospective partner, and then when enthusiasm is generated in that country, back off, show little interest and implicitly or explicitly express a need to be persuaded that it will be in US interests to participate.

This is what happened in the Canadian case,[14] and it has been occurring again with regard to Chile and Argentina (*Financial Post*, 10 September 1994; *Edmonton Journal*, 2 September 1994). It will be interesting to see how Chile responds under the circumstances.

2. Set forth conditions which the prospective partner must fulfil as *preconditions* for entering negotiations, when in fact such items could rightly be considered items that should be part of the negotiations themselves – things which the prospective partner might be prepared to give up in return for concessions from the United States.

This approach enables the United States to gain certain benefits ahead of time without giving up anything. Then they can go on with negotiations and extract *additional* concessions from partners in return for concessions from themselves. A good example of this is the demands put on Canada for greater patent protection for pharmaceuticals and some easing of foreign investment review procedures prior to entering FTA negotiations. The same type of thing has been occurring vis-à-vis Chile with regard to providing intellectual property protection on pharmaceuticals and computer software and other changes (Clark, 1994: 5). Certainly, for Canada and Latin America the gains from any increase in domestic pharmaceutical research expenditures are unlikely to come close to compensating for the higher drug costs that accrue to taxpayers.

3. Once negotiations commence, delay discussion of concessions that the other party is interested in obtaining until close to the deadline for conclusion of negotiations, pressure is on for a deal to be reached and the hopes of the other party are high that a deal will be reached. Then present unreasonable proposals in the hope that the other party will accept them, simply because it is now emotionally or otherwise committed to reaching an agreement.

This is, of course, the tactic of the car dealer. It was used by the United States in the FTA negotiations when it delayed discussing the definition of acceptable subsidies until nearly the closing date. Then its proposal would have meant that almost all Canadian production subsidies would have been countervailable whereas none of US ones would have been. It is not surprising that Canada could not go along with it.

This example leads directly to another US tactic.

4. When no intention exists of changing something, use delaying tactics which give the impression that something is going to be done, but which require next to nothing to happen.

Canada entered the FTA negotiations with its foremost desire being agreement on the definition of acceptable subsidies and cross-border pricing arrangements (dumping), so that Canadian products would not be constantly harassed by US allegations and actions. No agreement was reached, and instead provision was made in the FTA for the matter to be worked on over the ensuing 5–7 years. This work never really got off the ground, with the reason being given that it was best to wait and see what transpired in the Uruguay Round. The Uruguay Round did not resolve the matter and NAFTA provisions now effectively shelve the entire problem with no real commitment to do anything in the foreseeable future (see section 2 above).

5. To help gain acceptance in the partner country of negotiations being undertaken and for any agreement concluded, enlist the support of US multinationals operating in that country to convince the populace of the merits of it all.

Again, Canada certainly experienced this strategy in the FTA, particularly through the membership of US multinationals on the powerful lobby group, the Business Council on National Issues. Chile can expect to experience the same type of pressure in the Chilean–American Chamber of Commerce which has a well-established office in Santiago to work on free trade.

6. Make a list of the concessions they did not get into the first agreement, and at the next available opportunity pursue these.

In the US legislation that brought FTA into effect, a variety of desired concessions were set forth, including such items as greater liberalization of investment, protection of intellectual property rights, greater liberalization on telecommunications and the inclusion of more services. The United States then used these as part of the price Canada had to pay to be a party to the US–Mexico negotiations.

These US characteristics and approaches have been outlined because all too often the discussion among economists is limited to the narrow results of pure trade theory, or econometric or computable general equilibrium models, with insufficient attention being given to the political economy factors involved. Yet it is these political economy considerations which will often determine the long-run outcomes. Helleiner (1993) has made this point very well in pointing out that although pure trade theory suggests the small country will gain the most from a free trade deal, once the difference in bargaining power is factored in, the opposite is likely to be true.

Lessons for Latin America

The foregoing analysis gives rise to two key questions:

1. Should Latin American nations be trying to join NAFTA? and

2. If they do decide to negotiate for membership, how do they maximize the benefits and minimize the costs of such membership?

The broad answer to both questions is essentially the same. Membership should only be considered and net benefits will only be maximized if the nations involved view such membership *not* as their only option and their only hope for survival in our globalized world, but simply as one of a number of options they might exercise if the terms are sufficiently favourable.

If, however, they believe NAFTA membership should be negotiated at all costs, then it is likely that the outcome of negotiations will be far less favourable than if they had shown less eagerness and expressed more interest in following up one or more of their other options – such as entering trading arrangements with one another within Latin America, or developing closer ties with Europe or Asia, if negotiations for membership in NAFTA do not produce the results they want. Also, if the Latin American nations are to negotiate the best deal for themselves for membership in NAFTA, they would be well advised first to develop much closer ties with one another so that they can present a more united front. To do this it will be necessary for them to see one another not as rivals, but as partners working together in seeking a better world for their citizens. Above all, it will be important for them to assess very realistically the possible net gains from entering a deal with the United States. What has already been said above regarding the potential for export increases to the United States, and US attitudes and policies should serve to temper starry-eyed enthusiasm.

In addition, the Latin American nations should be developing detailed countervailing and anti-dumping duties, as well as safeguard laws, to parallel those in the United States, and have them in place *and be actively using them* prior to concluding any negotiations with the United States to enter NAFTA.

Also, these nations should be studying the Mexican experience very carefully, both with regard to such things as the impact of too rapid liberalization of agricultural trade and its effects on rural areas, and allowing virtually unrestrained capital flows, particularly of a portfolio and short-term variety. Inflows of such capital sustained the Mexican currency at an unrealistically high level, thereby helping to generate a large trade deficit, and ultimately they aggravated the outflow of funds when the balance of payments and financial crisis struck. There is much to be said for having some restraints on such flows in the form of a tax or other measure.

If the Latin American nations are not able to get concessions of this type, which they believe because of their smallness and/or stage of development are essential to their well-being, they should be prepared to walk away from the bargaining table and seek closer arrangements among themselves instead. They could do this much more readily if they had not initially hoodwinked themselves with overestimates of the potential net gains in exports and employment that they might achieve from somewhat greater access to the US market.

Another alternative South American countries might consider is negotiating separate agreements with Canada and/or Mexico. Each of these countries is likely to be more considerate of the perspectives which the Latin American countries bring to the bargaining table. At the very least, the rest of Latin America should be attempting to work cooperatively with Mexico and Canada to counterbalance US weight, rather than allowing themselves to be divided and conquered, so to speak.

In summary, the nations of Latin America need to see themselves as nations which together face a variety of opportunities waiting to be exploited. NAFTA in its most rigid form is only one of these.

4 NAFTA IN THE WORLD ECONOMY

Protectionist Blocs?

The question invariably arises: will the existing or an expanded NAFTA lead to the world being divided into three protectionist blocs under the leadership of the United States, the EU and Japan, respectively? Since the blocs already exist, the questions that remain are (1) how big will each one become? and (2) will each bloc become increasingly protectionist and inward-looking to the detriment of world trade generally?

Regarding the protectionist issue, the underlying US position has always been to protect and promote US industry, rather than bring about the well-being of the world economy (e.g. Lake,

1988, and references cited therein). Sometimes this has meant very high tariffs – such as in the nineteenth century, when the United States was building its industrial base to become competitive with Britain and Continental Europe, or in its post-World War II activity through the GATT, where domestic trade barriers have been reduced in return for greater access for American exports abroad.[15]

The question is whether current circumstances will push the United States to strengthen its protectionist wall or to reduce it in return for enhanced access to foreign markets outside NAFTA.

Certainly within the United States divergent views exist. Although it seems sometimes as though the increasingly protectionist view will prevail,[16] a number of forces will help to prevent this. From my perspective, the weight of evidence is that it is really not in the interests of the United States (or the EU or Japan) for the world trading and investment environment to collapse into highly protectionist solitudes as a consequence of an expanded NAFTA – or an expanded EU – for the following reasons.

First, with the exception of a couple of sectors such as automobiles, and clothing and textiles, an expansion of NAFTA is not expected to have major adverse (trade diversion) effects upon non-members. And to the extent that NAFTA results in some increased growth in member nations, any trade diversion that does occur may well be offset by increased imports to NAFTA from non-members (e.g. Wylie and Wylie, 1994). Therefore, little incentive will exist for non-member nations such as the EU or Japan to retaliate directly against any extensions to NAFTA.

Second, the United States is now the world's largest absolute debtor,[17] with net debts standing at between $508 and $556 billion, depending upon whether direct investment is valued at market value or current cost, respectively (*US Survey of Current Business*, June 1994). It continues to face annual current account deficits of over $100 billion. If it is ever going to be able to reverse its current account deficits and reduce its net international indebtedness, it will need access for its exports to other lands, so, although it will undoubtedly do everything possible to maximize its bargaining position, it will not want to see world trade and investment stifled.

Third, because the world, through trade and investment, has become increasingly integrated, the prosperity of the major trading nations depends much more upon the prosperity of one another than it did two or three decades ago. Business cycles, although not in perfect synchronization, are much more closely linked than they used to be, and not only the trade policies but also the monetary and fiscal policies of each of these nations have very important effects upon the others. It is in the interests of them all not to act in such a way that they bring down the rest. Increasing protectionism would do just that.

Fourth, multinational corporations (MNCs) are the dominant actors in today's trading and investment world, and it is very much in their interests to preserve a liberalized world trading and investment environment, because the magnitudes of the assets they hold and transfer internationally, and the volume of their world trade among parent companies, subsidiaries and affiliates, and with third parties – as they produce parts and components in a variety of countries and ship to other countries for assembly – are enormous.

For these reasons, I do not see NAFTA, or any additions thereto, being responsible for the world breaking up into highly protectionist blocs. There will be, or course, continuing pressures from some US firms to seek greater import protection, but this would occur whether NAFTA exists or not.[18]

Disadvantaged Groups

Who Are They? What Are The Problems?
A second and even more important area of concern relates to the changes taking place in trade and investment in the world economy of which NAFTA is only a part. The increase of income inequality as many are thrown out of work and others experience lower wages and reduced social benefits is a well-known phenomenon in many (not all) developed and developing countries (Robinson, 1993; 1994). Even where jobs are created by foreign capital, as in the maquiladoras in Mexico for example, they tend largely to be semi-skilled and unskilled ones (Kelly, 1987; Kopinek, 1994), and often they result in jobs elsewhere in the economy being destroyed as older factories are closed and/or agricultural production faces new competition from liberalized imports (Grinspun, 1993).

Where the work is of a more highly skilled nature, workers are often not rewarded commensurately, thereby preventing much of the labour force from sharing in the possible gains from new investment (Grinspun, 1993; Kopinek, 1994). We see, then, a growing divergence between the owners and managers of capital (and many professional people) on the one hand, and the labouring classes on the other.

In both developing and developed nations, the groups disadvantaged by structural shifts are almost invariably told by economists, businessmen and government officials that the changes are really for their benefit in the long run. But for many of them the particular long run involved may well be longer than their lifetimes.

Concomitantly, the scope for democratic decision-making may well be reduced as the smaller governments face increased policy restraints − restraints devised to free big business to act in their own profit- and growth-maximizing interests. This, plus the increase in income inequality, may well reduce the quality and stability of democracy (Muller, 1988).

Grinspun and Kreklewich see the NAFTA and other such economic integration agreements (like the EU) as 'a new form of conditionality that is being applied to restructure state–civil society relations in both industrialized and less-developed economies' (1993: 1). One of their comments is particularly perceptive:

> Conditioning frameworks, based on an international or transnational arrangement, are promulgated as if there were indeed a wide national and international consensus on what the policy objectives should be. This 'wide consensus' is really only achieved by different fractions of this transnational class, which is trying to dictate terms globally (or at least regionally). However, for public consumption the conditioning framework is packaged to appear as a national project. Thus, conditioning frameworks reconcile the policy needs of this transnational class with the political need to maintain the integrity and the illusion of the sovereignty of the nation-state. (ibid.: 12)

That there is validity to this argument can be seen from the results of a 1994 MORI poll for *The European* newspaper and quoted in *The Economist* (21 May 1994: 14), which indicates that substantially more people in Europe (49 per cent) were against a federal Europe than were in favour of it (32 per cent). And, perhaps surprisingly, this viewpoint was strongest in the stronger economies – Denmark (74 per cent), the Netherlands (73 per cent), Britain (68 per cent), Germany (67 per cent) and France (45 per cent). Yet, the Brussels bureaucrats and many in the halls of power in the individual countries are pushing forward with integration in spite of what the people may want. Do they actually have superior knowledge and wisdom based on definitive analyses and projections, or are they simply running on a bandwagon ideology that, as one writer put it, 'is a way of socializing the costs and privatizing the benefits of globalization' (Bernard, 1994: 88).

Another disadvantaged group consists of all those people who have jobs but are required to work longer hours and/or run faster and faster in order to 'keep up with the competition'. As a consequence, for many of these people work comes to dominate their lives completely, at the expense of family, friends and regular relaxation, posing a threat to human health and to the entire social structure built around the family. We need to think about these consequences as the current hectic pace of adjustment continues.

How Did We Get Here?
Essentially, our world seems to have come full circle since the early days of the industrial revolution when men, women and children worked long hours in unsafe, unhealthy working conditions for little pay, and businesses argued that they could not undertake improvements in working conditions and social benefits because to do so would make them uncompetitive.

A reaction to this heartless pursuit of profits and wealth occurred in the late nineteenth and early twentieth centuries on the European continent and in Britain with social legislation to improve working conditions and social benefits, which lasted in developed countries until well after the Second World War.

Gradually, however, a different type of problem arose. Governments in the Western developed world became ever larger and increasingly prone to looking after themselves in terms of salaries, benefits and pensions, while simultaneously buying off the populace with various goodies in order to stay in power. The populace in turn got into the habit on the one hand, of thinking that it was the government's job to 'fix' everything, and on the other hand, milking the system to obtain as large a share of benefits for themselves as they could.

Today we see a reaction to these phenomena particularly, though not only, in the English-speaking world led by the United States. It is typified by getting the government out of many activities by deregulating, privatizing, liberalizing international trade and by the reduction of government services. And it is underpinned by the ideology of 'letting the market work' – even if on occasion the market consists only of a few huge, world-wide, oligopolistic firms dominating a particular industry. The market has become god, and competition is its mate; we worship at the altar of ruthless efficiency and materialism. Workers are mere 'inputs', and are often dispensable in the pursuit of profits, wealth and power. Worker benefits are frequently minimized as well, for the same reasons.

We are back to many of the perspectives which dominated the industrial revolution. But we have also lost something in the process of coming full circle. The market ideology is generally not undergirded by a solid foundation of moral-ethical values. All too frequently the only thing that matters is 'winning', 'maximizing profits', 'looking after oneself', and the like. Of course, this latter set of 'values', if one dare call them that, also provides for ignoring the market too if 'winning' requires it. This is generally the prerogative of the rich and powerful, be they corporations or nations. We have seen it in the approaches the United States has used. And we see it in the observation of Kenichi Ohmae not many months ago when he suggested that if the European Union and Japan really liberalized their markets to world trade, they could experience 40 per cent unemployment.

What Do We Do Now?
There is a tendency on the part of many economists subscribing to the neoclassical view of the world and the competition-is-supreme ideology to dismiss completely any views or research which dare to question the nature and implications of this narrow theory and ideology. This is unfortunate, especially when the world is in such a convulsive state of change, for our end-goal should not be the triumph of a particular ideology, but human welfare maximization, not just at some later point, but during the process of instituting these changes.

It has been said that the prospect of imminent death concentrates the mind. I have often wondered whether it would also clarify or alter the thinking of economists and others, who adhere rigidly to their neoclassical analysis and ideology of the day, if they were told that they would have neither jobs nor welfare support until they came up with alternative ways of bringing about change in the world economy, which would minimize the suffering for the masses of people.

We should be asking ourselves some of the bigger questions instead of just assuming that the way we are proceeding will get us to where we want to go with the lowest possible amount of human adversity.

There are no easy answers to today's situation. A good beginning would be for economists to peer beyond the narrow confines of neoclassical theory and the current competition-is-supreme ideology to re-examine some of the other views of the so-called fathers of today's analysis. Adam Smith and his book, *The Theory of Moral Sentiments*, with its emphasis upon such basic virtues as honesty, generosity, kindness and respect for others, as counterweights to raw pursuit of self-interest, would be a good place for them to start. So would the work of John Bates Clark,[19] one of the originators of neoclassical marginal analysis. He wrote in 1887:

> Nothing could be wilder or fiercer than unrestricted struggle of millions of men for gain, and nothing more irrational than to present unrestricted struggle as a scientific ideal. . . . If competition were supreme, it would be supremely immoral; if it existed otherwise than by sufferance, it would be a demon.

Frank Knight, one of the leading figures at the University of Chicago in the early decades of the twentieth century, is thought-provoking. He believed that competition fails as a basis for human motive or action. In his words:

> Thus we appear to search in vain for any really ethical basis of approval for competition as a basis for an ideal type of human relations, or as a motive for action. It fails to harmonize either with the Pagan ideal of society as a community of friends or the Christian ideal of spiritual fellowship. Its only justification is that it is effective in getting things done; but any candid answer to the question, 'what things', compels the admission that they leave much to be desired. (Knight, 1935: 15)

Or, more recently, A.K. Sen has argued:

> Why should it be *uniquely* rational to pursue one's self-interest to the exclusion of everything else? ... To see any departure from self-interest maximization as evidence of irrationality must imply a rejection of the role of ethics in actual decision-taking ... (1987: 15)

In short, there is lots of good material around for us to build on as we think afresh of bringing about adjustments in the world in ways that place people above property and profits, and compassion above narrow economic efficiency. Social policy considerations will have to become more important as we proceed, not less so.

Let us hope that in NAFTA, as it is now or in some expanded form, there is room for this type of thinking.

2 Mercosur and Preferential Trade Liberalization in South America: Record, Issues and Prospects

Roberto Bouzas

Mercosur is a customs union encompassing 50 per cent of the population, 58 per cent of the gross domestic product and 40 per cent of the total foreign trade of the Latin American Integration Association (LAIA) (Table 2.1).[1] The four Mercosur countries, Argentina, Brazil, Paraguay and Uruguay, have a population of 200 million and an aggregate GDP of over US$800 billion. In 1994 their total foreign trade was over US$117 billion.

Table 2.1 Mercosur: Summary Information, 1994

	Argentina	Brazil	Paraguay	Uruguay	Merc-osur	Percentage of LAIA
Population (millions)	33.8	153.6	4.7	3.1	195.3	49.4
GDP (US$ billion)	270.8	532.3	6.6	14.1	823.8	57.7
GDP per capita (US$)	8004.0	3465.0	1400.0	4511.0	4218	na
Total exports (US$ billion)	15.2	43.3	1.2	1.8	61.6	43.8
Total imports (US$ billion)	19.4	32.0	2.0	2.7	56.1	36.7
Total foreign trade (US$ billion)	34.6	75.3	3.2	4.6	117.7	40.1
Foreign trade coefficient (X+M/GDP)	12.8	14.1	48.9	32.4	14.3	na

na: not applicable.

Source: World Bank (1994) and CEPAL (1994a).

Mercosur is a heterogeneous group: Brazil is a continental economy which contributes about two-thirds of regional output, with 80 per cent of the population and an extensive industrial base. Argentina, in turn, accounts for most of the remainder. Indeed, the two larger countries contribute 97 per cent of total population and output. Per capita GDP also differs markedly among the four partners: the relatively high per capita income of Argentina (US$8004) is almost six times Paraguay's (US$1400). Partly reflecting differences in country size, the national foreign trade coefficients are also disparate: two-way foreign trade represents 12.8 per cent of GDP in Argentina, 14.1 per cent in Brazil, and over 30 per cent in Uruguay and Paraguay (the smallest and relatively most open economies).

This chapter is divided into five sections. The first reviews Mercosur's record in the 1991/4 transition period. The second section addresses the issues and prospects raised by the establishment of the customs union as of January 1995. The third section deals with a number of areas which go beyond a 'minimalist' agenda (investment, financial services, government procurement and competition policy). The fourth section briefly reviews Mercosur's external trade agenda, particularly with regards to the North American Free Trade Agreement (NAFTA), LAIA and the European Union (EU). The final section summarizes some conclusions.

1 AN ASSESSMENT OF THE 1991/4 TRANSITION PERIOD

The Asunción Treaty signed on 26 March 1991 established that by 1 January 1995 Argentina, Brazil, Paraguay and Uruguay would have completed the transition towards a common market (Mercosur). The two main instruments placed in motion at the time were a four-year Trade Liberalization Programme (TLP) and a commitment to implement a Common External Tariff (CET) by January 1995. The treaty also established the objective to coordinate sectoral and macroeconomic policies, but no specific procedures or calendars were set.

The TLP included two main components, namely: (1) a linear and automatic import tariff reduction programme, and (2) a commitment to remove all non-tariff barriers (NTBs) to intra-regional trade. Implementation of the TLP would thus lead to the establishment of a free trade area among the four countries by January 1995. The CET, in turn, would be negotiated during the transition period and enforced as of January 1995. The Asunción Treaty created two inter-governmental bodies: the Common Market Council (CMC) and the Common Market Group (CMG). The CMC, composed of the four countries' ministers of foreign relations and economics, was the body in charge of providing political leadership to the process. The CMG was the executive agency in charge of overseeing and implementing the treaty, enforcing CMC decisions and establishing the schedule to move towards the common market. The treaty established that during the transition period decisions would be taken by consensus. Member countries also made a commitment to decide upon a permanent governing structure by year-end 1994. Three annexes to the treaty defined a rules of origin regime, a dispute settlement mechanism and escape clause procedures applicable to the transition period.

Preferential Trade Liberalization

Unilateral trade liberalization by member countries provided a favourable background to the success of the Trade Liberalization Programme. Starting from a 47 per cent preference margin in March 1991, the TLP established a programme for tariff reduction in semi-annual instalments to reach a 100 per cent preference margin by year-end 1994. The TLP also authorized countries to exempt a limited number of goods from the tariff liberalization schedule,[2] with the number of products included in such lists to be cut by 20 per cent each year until completion of the free trade zone by the end of 1994.[3] By late 1994 the preference margin for intra-regional trade was more than 90 per cent, and the two largest partners had only about 80 tariff items covered by the exemptions regime.

Progress in removing non-tariff barriers (NTBs) was slower and less uniform across countries. Again, the broader environment of unilateral trade liberalization and trade policy reform greatly contributed to less intrusive border NTBs. Notwithstanding its overall liberalizing trend, the Brazilian trade regime maintained a number of border restrictions on individual products and activities (such as prior authorization to import wheat flour and chemicals, or prohibitions on certain kinds of seeds, unbottled wine and leisure vessels). Furthermore, a number of non-border NTBs (such as government procurement practices) remained in force.

The Argentine record was somewhat different. Although the country underwent a rapid trade liberalization after 1989, by 1992 a number of *ad hoc* measures had partly reversed the trend. In response to an import surge Argentine authorities raised the statistical surcharge from 3 per cent to 10 per cent on a non-discriminatory basis in mid-1992. This decision angered Mercosur partners, and Argentina eventually exempted all Paraguayan and certain Uruguayan imports from the higher surcharge, but continued to levy it upon fast-growing imports from Brazil. Similarly, rapid import growth in 1993 and 1994 led Argentine economic authorities to impose non-discriminatory specific duties and quotas on selected paper and textile products and to make extensive use of anti-dumping procedures, which included goods purchased from Brazil. Import quotas were also established under the provisions of the Asunción Treaty safeguard clause.[4]

Trade and Investment Flows

Accompanying the unilateral and preferential removal of tariffs and border NTBs, intra-Mercosur trade flows increased rapidly in the transition period. In effect, the value of intra-regional total exports jumped from US$4.1 billion in 1990 to a total of US$11.6 billion in 1994 and up from just US$2.6 billion in 1986. Although this rapid growth has been partly stimulated by the easy credit conditions and real exchange rate appreciations of the early 1990s, the fact that the rate of growth of intra-regional imports has outpaced that of total purchases abroad suggests that growing trade interactions have had more solid foundations than merely short-term exchange rate movements or transient import booms (Table 2.2). Trade intensity indices greater than one also suggest significant structural trade interaction among Mercosur partners. The increase in these indices in the 1990–3 period (particularly for trade between the two largest partners) indicates a consistent expansion of trade interactions[5] (Table 2.3).

Traditionally, Argentina and Brazil have been important trade partners for the smaller economies of the region: indeed, between a third and a half of total Paraguayan and Uruguayan two-way

Table 2.2 Mercosur Export/Import Trade, 1990–4

	Mercosur Value (US$ million)					Percentage annual rate of growth (%)	World Value (US$ million)					Percentage annual rate of growth (%)
	1990	1991	1992	1993	1994		1990	1991	1992	1993	1994	
Exports:												
Argentina	1,833	1,977	2,327	3,684	4,737	26.8	12,352	11,964	12,235	13,117	15,739	6.2
Brazil	1,318	2,309	4,128	5,397	5,921	45.6	31,391	31,636	36,207	38,617	43,558	8.5
Paraguay	379	259	246	287	151[a]	−8.9[b]	959	737	657	694	413[a]	−10.0[b]
Uruguay	591	552	622	699	899	11.1	1,693	1,605	1,703	1,645	1,913	3.1
Imports:												
Argentina	876	1,805	3,765	4,214	5,129	55.6	4,079	8,276	14,872	16,784	21,544	51.6
Brazil	2,327	2,268	2,215	3,329	4,658	18.9	20,651	21,042	20,500	25,652	33,549	12.9
Paraguay	367	397	475	571	342[a]	15.8[b]	1,352	1,460	1,422	1,689	945[a]	7.7[b]
Uruguay	535	663	883	1,125	1,371	26.5	1,343	1,636	2,045	2,324	2,773	19.9

Notes: (a) First semester.
(b) 1990/3.

Source: INTAL (1995).

Table 2.3 Mercosur: Trade Intensity Indices[a]

	Argentina	Brazil	Paraguay	Uruguay
1986				
Argentina		13.56	35.27	44.93
Brazil	9.88		63.51	32.72
Paraguay	66.46	52.68		65.67
Uruguay	36.60	35.05	14.91	
1990				
Argentina		17.58	30.33	51.52
Brazil	17.18		30.62	22.61
Paraguay	48.70	49.76		29.23
Uruguay	40.48	45.26	9.66	
1993				
Argentina		28.34	59.64	61.85
Brazil	20.70		54.01	31.52
Paraguay	19.75	39.59		15.77
Uruguay	38.30	30.42	21.97	
Trade intensity change 1986/93				
Argentina		14.77	24.37	16.91
Brazil	10.82		−9.50	−1.20
Paraguay	−46.71	−13.09		−49.90
Uruguay	1.70	−4.63	7.07	
Trade intensity change 1990/3				
Argentina		10.76	29.31	10.33
Brazil	3.52		23.38	8.91
Paraguay	−28.96	−10.17		−13.46
Uruguay	−2.18	−14.85	12.32	

Note: (a) The trade intensity index measures the share of country i's exports to country j in i's total exports (X_{ij}/X_i) relative to the share of j's imports in world net imports $(M_j/M_w - M_i)$. An index above (below) unity indicates that the countries have a greater (smaller) trade than expected on the base of the partner's share in world imports.

Source: United Nations (1994)

trade flows take place with their larger Mercosur partners. Although trade concentration is less marked in the case of Argentina and Brazil, the reciprocal relative importance of these two countries has increased markedly in recent years. The shift has been more marked as regards the role of Argentina as a supplier of Brazilian imports and export outlet for Brazilian exports: in the 1990–3 period Argentina jumped from fifth to second place among the largest suppliers of Brazilian purchases abroad (only surpassed by the United States). Argentina also went up from being the tenth to the second largest market for Brazilian exports. In the same period Brazil remained Argentina's second largest supplier and became the most important market (up from second place at the turn of the decade).

One feature of recent Argentine–Brazilian trade flows has been the rapid growth of manufacturing trade (Tables 2.4 and 2.5). Lucangeli (1993) classifies Argentine–Brazilian trade in three broad categories, namely: (1) products in which one of the countries has an absolute advantage, which account for about one third of the value of total trade and display low indices of intra-industry trade (mainly food products and raw materials such as grains, fruits, vegetables, iron ore, selected seeds and oils); (2) manufactures with relatively high and stable intra-industry trade indices (particularly chemicals, machinery, transport equipment

Table 2.4   Argentine/Brazilian Total Trade Flows, 1984–93
(percentage and US$ billion)

Products	1984	1986	1988	1990	1991	1992	1993
Food and beverages (CUCI 0+1+22+4)	31.3	38.7	21.6	40.9	32.4	23.3	22.0
Agricultural raw materials (CUCI 2-22-27-28)	2.9	2.2	2.7	1.1	0.8	1.1	0.9
Oils and fuels (CUCI 3)	2.8	1.7	3.0	0.7	1.3	2.5	9.1
Minerals and metals (CUCI 27+28+68)	6.4	8.7	7.9	6.9	5.0	3.9	3.2
Manufactures (CUCI 5+6+7+8-68)	56.3	48.4	64.8	49.4	61.6	70.1	64.7
Non-classified (CUCI 9)	0.3	0.3	0.0	1.0	0.0	0.0	0.0
Total	100.0	100.0	100.0	100.0	100.0	100.0	100.0
Value (US$ billion)	1.329	1.376	1.579	2.059	2.974	4.280	6.300

Source: Data derived from Lucangeli (1993).

Table 2.5 Argentine/Brazilian Intra-industry Trade, 1984–93
(as a percentage of total trade)

Products	1984	1986	1988	1990	1991	1992	1993
Food products	20.6	12.1	12.3	3.2	11.2	15.4	13.5
Beverages and tobacco	64.3	79.0	53.6	51.8	50.0	24.7	27.8
Non-edible crude material	5.2	22.1	31.4	23.0	11.7	9.3	14.0
Oils and fuels	68.4	0.8	0.0	74.9	40.5	47.2	31.4
Edible oils	0.0	0.1	1.1	5.0	0.2	8.2	11.6
Chemicals	18.2	31.7	32.4	67.0	65.7	62.3	49.6
Manufactures classfied by material	6.0	8.2	13.6	34.4	25.7	17.7	27.9
Machinery and transport equipment	30.9	52.9	45.0	65.8	60.2	34.8	60.9
Miscellaneous manufactures	55.8	63.8	51.4	39.7	73.5	32.3	37.9
Total	18.0	23.4	26.2	37.8	35.6	28.5	38.8
Value (US$ million)	239.0	322.0	413.0	777.0	1,059.0	1,222.0	2,440.0

Source: Lucangeli (1993).

and photographic materials); and (3) miscellaneous manufactures and selected raw materials with volatile intra-industry trade indices and flows which are highly sensitive to prevailing macro-economic conditions (mainly dairy products, processed foods, textile and garments, paper, cardboard and wood products). Intra-industry trade seems to be significant in the chemical, machinery and transport sectors. As is well known, expansion of intra-industry trade is welcome because it reduces adjustment costs and allows both parties to reap the benefits of a broader variety of products and economies of scale.

The interaction between investment flows into and within the region and the prospect of a larger regional market are more difficult to identify. Foreign investment flows into the region have been mainly related to privatization programmes and, particularly in Argentina, rapid growth of domestic demand. Yet there is evidence that, at least in Argentina, Mercosur has been a contributing factor to a number of new investment endeavours. The automobile industry is a case in point, although it is difficult to separate incentives which stem from the integration process from those linked to the special sectoral promotion regime currently in operation. In fact, the Argentine automobile industry has been under a process of 'globalization' since the mid-1980s, stimulated by production specialization and complementarity with the larger and relatively more modern Brazilian car industry. In other sectors there is no direct or conclusive evidence that investment flows have been aimed at exploiting the advantages of a larger regional market (Chudnovsky et al., 1994). But the recent upsurge in foreign investment in sectors such as the food and paper industries may be laying the basis for future export expansion, even if their driving force so far has been rapid domestic demand growth rather than market enlargement.

Similarly, although no boom in intra-regional investment flows has taken place, since 1991 there has been unprecedented activity throughout the region involving both affiliates of foreign multinationals and domestic firms. By late 1994 there were 215 bilateral inter- and intra-firm initiatives, 43 per cent of which had direct production implications (Table 2.6). More than 300 Brazilian firms had some kind of investment commitment in Argentina, in contrast to just over 30 Argentine firms in Brazil. Brazilian firms engaging in intra-regional investment operate in diverse sectors and include some with a long-standing internationalization experience and others which have made their first inroads into investing in foreign markets through Mercosur, and particularly Argentina (Goulart et al., 1994).

Trade Liberalization and Macroeconomic Performance

Mercosur's unilateral and preferential trade liberalization process took place in a climate of macroeconomic instability, particularly in the two largest partners (Table 2.7). It is well known that trade liberalization (unilateral as well as preferential) may be endangered by excessive macroeconomic volatility. Indeed, unstable macroeconomic conditions may cause large shifts in competitiveness and give rise to destabilizing trade flows and irresistible demands for protection. The two largest Mercosur partners have displayed not only volatile but also divergent macroeconomic performances, and this asynchronism has been partly reflected in unstable bilateral real exchange rates and divergent domestic business cycles.

Table 2.6 Argentine /Brazilian Inter- and Intra-firm Initiatives (by November 1994)

	Number	Number
With trade implictions		37
Trade agreements	18	
Distribution agreements	7	
Offices/Tradings	12	
With productive implications		92
New plants	23	
Joint ventures	15	
Joint ventures/new plants	9	
Acquisitions	17	
Participation in capital	3	
Productive complementation	17	
Technological information	3	
Regionalization	5	
Services		86
Operational or complementation agreements	21	
Participation in capital	9	
Joint ventures	14	
Franchising	10	
Representations	2	
Affiliates	14	
Acquisitions	3	
Associations to participate in public bids	8	
Others	5	
Total		215

Source: Embajada de Argentina en Brasil (1994).

At the initial stages of Mercosur there was a considerable academic and policy debate as to the prospects of preferential trade liberalization among countries with highly unstable macroeconomic environments. A frequently heard argument was that, in order to promote rapid rates of growth in trade, closer macroeconomic coordination was required. Yet incentives to do

Table 2.7 Mercosur: Macroeconomic Indicators, 1986–94

	Argentina	Brazil	Paraguay	Uruguay
GDP growth rate[a]				
(% annual average)	3.2	2.0	3.4	3.9
(Variation coefficient)	149.4	169.6	59.0	79.2
Real exchange rate[b]				
(average 1986=100)	91.7	76.9	85.0	93.0
(Variation coefficient)	13.1	18.0	21.2	6.6
Fiscal deficit/GDP[c]				
(percentage average)	2.3	2.4	−1.3	0.9
(Variation coefficient)	108.3	134.9	125.6	155.1
Inflation				
(annual average)	780.5	1,144.7	23.8	72.6
(Variation coefficient)	194.6	63.5	38.8	32.9

Notes: (a) GDP for year 1994 are CEPAL estimates.
(b) Deflated by WPI. Data for Paraguay and Uruguay is 1986–93.
(c) Argentina: Non-financial central government. Brazil: Operational deficit non-financial public sector. Paraguay and Uruguay: central government. Data corresponds to 1987–93, except for Argentina (1987–94).
Source: CEPAL (1994a); CEI (1994).

so were very limited due to the relatively low level of economic interdependence at the outset of the integration process. This problem was temporarily eased by a combination of favourable circumstances. One was the relatively fluid access to international capital markets, which eased the financing of growing current account deficits (particularly in Argentina). Another was the fact that trade expanded rapidly both ways, thereby helping to maintain the momentum of the TLP. In effect, on the Argentina side rapid growth of imports (on aggregate terms and from Brazil in particular) after the Convertibility Plan (1991) was partly compensated by the fact that Brazil was also one of the fastest growing markets for Argentine exports. Conversely, Brazilian authorities were more ready to accept a pragmatic implementation of trade remedy laws or *ad hoc* measures on the part of Argentine authorities because total exports were growing rapidly anyway. Rapid expansion of two-way trade flows henceforth became a self-reinforcing mechanism.

At least temporarily, the implementation of the Plan Real in Brazil in 1994 brought about some degree of macroeconomic convergence among the two largest partners. As might have been expected with two countries of relatively tenuous economic interdependence, macroeconomic convergence was 'exogenous' to the integration process and mainly driven by domestic considerations. Yet 1994 can be regarded as a turning point in the favourable external economic environment which had prevailed since the early 1990s. The effect of rising international interest rates and the Mexican foreign exchange crisis of December 1994 severely restricted access to international capital markets. The fragile current account position of Argentina and the still precarious stabilization programme in Brazil have the potential of further macroeconomic divergence in the future. This may place renewed pressure upon the regional economic integration process, precisely at a time when flexibility has been constrained by the implementation of common trade policies. The rapid expansion of trade and investment interactions in the transition period may give cause to be reasonably optimistic that the flexibility required to accommodate macroeconomic disturbances will not lead to a reversal of the process of regional economic integration.[6]

2 THE CUSTOMS UNION: ISSUES AND PROSPECTS

After protracted negotiations, the Ouro Preto presidential meeting of December 1994 confirmed the setting up of a customs union as of January 1995. Compliance with the original commitment had been threatened by divergent national preferences as to the level and structure of the CET and the Argentine government's reluctance to bind its trade policy to that of Brazil.

Market Access Issues

Establishment of the customs union will not be immediately accompanied by unrestricted free trade among member countries. There will be a limited number of exceptions to intra-regional free trade included in the so-called 'convergence scheme' (régimen de adecuación). The scheme will enable countries to exempt a limited number of products from duty-free treatment until 1999, although Paraguay and Uruguay will have one

Table 2.8 Mercosur: Exemptions to the Free Trade Area

Mechanism	Argentina	Brazil	Paraguay	Uruguay
'Convergence regime'				
Tariff items	223	29	272	1018
Products[a]	Steel products (57%), textile products (19%), paper (11%), shoes (6%) Others include: tyres, wood products, canned peaches, refrigerators, orange juice, coffee and furniture.	Wool fabrics, canned peaches, rubber manufactures, wines	Textiles (57%), agricultural products (10%) Others include: shoes, steel products, wood, furs and skins, furniture	Textiles (22%) Chemical and pharmaceutical products (16%) steel products (11%), electric appliances and machinery (8%), transport equipment (8%), plastics (7%), food products (6%)
Initial preferences	Duty-free quotas, 10% initial margin of preference	Duty-free quotas, 20% initial margin of preference	10% initial margin of preference starting 1996	No initial margin of preference for 250 items
Duty-free as of	1.1.1999	1.1.1999	1.1.2000	1.1.2000
Finished vehicles and parts				
Tariff items		To be defined		
Agreements	Bilaterals agreements between Argentina and Brazil, Argentina and Uruguay and Brazil and Uruguay. Ad hoc group to elaborate proposal for intra-regional free trade before 1997.			
Duty-free as of	1.1.2000	1.1.2000	1.1.2000	1.1.2000
Sugar				
Tariff items	4	4	4	4
Agreements	*Ad hoc* group to propose a convergence regime. National policies maintained until approval of convergence regime			
Duty-free as of	1.1.2001	1.1.2001	1.1.2001	1.1.2001

Note: (a) The percentage indicates the number of tariff lines as a percentage of total tariff items included in the 'convergence regime'.

Source: Own calculations on the basis of official documents.

additional year to comply (Table 2.8). Intra-regional trade in these products will initially pay national tariff rates,[7] but these will automatically fall in annual instalments.

Table 2.9 Mercosur: Exemptions to the Customs Union

Mechanism	Argentina	Brazil	Paraguay	Uruguay
Goods converging towards the CET				
Capital goods				
Tariff items	approx.1000	approx.1000	approx.1000	approx.1000
Maximum CET	14%	14%	14%	14%
Convergence by	1.1.2001	1.1.2001	1.1.2001	1.1.2001
Informatics and telecommunications				
Tariff items	approx.300	approx.300	approx.300	approx.300
Maximum CET	16%	16%	16%	16%
Convergence by	1.1.2006	1.1.2006	1.1.2006	1.1.2006

National exemption lists
(A total of 300 tariff items can be included, 399 for Paraguay. Convergence by 2001 for Argentina, Brazil and Uruguay. Convergence by 2006 for Paraguay. Excludes exemptions as a result of the 'convergence regime', except for Argentina)

	Argentina	Brazil	Paraguay	Uruguay
Tariff items	471	286	214	212
Products[a]	Chemicals (29%-A) Steel products (23%-D), Electric materials and electric appliances (20%-D), Paper and shoes (11%-D), Plastics (4%-D)	Chemicals (31%-A/D), Petroleum derivatives (18%-D), Textiles inputs (11%-A), Stone and clay manufacturing (8%-A), Skins and furs (5%-A)	Chemicals (54%-A), Textiles (11%-A), Electric materials and machinery (A), Steel products (9%-A)	Chemicals (69%-A), Plastic materials (16%-A)

Notes: (a) The percentage indicates the number of tariff lines as a percentage of total exempted tariff items.
A = (ascendant).
D = (descendant).

Source: Own calculations on the basis of official documents.

In order to qualify for exemption under the 'convergence scheme', products had either to be previously included in national exemption lists or subject to Mercosur safeguard clause procedures. The objective of the 'convergence scheme' is to give time for sensitive domestic sectors to adapt to the new competitive conditions in the subregion. Its main innovation as compared to the exemption lists implemented in the transition period is that protection will fall progressively over a four-year period.

Since a number of products will be temporarily exempted from the CET, rules of origin will have to be enforced to prevent deflection of trade.[8] The general rule of origin in Mercosur is a change in tariff classification, yet selected products will have to comply with a 60 per cent value-added regional content requirement and/or specific requirements (such as chemicals, steel, telecommunications and information technology).

Treatment of NTBs poses a tricky challenge due to lack of transparency and the legislative regulatory changes which are frequently required to implement CMG decisions.[9] A technical committee will oversee the process of identification and elimination or harmonization of NTBs. If the committee identifies a non-declared NTB, the country in question will have a maximum of six months to remove it. The four countries also eliminated designated NTBs by year-end 1994.[10]

Uruguay was able to maintain a special treatment until year 2001 for products included in its bilateral preferential arrangements with Argentina (CAUCE) and Brazil (PEC). Uruguay's main advantage is that products currently receiving the benefits of bilateral preferential arrangements will have to comply with a 50 per cent regional content clause, in contrast to the general 60 per cent rule. Convergence will also take place over the transition period.

Member countries will continue to enforce domestic anti-dumping legislation for intra-regional trade until a common statute on competition is agreed upon. In 1995 the technical committee on competition policy agreed on a protocol referring the issue to domestic legislation. Yet this has not been operative because neither Paraguay nor Uruguay have domestic competition legislation in force. In the meantime, they will continue to make use of the existing arrangement to exchange information.

Sectoral Issues

Automobile and sugar industries will receive special treatment for a limited period and will be temporarily excluded from common trade policies. Other sectors such as capital goods and information and telecommunication products (about 1300 tariff items) will also have differential treatment in so far as they will be excluded from the CET (see below). Other sensitive products included in national exemption lists (such as textiles) are also likely to have a special common regime developed in the near future.

Automobiles
Argentina and Brazil have established car industries, but with significant structural differences. Whereas car output in Brazil is 1.5 million units per year, Argentina produces just 400 000 vehicles.[11] There are also important differences between the two countries' regulatory frameworks. Brazil levies a 70 per cent tariff on imported vehicles, while domestically produced automobiles of less than 1000 cc enjoy preferential tax treatment. There are also 200 tariff items (strategic inputs) which can be imported duty-free.

Argentina has a more elaborate contractual programme scheduled to remain in force until 1999. The Argentine programme includes local content requirements (60 per cent), firms' commitments to invest and rationalize, and a three-tier import regime protecting the domestic market and established manufacturers' right to import at preferential tariff rates.

Argentina's national content requirements influence investment decisions, and the ability of established manufacturers to import at preferential tariff rates punctures Brazilian producers' preferences in the Argentine market. In the 1991/4 transition period Protocol 21 between Argentina and Brazil regulated sectoral bilateral trade through duty-free quotas. The agreed formula for governing bilateral automobile trade from January 1995 onwards includes a transitory regime until the year 2000. In the transition period intra-regional trade will be freed, but Argentina will maintain quotas on imports from the rest of the world, as well as the requirement of a foreign exchange balance for established manufacturers. Brazilian producers will have preferential access to the Argentine market, since each dollar of Argentine exports to the Brazilian market will be valued at a 1.20 rate, to account for the foreign exchange balance. Brazilian and Argentine auto-part producers will be considered national in both markets, which means that Argentine autoparts will benefit from national treatment (preferential tax treatment) in the production of the so-called 'popular car' in Brazil.

A technical committee convened by the Mercosur Trade Commission (MTC) will work out a proposal to liberalize intra-regional trade, establish the CET, eliminate domestic incentives which distort competition and set up a transition mechanism for moving from existing national regimes to a regional one. This proposal should be ready before 1997 and be enforced by the year 2000.

Capital Goods, Information Technology and Telecommunication Products
Capital goods and information and telecommunication products were a stumbling block to an agreement on the CET. Whereas Brazilian negotiators preferred relatively high tariff rates (Brazil has established producers), Argentine negotiators were reluctant to abandon zero tariff rates for capital goods imports on the grounds that Argentina required duty-free capital goods imports to modernize firms' plant and equipment.

The capital goods issue was particularly sensitive because Argentina had unilaterally reduced tariff rates on capital goods in 1992, thus contravening the Asunción Treaty. Argentina had also rejected the Brazilian proposal to allow exceptions only for above-CET rates. The final agreement included exemptions both for above and below-CET rates, thereby enabling Argentina to maintain its zero tariff rate for capital good imports, and in order to compensate for the erosion of preferences, Brazilian capital goods producers will receive a 10 per cent subsidy (5 per cent lower than that received by domestic producers). However, implementation of the agreement is dubious because of its budgetary implications, cumbersome administrative procedures and opposition from Argentine producers.[12]

The agreed CET includes a maximum 14 per cent tariff rate for capital goods, to come into force by 2001, and a maximum 16 per cent tariff rate for information and telecommunication products to become effective in 2006. Convergence will be gradual and starts from national rates both lower and higher than the agreed CET.

Agriculture

Sugar will also be temporarily exempted from common trade policies. The sugar sector is heavily distorted by subsidies to the Pro-Alcool programme in Brazil and high protection in Argentina (sugar imports pay specific duties to compensate for the high production costs of domestic producers). Argentina will maintain its national trade regime for sugar imports, but industrial users are likely to have a duty-free quota for sugar imports from Brazil to compensate for higher domestic prices.

A technical group will be in charge of defining a convergence scheme to run until 2001, which is expected to include gradual liberalization of intra-regional trade and neutralization of distortions produced by asymmetrical national policies. Brazil has already committed the removal of sectoral subsidies over a ten-year period. Meanwhile, member countries will be authorized to maintain national tariff policies for intra- and extra-regional sugar industry trade.

Wheat trade will also be governed by special transitory rules to compensate for the large distortions which prevail in the international market, considering that Argentina is a non-subsidizing low-cost producer and Brazil a net importer. Special regulations governing wheat trade illustrate the importance of establishing and enforcing a common regime to deal with third parties' unfair trade practices. Since January 1995, and parallel to the period in which the Argentine harvest is sold, Brazil has levied a transitory 10 per cent surcharge on wheat imports from third party countries. The 10 per cent CET plus the 10 per cent temporary import surcharge should be sufficient to compensate for price differentials caused by production and export subsidies. A permanent regime will be negotiated in the future.

Textiles

A technical committee will assess the advantages of developing a common import policy for the textile sector, beyond implementation of the CET. Most textile products are in national convergence or exemption lists. While a common import regime is enforced, countries will maintain national tariff rates and Argentina will not levy specific duties on intra-regional trade. Argentina will continue to levy specific duties on textile imports from third countries and charge a 30 per cent tariff rate for textile imports from Mercosur partners included in the 'convergence scheme'.

All textile products included in the Argentine 'convergence scheme' have duty-free quotas for imports from Mercosur countries.

Common Trade Rules

In the first stage of Mercosur, the main common trade policy instrument will be the CET, enforced from January 1995 onwards. Yet agreement on a common external tariff (CET) was not easy to achieve. Whereas Brazilian negotiators initially preferred relatively high tariff rates (35 per cent) for capital goods and information and telecommunication products, the smaller partners (including Argentina) pushed for lower tariffs, particularly for capital goods. In an anticipatory move, in 1992 Argentine authorities had unilaterally zeroed import duties on capital goods, thereby eliminating the preference margin in favour of Brazil.

The agreed CET includes eleven tariff levels with a 0 per cent minimum and a 20 per cent maximum tariff rate. About 85 per cent of total tariff lines had their CET operational by January 1995. The remainder, including capital goods and information and telecommunication products will keep national tariff rates vis-à-vis third countries, but will converge automatically by 2001 (capital goods) and 2006 (information and telecommunication products).

Apart from capital goods and information and telecommunication products, member countries were allowed exemptions from the CET up to a maximum of 300 tariff lines until 31 December 2000.[13] At the time of writing Argentina had already designated its list of exemptions, mostly composed of chemicals (with lower than CET tariff rates) and steel products, electrical appliances and electric material, paper, shoes and plastics (all with above-CET tariff rates). Brazil in turn designated 286 products, mostly chemicals (with above- and below-CET tariff rates), petroleum derivatives (above-CET tariff rates) and textile inputs, stone and china manufactures and skins and furs (with below-CET tariff rates). In March 1995 Brazil widened the list to include automobiles and domestic electrical appliances, which will pay above-CET tariff rates.[14]

The new CET will represent a significant reduction in average protection for Argentina, particularly if the national tariff is taken inclusive of the statistical import surcharge. The transition will be smoother in the case of Brazil. Average tariff rates in Argentina prior to the implementation of the CET was 19 per cent (including the statistical surcharge), whereas the average CET is just over 12 per cent. Only 13 per cent of products had tariffs lower than those in force in January 1995, whereas 40 per cent of tariff lines reduced their rates by between 8 per cent and 13 per cent (products most affected are paper, leather and wood). In contrast, Brazil's average tariff prior to the CET was 14 per cent and similar to the CET average.

Member countries will also develop a common regime for anti-dumping and countervailing duties applicable to imports from the rest of the world, following GATT guidelines. National anti-dumping regimes will continue in the meantime. Member countries have agreed to keep certain GATT-compatible export incentives, until tax policies are harmonized. A bilateral agreement between Argentina and Brazil allowed the main-tenance of special customs zones in Manaos and Tierra del Fuego until 2013. Imports from special customs zones, export-process-ing areas and duty-free zones (except Manaos and Tierra del Fuego) will pay the CET or the national tariff (if the pro-duct is on the exemption list) when exported to a partner country.

Mercosur countries also agreed on a common safeguards scheme. If rising imports cause, or threaten to cause, damage to domestic producers in one country or in the region as a whole, the Trade Commission (see below) may impose safeguard measures prior to launching an investigation. Under certain circumstances provisional safeguard measures could be applied by the national chapters of the Commission for a maximum of 200 days. Safeguards will be non-discriminatory and can take the form of either higher tariffs or quotas, but they may not reduce the volume of imports below the average for the last three years. Safeguards will be applicable for four years, with an extension to a maximum of eight years.

Governance and Dispute Settlement

For the time being, Mercosur will maintain an inter-government-al rather than a supranational governing structure. The Common

Market Council (CMC), comprising the foreign relations and economics ministers, will remain as the governing body with legal power to negotiate with third parties, and the Common Market Group (CMG) will stay on as the executive body. A four-party Trade Commission was created to oversee implementation of common trade rules and policies as regards intra-regional as well as extra-regional trade relations. The Trade Commission will also be in charge of implementing the common safeguards mechanism, empowered to establish specific rules of origin requirements, review existing ones and modify the CET. Mercosur will also set up a Joint Parliamentary Commission, an Economic and Social Consultative Forum and an Administrative Secretariat based in Montevideo. All directives (decisions about trade policy) and proposals will be adopted by consensus.

Dispute settlement procedures implemented by the Asunción Treaty include three mechanisms: (1) 'direct negotiations' between the parties, (2) an analysis of the dispute by the CMG (maximum of 60 days), and (3) an analysis of the dispute by the CMC. In late 1991 specific procedures were detailed in the Brasilia Protocol for Dispute Settlement. The Brasilia Protocol significantly expanded the scope of issues which can be dealt with, from disputes about the implementation of the treaty to those arising out of non-compliance and problems of interpretations.[15]

Resolutions are definitive and obligatory. If one state refuses to comply, the affected party can adopt temporary compensatory measures. The Brasilia Protocol also established that the national section of the CMG will be the mechanism for individuals to make claims regarding trade issues.

3 'DEEPENING': BEYOND A 'MINIMALIST' AGENDA

The above discussion suggests that even if a minimalist approach is followed, Mercosur has an intensive negotiating agenda ahead. This agenda revolves around the issue of an orderly completion of the customs union, including the thorny issue of NTBs and common trade rules. The issues involved are sufficiently complex to justify no more than a cautious optimism. Yet sustained progress towards the completion of the customs union is unlikely to take place if negotiations do not go beyond a 'minimalist' agenda. This more ambitious agenda includes non-border practices influencing the locational advantages of firms, investment and service sector regulations.

Investment

In January 1994 the four Mercosur countries signed a reciprocal promotion and protection investment agreement (Colonia Protocol) by which they committed themselves to provide national treatment to investors from within the region. The Colonia Protocol included a most favoured nation (MFN) obligation ensuring that regional investors are treated as favourably as any other foreign investor. As a general rule, the agreement also prohibited the use of performance requirements.

Member countries have identified a number of transitory exceptions in coverage, yet of unspecified duration. Argentina has reserved the right to maintain or establish exemptions in border real estate, air transportation, shipbuilding, nuclear power generation, uranium mining, insurance and fisheries. The Brazilian list of exemptions is longer. It includes exploration and exploitation of minerals, hydroelectric power, health care, radio frequencies and telecommunications, rural property, banking and insurance services, construction and shipping. Brazil also reserved the right to preserve the exemption to government procurement established by the 1988 Constitutional reform. Both countries have reserved the right temporarily to maintain performance requirements for the automobile sector.

Common investment regulations outlaw expropriation, except on public interest grounds and undertaken on a non-discriminatory basis with due process and prompt payment of a fair compensation. The Colonia Protocol also forbids restrictions on capital repatriation and profit remittances in convertible currencies.

The Brasilia Protocol was designated as the dispute settlement mechanism among Mercosur member countries (see above). If the dispute is between an individual investor and the host country government, the investor may seek redress in a host country court, an international arbitration mechanism or a dispute settlement mechanism for individuals (to be set up). The investor's choice will be definitive and rulings will be indisputable and obligatory.

The investment protocol meant that the Brazilian position became more flexible as compared to other bilateral treaties. However, more significant changes are likely to come out of the Constitutional reform process launched in early 1995. For Argentina the Colonia Protocol did not introduce innovations because the foreign investment regime has been generously liberalized in recent years.

Financial Services

Although the Asunción Treaty establishes free trade in goods and services, there is no calendar or provision regarding the means of advancing liberalization in the service sector. In particular, in the financial services sector there are large regulatory asymmetries between Mercosur countries. Whereas the Argentine financial market has undergone far-reaching liberalization in recent years, the Brazilian regime is still restrictive. Furthermore, a number of Brazilian regulations are currently part of the 1988 Constitution.[16] These limit the number of foreign banks established in the country, whereas the Argentine regime for the banking sector is very liberal.

As far as regulatory policies are concerned, member countries have agreed to adopt the Basle Committee rules for minimum capital requirements, but implementation is still pending in the case of Paraguay. The four countries' regulatory authorities are also negotiating the implementation of a consolidated regime for banking supervision, debtors' rating and precautionary reserves.

Regulatory asymmetries are also prevalent in the insurance market. The Argentine insurance market is temporarily closed to the establishment of new firms (except for retirement and reinsurance firms), but existing companies can be purchased by domestic and foreign firms, with national treatment as the rule. In contrast, the Brazilian insurance market is more heavily regulated with a state monopoly in the reinsurance business.

Government Procurement

Government procurement regulations also vary among Mercosur countries. Whereas the Argentine regime is open and the rule is national treatment, in Brazil preferences for domestic suppliers prevail. Article 171 of the Constitution authorizes preferential treatment for Brazilian firms of 'national' capital. Executive Order No. 2300 regulating state procurement establishes that domestic producers will have preference whenever price, quality and time conditions are comparable to those of foreign suppliers. Regulations governing some state firms' procurement even state that purchases are open only to domestic bidders (Telebras for telecommunications equipment and Petrobras for petroleum inputs). Executive order No. 666 also stipulates that the transportation of imported goods, purchased by the state, be transported in Brazilian vessels, although the impact of this regulation is being eroded by privatization.

Competition Policy

The Trade Commission will have to propose a Competition Defence Statute to the CMG. The CMG will then decide whether the statute will become a reference for national legislations (provide common parameters) or be implemented as a protocol.

The basic harmonization principles include the usual prohibition of practices affecting competition and free market access (organized practices and abuse of dominant position). Operations between firms with more than 20 per cent market share will be reviewed by member countries. The Trade Commission will also establish a Technical Committee in charge of identifying public policies which may influence competitive conditions in the region.

4 MERCOSUR'S FOREIGN TRADE RELATIONS: NAFTA, LAIA AND BEYOND

The regional and commodity composition of Mercosur foreign trade gives a high priority to multilateralism. Yet the prevailing international scenario suggests that regional initiatives will continue to play a key role in Mercosur external trade relations. In particular, 'regionalism' is likely to be instrumental in shaping relations with the rest of the Western Hemisphere and the European countries. In practice, this means relations with NAFTA, LAIA and the European Union.

The North American Free Trade Agreement

The establishment of NAFTA and the announcement by the Bush and Clinton administrations that additional free trade agreements could be negotiated with other countries in the Western Hemisphere initially gave rise to disparate reactions among Mercosur members (Bouzas, 1994). For Paraguay and Uruguay the issue passed largely unnoticed, with public attention and bureaucratic energies channelled towards the more immediately relevant subregional process of preferential trade liberalization. In the two largest partners reactions differed markedly. Whereas in Brazil the option of negotiating a free trade agreement with either NAFTA or the United States was generally viewed with scepticism, in Argentina it gave rise to positive reactions (at least in official circles) and public discussion. At one point, divergences between the two largest partners threatened to block progress towards the customs union. However, implementation of the customs union in January 1995 buried the issue, at least for the time being.

Contending points of view between the Argentine and Brazilian governments have been explained by contrasting policy 'preferences', with the latter allegedly being more reticent towards unilateral trade liberalization and more prudent as regards a preferential trade agreement with the United States. Although such differences played an undeniable role, a number of underlying structural factors are probably more relevant. If so, even in a scenario of closer 'policy convergence' between the two largest Mercosur partners (as one might expect in the future), a number of differences are likely to remain on how to approach prospective negotiations with the United States and/or NAFTA.

Notwithstanding the smaller countries' high trade concentration with their larger neighbours, all Mercosur partners share the common feature of being 'global traders'.[17] Indeed, the United States is not a 'natural' trade partner (at least to the extent it can be so considered in the case of Mexico and the Caribbean basin economies), but it is an important supplier and outlet for Mercosur imports and exports. This is certainly the case for Brazilian exports, a quarter of which go to the US market. More importantly, Mercosur exports to the United States are biased towards manufactured products, thus expanding the scope for dynamic gains.

Improved and predictable market access is a shared objective for Mercosur countries. Yet its national relevance is subject to two qualifications. The first is the contrasting influence of supply and market access conditions on the performance of each country's exports to the United States. Indeed, whereas US market access conditions (particularly NTBs and contingent protection) seem to play an important role in the case of Brazilian exports, supply constraints seem to be more decisive in the case of the two smaller countries, and to a large degree Argentina (Barboza et al., 1994).

The second caveat relates to the difficulties in removing, bilaterally, many of the trade restrictions which affect Mercosur exports to the US market, particularly in agricultural products. Issues involved (like export and production subsidies) are largely 'systemic' and can only be adequately dealt with on a multilateral basis.

Mercosur countries also share similar 'defensive' incentives regarding their trade relations with the United States, but again their importance differs from country to country. Brazilian exports seem to be the most harmed by NAFTA preferences. Although recent estimates find that the static effect on Brazilian exports, of Mexico's accession to NAFTA, is moderate, the effect on Brazilian exports of the removal of US NTBs on imports of Mexican fruits, steel products, machinery, automobiles and textiles may change this conclusion in the medium term, particularly when investment decisions are taken into account (da Motta Veiga, 1994). The estimated effect on Argentine exports is more modest. Nogues (1993) argues that the competitive condition of about a third of Argentine exports to the United States may be negatively affected by NAFTA, but other estimates suggest that in absolute terms the effect will not be substantial.[18] It is interesting to point out that in the case of Argentina, exports displaced in the Mexican market are more important relative to total exports that those displaced from the US market.

Yet access conditions to other regional markets could deteriorate if NAFTA expands further through bilateral agreements. Again, these effects are more significant in the case of Brazil, but they also play a role in Argentina. For Paraguay and Uruguay the risk of preference erosion in the subregional market is probably the most important.

The divergent nature of Mercosur incentives to negotiate an FTA with NAFTA can be explained on two grounds. One is the size of transition and adjustment costs involved in preferential trade liberalization with the United States. The other is the prevailing divergences as regards the treatment of non-border issues, 'new issues' (investment, services and intellectual property) and so-called 'brand new' issues (environment and labour standards).

Asymmetrical incentives arising out of divergent transition costs can be explained by two facts, one structural and the other policy-related. The structural fact is the difference in the degree of complexity of national productive structures. Brazil has a more sophisticated productive structure, suggesting high transition costs in the short run. Yet this also increases the potential for reaping dynamic gains in the medium to long term.[19] The policy-related fact (not completely independent from the latter) is the divergence in prevailing levels of legal protection. However, this obstacle will progressively disappear once the CET is implemented in January 1995.[20]

Differences stemming out of non-border practices, 'new issues' and 'brand new issues' should also be taken into consideration. The two smaller economies are reported to have few conflicts with the United States on these issues, although enforcement may turn out to be a problem (particularly in the case of Paraguay). As far as Argentina is concerned, the reform process undertaken in the past few years has ironed out many of the pre-existing differences. In fact, the only pending issue is intellectual property rights protection, currently under congressional consideration.

For Brazil, in contrast, this extended agenda poses more complex problems. Harmonization of non-border practices, 'new issues' and 'brand new issues' along US-sponsored lines would demand substantial changes in domestic practices. Brazil has a heavily regulated service sector and foreign investment regime. Non-border obstacles to trade are also extensive, particularly as a result of public monopolies and government procurement. The environmental and labour agenda is also likely to cause irritation, as shown by recent experience (particularly in the environmental field). However, some of these issues will have to be tackled by Mercosur in the near future. Intra-regional negotiations may thus contribute towards paving the way for future negotiations with the United States.

In summary, not all Mercosur countries find a preferential trade agreement with the United States or NAFTA equally desirable. For the smaller partners the main issue is subregional trade liberalization. Their main incentives vis-à-vis the United States are defensive: to make sure that preferences in the subregional market are not being unilaterally eroded. For Brazil the balance is different: exports from Brazil are likely to gain most in terms of market access from preferential trade liberalization vis-à-vis the United States, and it is also the country most seriously threatened by trade diversion in North American markets. Brazilian exports may also suffer in regional markets if NAFTA expands to other countries in Latin America. Brazil's reluctance to enter into negotiations with the United States and/or NAFTA stems from a widespread belief that adjustment and macroeconomic issues posed by trade liberalization have not received adequate attention in NAFTA, and are unlikely to do so in the future (da Motta Veiga, 1994).

Finally, the case of Argentina is a peculiar one. Although market access is not a key issue in US–Argentine trade relations, the Argentine government has at certain times appeared excited by the prospect of free trade negotiations with the United States and/or NAFTA. The main incentive seems to have been to consolidate (lock in) economic reforms and obtain a 'seal of approval' for domestic policies. The objective of strengthening their negotiating stance vis-à-vis Brazil may have also played a role.

Frequently the case is made that assessing the impact of a preferential agreement with the United States and/or NAFTA, only taking trade flows into consideration, is highly unsatisfactory. Yet the idea that the smaller Mercosur countries (including Argentina) would benefit greatly from direct investment inflows, if a preferential agreement is negotiated with the United States, is unconvincing. Localization disadvantages (vis-à-vis Mexico) and a pre-existing US agreement with Mexico seem two powerful reasons.

The Latin American Integration Association

Mercosur is a key player in intra-Latin American trade relations. Mercosur countries contribute approximately 40 per cent of total LAIA two-way trade flows, while intra-Mercosur trade amounts to over two-thirds of intra-LAIA export–import trade. This makes Mercosur a key player in the process of preferential trade liberalization in the Western Hemisphere.

Since its inception, Mercosur has left a door open to the early inclusion of Chile. Article 20 of the Asunción Treaty established that Mercosur would be open for other LAIA members to join after a five-year waiting period (countries not part of subregional or extra-regional agreements may join immediately). Notwithstanding this tailor-made clause, successive Chilean governments have been reluctant to join Mercosur, allegedly on the grounds of divergent trade policies and Mercosur's unstable macroeconomic record.

The establishment of Mercosur as a customs union as of January 1995 implies that all bilateral preferential arrangements will expire, although existing agreements have been extended until 30 June 1995, in order to conclude negotiations with partner countries. Mercosur has already made an offer to its LAIA partners, the main points being:

1. to 'multilateralize' pre-existing bilateral preferences unless there is expressed opposition from one of Mercosur partners;
2. the remainder will receive a minimum generalized preference of 40 per cent;
3. definition of a timetable to increase preference margins automatically and linearly;
4. definition of a list of exempted products and agreement on a phase-out calendar;
5. definition of a list of sensitive products to receive a preference lower than the minimum (30 per cent) for a period of three years. After this waiting period, products will be included in the general programme if NTBs have been harmonized or eliminated;
6. an agreement on rules of origin, safeguards, dispute resolution, duty-free zones, customs valuation, export incentives, special customs regimes, harmonization of technical and sanitary standards and unfair trade practices;
7. automatic extension of benefits negotiated with extra-regional members.

The two most demanding cases ahead are the negotiations with Mexico and Chile. Negotiations with Mexico will be problematic as a fallout of NAFTA. Article 44 of the LAIA treaty established that member countries should automatically extend preferences granted to extra-regional parties, yet Mexico did not extend to LAIA members preferences granted to Canada and the United States. The implications of this refusal were addressed in mid-1994 when an interpretative protocol of LAIA article 44 was signed. This established that a LAIA member country could request a temporary suspension of its obligations under article 44, in exchange for a commitment to hold bilateral negotiations with LAIA partners aimed at maintaining a level of concessions as favourable as that prior to the new agreement. The protocol established a predetermined negotiating calendar, including the creation of a Special Group to determine appropriate compensation if no agreement is reached. Mexico has not started negotiations yet.

The issues at stake with Chile are more substantive. Mercosur countries (particularly Argentina) have insisted on seeking alternatives for incorporating Chile into Mercosur. Yet these efforts have been counteracted by other partners' reluctance to accept a special mechanism for Chile's accession, and Chile's refusal to commit to the CET. It is likely that Chile will have to 'pay a price' (probably non-participation in governing bodies or a more lengthy tariff removal process) for not joining the customs union. Mercosur is an attractive market for Chilean exports, not only because of the value of trade but also because of its composition: Chile sells most of its manufactured exports to the subregion and the share of products traded with preferences is higher for Chilean exports to Mercosur than for Mercosur exports to Chile.[21]

In mid-1994 the Brazilian government proposed launching negotiations to create a South American Free Trade Area (SAFTA), based on convergence between Mercosur, the Andean Pact and Chile. The proposal offered negotiations to establish a calendar for automatic, linear and progressive tariff reductions on a minimum 80 per cent of total tariff lines, as well as the removal of NTBs. Exceptions would be incorporated gradually into the liberalization process. If it materializes, SAFTA may play a key role in the process of regional trade liberalization in the Western Hemisphere.

The European Union

The European Union (EU) is one of the prospective partners for bilateral trade negotiations with Mercosur. The June 1994 European Council meeting in Corfu decided to strengthen relations with Mercosur countries, subject to two conditions: the establishment of a CET and the definition of a common representation to negotiate with the EU. Both requirements were met with the establishment of the customs union on January 1995.

The stages of the negotiation would involve signing an inter-regional framework agreement for economic and trade co-operation in late 1995, to be followed by a free trade agreement by 2001. The reasons for EU's interest in Mercosur are grounded on trade and broader 'foreign policy' interests. Mercosur countries are the most important trade and investment partners for the EU in Latin America. Furthermore, an agreement with Mercosur may ensure the EU a more effective presence in the southern part of the Americas to counterbalance the mounting influence of the United States after NAFTA and the proposed hemispheric free trade area. Furthermore, the fact that Mercosur has adopted the structure of a customs union rather than a free trade area makes it more similar – notwithstanding all the differences – to the EU structure.

However, the negotiating agenda is likely to be extremely difficult to deal with. In early 1995 the EU finally agreed not to exclude any sector from the negotiations. Initially, there was a strong EU preference to negotiate a free trade area solely in industrial products. This aim would both have failed to meet the WTO article 24 test of including 'substantially all trade' as well as failing to meet Mercosur expectations, which certainly include extending negotiations to agricultural products. This is likely to slow down the process of reciprocal trade liberalization, but with the benefit of a more substantial product coverage.

CONCLUSIONS

Mercosur's record has been remarkable by past standards. Trade flows have expanded rapidly and investment flows have displayed some signs of responsiveness. Furthermore, since part of the trade expansion has been intra-industry (where scale economies are more likely to be achieved) trade diversion may not have been a net welfare cost to consumers.

Domestic conditions (unilateral trade liberalization) and the international environment (the resurgence of preferential trade arrangements) undeniably played a role throughout the process. In this context, closer trade relations between traditionally inward-looking, natural trade partners have boomed. Macroeconomic instability was not detrimental to mounting trade interaction due to *ad hoc* factors such as readily available external finance and rapid growth of two-way trade flows. But the favourable external financial environment of the early 1990s has now disappeared. From 1995 onwards divergent macroeconomic paths are likely to influence aggregate trade flows more forcefully.

However, if Brazil is able to stabilize its economy successfully and Argentina avoids a full-blown financial crisis, Mercosur offers grounds for reasonable optimism. While the relatively low import coefficient of the Brazilian economy is set to increase, the attractive preference margin enjoyed by its Mercosur partners is likely to lead to a fast expansion of intra-regional trade.

The institutional area is one in which Mercosur will have to make smooth progress in the future. The reluctance to create supranational agencies seems understandable given the previous experience of Latin America and the fact that supranationality is no substitute for weak political commitment and feeble interdependence. Yet if the customs union and an 'expanding' agenda are to be successfully pursued, a gradually larger share of issues will have to be dealt with by supranational mechanisms rather than inter-governmental negotiations.

The conduct of Mercosur's external trade relations will be a proof of its coherence and commitment to the future. It has a complex agenda of negotiations with LAIA and, if the Miami commitments materialize, with the rest of the Western Hemisphere (particularly NAFTA). An agreed procedure for advancing towards harmonization of subregional preferential trade arrangements in the Western Hemisphere would demand the active participation of both NAFTA and Mercosur, the two largest trading groups in the region. For this to be occur, Mercosur will have gradually to iron out internal conflicts based on the economic sense of the natural partnership which binds its members together.

3 The G3 and the Road To Continental Integration

Juan José Echavarría

1 INTRODUCTION

Like many other Latin American countries, Mexico, Venezuela and Colombia have undertaken far-reaching reforms aimed at giving leading roles to the external sector and foreign investment in the economic growth process. The reforms in Mexico took place from 1985 onwards, Colombia's and Venezuela's in 1989–94. The three countries partly dismantled their quantitative restrictions on imports, substantially reduced tariffs and introduced (amongst other things) significant reforms in labour and transport legislation, as well as in the fields of science and technology and in the treatment of foreign investment. Mexico also carried out a massive programme to privatize state enterprises.[1] It is no coincidence that Venezuela (1990) and Mexico (1986) joined the GATT in this period.

In each of the three countries total exports have grown,[2] especially in non-traditional products and manufactures, where GDP shares have risen to unprecedented levels.[3] Of special relevance to this chapter is the fact that in all three countries exports to 'natural trading partners' have expanded relatively more than those to the rest of the world.

In addition, there has been a marked increase in foreign investment: direct investment flows to Mexico increased fourfold in the post-1985 period compared with 1970–85, while those to Colombia in 1990–3 tripled with respect to 1970–90. Venezuela's net investment flows have been particularly variable, but extremely high values were recorded between 1991 and 1994.

Complementary to this strategy, the three countries have pursued a particularly aggressive policy towards integration. Mexico has signed free trade agreements with the United States and Canada (NAFTA), Chile, Bolivia and Costa Rica, while Colombia and Venezuela have agreements with Chile, CARI-

90

COM, Panama and Central America (still to be finalized). In addition, all trade barriers have been eliminated between Colombia, Venezuela and Ecuador in the framework of the Andean Pact. In addition, in June 1994 Colombia, Mexico and Venezuela signed the Group of Three Agreement (G3), which came into force on 1 January 1995.

In the G3, obstacles related to distance are minimized by freeing transport (services in general) in the three countries, by reducing the significance of excluded products and by eliminating non-tariff barriers between members. However, significant exceptions remain in the agriculture and automobile sectors. The G3 places no obstacles whatsoever on members continuing to open up their economies to third-party countries or entering into new processes of integration with simple and transparent accession clauses.

The G3 belongs to the new generation of agreements in Latin America, and its goals are entirely consistent with what ECLAC (1994: 52) calls 'open integration'. The agreement is important for the benefits which will derive from increased trade flows between members, but in Colombia and Venezuela it has also been seen as a 'bridging' agreement on the road to hemispheric integration: the G3 could provide training for negotiators in government and in the private sector (in an intensive process of collaboration), which eventually could be useful for a possible future admission to NAFTA. Also, other countries interested in a similar process leading towards hemispheric integration might join. Finally, it was thought that some of the agreements reached by Venezuela and Colombia in the G3 framework could be transferred, with suitable modifications, to the Andean Pact.

Based on the experience of the G3, some of the obstacles which should arise on the road to hemispheric integration are discussed. As well as the conflictive negotiations on environmental issues and labour standards (absent from the G3), the results in terms of asymmetries, safeguards and rules of origin were what most provoked opposition from the most influential trade associations in Colombia (and in Venezuela in certain phases of the negotiations).

'Ghosts of the past' also played an important role, and in each country there were demands for the new agreements to respect certain clauses previously agreed with other countries. In the context of the G3, the private sectors in Colombia and Venezuela continuously sought the inclusion of an exchange rate safeguard such as that existing in the Andean Pact, and the recent devaluation in Mexico has revived this discussion.

In the particular case of Colombia and Venezuela it seems obvious to continue along the road to hemispheric integration, when one considers that the benefits obtained are substantial and that in a few years' time producers will feel the full force of competition from Mexican goods made (inside NAFTA) to international standards of efficiency. Integration will provide an insurance against possible protectionist measures in the countries of the hemisphere, it will enhance the two countries' bargaining power and it will facilitate the 'importing of stable institutions'. It will constitute a central element in the region's development strategy, since countries excluded from trade blocs will be the principal losers of the future.

2 TRADE FLOWS, COMPARATIVE ADVANTAGE AND PROTECTION

The potential benefits of the agreements depend, among other things, on the creation of new trade flows, on tariff reductions between members being considerable and on the agreement leading to a pattern of specialization similar to what would be the outcome in an open economy. On the basis of these parameters it is possible to state that the benefits of the G3 will be considerable in the medium term.

Trade flows within the G3 (first factor) will possibly increase significantly in the coming years, considering that trade at the moment is minimal, that the pattern of exports between the three countries is radically different from the pattern of exports to the rest of the world, that transport and other services are also being freed at the same time, and that the tariff reduction will be considerable.

As well as this, the G3 offers an ideal situation for specialization in countries such as Colombia and Venezuela: adjustment costs will be low during the early years, as liberalization with Mexico will take place gradually over a 10–13-year period, and the weight of intra-industry trade will remain high in the early years, so the new trade flows will not have a big impact on the distribution of income or on the reallocation of resources between sectors.[4]

It is suggested that adjustment costs and the gains generated through the reallocation of resources will be greater in Venezuela than in Colombia, as the structures of production in Colombia and Mexico are highly complementary, while Venezuela and Mexico have similar comparative advantages with respect to the rest of the world.

Present and Future Trade Flows

Trade within the G3 is very limited at the present time, accounting for scarcely 2 per cent of total exports.[5] Mexico does not even figure among the top ten trading partners of Venezuela or Colombia (and vice versa).[6] None the less the past ten years have seen big changes: Colombian exports to Mexico and to Venezuela have increased fourfold and sixfold respectively between 1986 and 1992, and exports from Venezuela to Mexico increased 38 times in the same period. This would suggest that there is high trade potential, which may intensify in the coming years. What will be the dynamic pattern of future sectoral flows? The analysis of each country's comparative advantages with respect to Colombia indicates that Mexico and Venezuela will compete to sell inputs and capital goods to Colombian producers.

The pattern of Colombian and Mexican exports to the G3 differs radically from their sales to the rest of the world (this is less so in the case of Venezuela). Thus, while 66 per cent, 44 per cent and 85 per cent of total Colombian, Mexican and Venezuelan exports, respectively, are based on agriculture and mining, the shares of these sectors only amount to 21 per cent, 2 per cent and 13 per cent of their respective sales within the G3. Intra-industry trade also seems to be disproportionately high, with a substantial weight in chemicals, plastic and rubber products and in machinery and textiles.[7] This result is not surprising when one considers their relative similarity in capital:labour ratios, but the trend of intra-industry trade is difficult to predict, depending in the majority of cases on simple historical accident.

Table 3.1 shows the 15 (out of 98) tariff chapters in which Colombia has advantages and disadvantages compared to Mexico and Venezuela, based on each country's current exports worldwide[8] with respect to the three countries is relatively similar to its

Table 3.1 Bilateral Comparative Advantages with respect to Mexico, Venezuela and Chile

Colombia's comparative advantages with respect to:

No.	Mexico Chapter	Mexico Description	Mexico Index	Venezuela Index	Venezuela Chapter	Venezuela Description	Chile Index	Chile Chapter	Chile Description
1	62	Clothing: garments	2.92	3.82	46	Basketwork	3.50	42	Leather goods
2	61	Knitwear	2.67	3.80	42	Leather goods	3.36	09	Coffee, tea and spices
3	11	Flours	2.66	3.53	65	Felt hats	3.29	65	Felt hats
4	42	Leather goods	2.57	3.49	17	Sugar and pastry goods	3.25	63	Household linen
5	49	Printed materials	2.46	3.32	62	Clothing: garments	3.09	27	Fuels
6	17	Sugar and pastry goods	2.41	3.32	63	Household linen	2.98	46	Basketwork
7	97	Art materials	2.38	3.24	61	Knitwear	2.61	97	Art materials
8	21	Coffee extracts	2.33	2.89	01	Live animals	2.56	61	Knitwear
9	24	Tobacco	2.29	2.76	64	Footwear	2.48	59	Industrial textiles
10	02	Meats	2.28	2.74	49	Printed materials	2.22	17	Sugar and pastry goods
11	59	Industrial textiles	2.26	2.66	11	Flours	2.19	52	Cotton
12	46	Basketwork	2.26	2.44	97	Art materials	2.15	62	Clothing: garments
13	18	Cocoa	2.23	2.41	58	Other textile products	2.15	57	Rugs and floor mats
14	58	Other textile products	2.20	2.36	94	Diverse manufactures	2.11	58	Other textile products
15	63	Household linen	2.15	2.26	06	Live plants	2.10	35	Enzymes

Each country's comparative advantages with respect to Colombia

	Mexico			Venezuela			Chile		
No.	Chapter	Description	Index	Chapter	Description	Index	Chapter	Description	Index
1	79	Zinc metalwork	0.31	76	Aluminium metalwork	0.38	47	Paper pulp	0.25
2	78	Lead metalwork	0.36	16	Meat and shellfish preserves	0.41	74	Copper metalwork	0.28
3	74	Copper metalwork	0.42	98	Vehicle parts	0.50	23	Fodder	0.29
4	87	Automobiles & other vehicles	0.42	72	Iron and steel	0.67	43	Skins and hides	0.31
5	07	Vegetables	0.49	12	Fodder	0.74	13	Vegetable extracts	0.32
6	31	Fertilizers	0.56	34	Soap	0.74	12	Fodder	0.34
7	13	Vegetable extracts	0.58	05	Other items of animal origin	0.77	16	Meat & shellfish preserves	0.42
8	34	Soaps	0.62	29	Basic organic chemicals	0.79	81	Other metal work	0.42
9	28	Basic inorganic chemicals	0.65	28	Basic inorganic chemicals	0.88	22	Beverages	0.44
10	37	Photography	0.66	74	Copper metalwork	0.88	07	Vegetables	0.46
11	43	Skins and hides	0.66	51	Wool	0.89	98	Vehicle parts	0.50
12	22	Beverages	0.67	31	Fertilizers	0.90	51	Wool	0.54
13	29	Basic organic chemicals	0.69	10	Cereals	0.92	28	Basic inorganic chemicals	0.56
14	53	Flax & other textile fibres	0.70	23	Animal food	0.93	26	Metals	0.56
15	89	Wood chips (?)	0.71	79	Zinc metalwork	0.93	44	Wood	0.60

Notes: The indicator of comparative advantage is described in the text. It may take a value between 0.25 and 4. High CV values indicate that Colombia possesses a comparative advantage in that sector and vice versa (the advantage is with the other country when the number is low).

advantages worldwide: Colombia will export textiles and clothing, leather manufactures, printed and art materials, pastry
products, coffee extracts and certain agricultural products (flour,
sugar, tobacco, meat and cocoa).[9]

The analysis of Colombia's relative disadvantages (the second
part of the table) is interesting for a number of reasons. In the
first place, it clearly explains the strong opposition of sectors such
as chemicals and petrochemicals to the signing of the G3 (see
below), although their fear of imports from Mexico seems exag-
gerated when one remembers that the country already imports
these products from Venezuela with low transport costs and zero
tariffs. Secondly, the analysis suggests a high degree of complementarity between the structures of production in Colombia
and Mexico, and a high degree of substitution between Venezuela and Mexico. This means that Mexican and Venezuelan
producers will compete to provide low-cost inputs to Colombia.

Mexico and Venezuela have comparative advantages in common in basic chemicals (both organic and inorganic), in fertilizers
and soaps, copper metalwork (also in Chile) and zinc metalwork.
Mexico and Chile share comparative advantages in vegetable
extracts and vegetables, in skins and in beverages. Chile and
Venezuela have advantages in common in fodder and animal
foods, in meat and shellfish, in wool and vehicle parts. Of course,
there are also advantages which are not shared. Mexico alone has
advantages in flax, photography, lead metalwork, automobiles
and in wood chips, while Venezuela has advantages in 'other
items of animal origin', in cereals, in iron and steel and in
aluminium metalwork.

Protection Levels in Colombia, Mexico and Venezuela

Although Colombia, Venezuela and Mexico have undertaken far-
reaching reforms to reduce the protection of their external sector,
and in each case average nominal tariff rates are all below 14 per
cent,[10] there are still sectors which enjoy high nominal and
effective tariff levels. Table 3.2 shows that the maximum tariff
and its variance are greater in Colombia and Venezuela than in
Mexico.[11]

In addition, the analysis of effective tariff rates indicates high
levels of protection in different subsectors. Thus the average
effective tariff is above 20 per cent in Colombia–Venezuela and

Table 3.2 Nominal and Effective Tariff Rates in Colombia, Venezuela and Mexico

Nominal Tariff CIIU Sector 2	Colombia and Venezuela				Mexico			
	Average	CV	Range max.	min.	Average	CV	Range max.	min.
11 Agriculture and hunting	8.1	38.5	20	5	10.7	61.3	20	0
12 Forestry and wood extraction	6.8	39.4	15	5	11.2	32.9	20	0
13 Fishing	15.4	43.2	20	5	18.7	18.9	20	10
21 Exploitation of coal mines	5.0	0.0	5	5	10.0	0.0	10	10
22 Petroleum and gas production	10.0	–	10	10	10.0	–	10	10
23 Metallic mineral mining	5.0	0.0	5	5	8.9	33.6	10	0
29 Other mineral mining	5.5	26.5	10	5	9.7	35.8	20	0
31 Food, beverages and tobacco	16.0	31.0	20	5	16.5	36.1	20	0
32 Textiles, clothing and leather	18.1	21.1	20	5	17.3	20.7	20	5
33 Wood and wood products	15.4	28.5	20	5	15.3	23.6	20	0
34 Paper, printing and publishing	12.4	52.9	20	0	9.4	44.2	20	0
35 Chemical products	9.9	57.6	20	5	12.3	34.0	20	0
36 Non-metallic minerals	13.3	34.5	20	5	15.3	26.8	20	0
37 Basic metals	9.3	46.8	15	5	10.8	27.9	20	0
38 Machinery and equipment	12.2	59.8	35	0	14.1	30.8	20	0
39 Other manufacturing industry	15.4	38.2	20	5	16.3	28.5	20	0
Total	11.5	54.6	35	0	13.4	35.6	20	0
Industry								
Simple average	12.8				14.3			
Weighted average	14.9				13.9			

Table 3.2 contd
Effective Tariff CIIU Sector 2

		Colombia and Venezuela				Mexico			
		Average	CV	Range max.	Range min.	Average	CV	Range max.	Range min.
11	Agriculture and hunting	-5.4	87.4	148.2	-28.7	18.9	107.6	149.7	-42.0
12	Forestry and wood extraction	5.9	119.2	20.4	2.9	15.7	68.0	60.2	-1.1
13	Fishing	30.7	62.0	44.2	2.8	32.2	30.3	38.0	11.1
21	Exploitation of coal mines	6.2	0.0	6.2	6.2	12.8	0.0	12.8	12.8
22	Petroleum and gas production	15.5	–	15.5	15.5	15.1	–	15.1	15.1
23	Metallic mineral mining	6.6	4.2	6.8	5.4	12.1	49.0	14.3	-7.9
29	Other mineral mining	7.5	61.2	26.4	2.7	14.3	54.9	42.4	-3.6
31	Food, beverages and tobacco	43.7	85.6	223.2	-54.8	31.2	99.4	235.2	-153.6
32	Textiles, clothing and leather	32.5	37.0	79.3	-60.4	31.5	36.6	76.7	-4.9
33	Wood and wood products	28.4	43.2	49.5	-9.3	25.3	41.2	60.2	-20.1
34	Paper, printing and publishing	19.0	86.0	44.6	-12.1	13.2	72.5	45.3	-12.1
35	Chemical products	16.6	99.1	60.5	-45.8	19.8	63.1	59.3	-22.3
36	Non-metallic minerals	21.7	47.4	66.7	-0.5	23.2	36.2	42.4	-4.9
37	Basic metals	15.7	82.0	71.9	-53.1	17.4	63.7	85.3	-48.0
38	Machinery and equipment	23.0	121.5	123.1	-15.5	23.6	56.4	58.0	-28.9
39	Other manufacturing industry	26.7	56.4	60.4	-3.8	27.4	43.3	59.0	-12.7
	Total Industry	20.9	106.8	223.2	-60.4	23.2	77.2	235.2	-153.3
	Simple average	23.2				24.3			
	Weighted average	36.3				23.7			

Note: CV: Coefficient of variation
Methodology: The tariff for Colombia and Venezuela corresponds to that tentatively agreed to in the Andean Pact Common External Tariff negotiations. Changes were made to this tariff before it was finally approved. The Effective Protection Indexes were calculated on the basis of the Andean Input–Output matrix for each item. For the calculation of nominal and effective tariffs, the simple arithmetic mean of the positions for each 3-digit CIIU sector was obtained. Then the 2-digit weighted average was calculated, weighted by the value added in each subsector. The maximum and minimum values were obtained on the basis of nominal and effective protection at the CIIU 4-digit level.

in Mexico, with rates higher than 30 per cent in subsectors 13 (fishing), 31 (food, beverages and tobacco) and 32 (textiles and clothing). These values are considerably higher when the tariff structure is analysed at a less aggregated level (SITC, 4 digits), with values above 70 per cent (in both cases) in subsectors of agriculture and hunting, in food, beverages and tobacco, in textiles and leather, as well as in basic metals and machinery and equipment.

Along with Ecuador, Colombia and Venezuela have implemented a complicated programme to stabilize and support (protect) agricultural prices, involving more than 100 products.[12] The implicit surcharges will depend on the trend of international prices, but Reyes and Ramirez (1994) obtain surcharges which vary between 53 per cent and 100 per cent (depending on the year and the product) from a simulation of the system carried out for the periods 1976–93. In October 1993, Mexico replaced agricultural price-support mechanisms with direct subsidies granted by Procampo in those areas presently sown with wheat and maize, beans, rice, cotton, soya, barley and sorghum. The amount paid is determined on the basis of average output per hectare, kept constant in real terms for 10 years, to phase out gradually during years 11–15 (Valdés and Hjort, 1994).

As regards the automobile sector, Resolution 355 of the Andean Pact (or Complementarity Agreement, September 1993) set a common external tariff of 35 per cent and 15 per cent for the two categories considered, and stipulated specific rules of origin requirements as well as regional content percentages of 40 per cent and 30 per cent. Mexican legislation is still more protectionist, since the 'Automobile Decree' set agreements for trade compensation (quotas) among American, Canadian and Mexican producers for all of the sector's products, except for trucks of 15 tons and complete buses.

3 GENERAL CHARACTERISTICS OF THE G3

The agreement covers both goods and services, and contains clear and simple rules of accession (which are facilitated by an automatic and linear process of tariff reduction, with few exceptions). There are no restrictions on members liberalizing unilaterally or entering into future integration negotiations with other countries, and it noticeably reduces so-called unfair trade practices.

Description of the Agreement

The origins of the G3 date back to the beginning of 1991, when the presidents of the three countries agreed to strengthen the links between them and develop a common policy in the Caribbean (The Guadalajara Act). Later it was thought advisable to create a free trade zone, and throughout 1991 negotiations were held with a view to a 'traditional' type of agreement (with similar characteristics to those signed by Chile with Colombia, Mexico and Venezuela) and a practically definitive text was ready in May 1992.

Nevertheless, once the NAFTA negotiations had ended in August 1992, Mexico changed its mind and proposed negotiating an agreement with a scope similar to that of NAFTA. Colombia and Venezuela finally accepted, in view of the possibilities for expanded trade with Mexico, and with the idea that the G3 could be a bridging agreement on the road to hemispheric integration. It would prepare the country for future negotiations with NAFTA and with other regional blocs, and it could put forward a bloc strategy which Caribbean or Central American countries could join. It was also believed that the agreements reached between Colombia and Venezuela could later be discussed in the context of the Andean Pact. Eight rounds of negotiations were held in 1993, and four more between January and May 1994; the agreement was signed in Cartagena on 13 June 1994.

The structure of the G3 is similar to NAFTA. Its 23 chapters deal with the issues of national treatment and market access for goods (Chapter 23), the automobile sector (4), the agriculture sector including plant and animal hygiene (5), rules of origin (6), customs procedures (7), safeguards (8), unfair international trading practices (9), general principles governing services trade (10), telecommunications (11), financial services (12), temporary entry of business people (13), technical norms (14), public sector acquisitions (15), policies towards public sector companies (16), investment (17), intellectual property (18) and dispute resolution (19). As well as this there are two preliminary chapters of a general nature dealing with initial arrangements (1), and general definitions (2), and three final chapters on the administration of the treaty (20), transparency (21), exceptions (22) and final provisions (23).

The general characteristics of the G3, which distinguish it from other Latin American agreements, include the following:

- Unlike other treaties in force in Latin America, there is no intention of turning the G3 into a customs union (with the consequences for rules of origin discussed below).
- It is relatively easy for a country to withdraw from the agreement, by simply giving six months' notice. This is in contrast to certain past agreements which contained clauses which practically prevented withdrawal: in the Central American Common Market, for example, it was originally stipulated that no signatory country could withdraw in the first 20 years, and that once this period had elapsed the obligations would remain for a further five years. This latter clause also exists in the Andean Pact.
- Unlike the LAIA or the Andean Pact, any member may enter into free trade negotiations with any other country or bloc without any kind of penalty.
- The agreement includes very broad accession clauses.
- Disputes are resolved through the setting up of panels, whose decisions the parties are obliged to comply with.

It is also interesting to note that the G3 comprises two bilateral agreements with Mexico, since many of the relations between Colombia and Venzuela continue to be governed by Andean Pact rules. In spite of this, the two latter countries decided to adopt those disciplines of the G3 which were not sufficiently developed in the other agreement: plant and animal hygiene rules, customs procedures, certain services (telecommunications, financial services and temporary entry), technical standards, state acquisitions, investment and dispute resolution.

Tariff Reduction, Quotas and Unfair Practices

Tariff Reduction
It was originally intended to negotiate tariff reduction lists product by product (as in NAFTA), but after long and fruitless discussions the presidents of the three countries decided on a single tariff reduction programme over a 10-year period, except for the automobile industry, which was given 13 years. Mexico,

however, maintains significant quantitative restrictions in the automobile sector, for which reason the tariff reductions will have no effect on imports (although they will do in Colombia and Venezuela), and the three countries keep special agricultural policies, which led to the permanent exclusion of various products from this sector. In the final rounds of negotiation Colombia and Mexico (but not Venezuela) decided to speed up the process and reduce it to less than ten years for a significant group of goods.

Table 3.3 sets out the final results of the G3 negotiations between Colombia and Mexico, indicating the weight of the goods included in each list in terms of exports to the other country and to the rest of the world. The table clearly demonstrates that the significance of the excluded products is minimal: Colombia excluded 0.8 per cent of its imports from Mexico (1.9 per cent or 2.6 per cent when Mexico's exports worldwide are considered, with and without oil), and Mexico excluded 1.8 per cent (9.2 per cent or 1.8 per cent, for exports worldwide with and without oil). All the exceptions belong to the 'agriculture and hunting' or the 'food, drinks and tobacco' sectors. In the final round of negotiations textiles and clothing were also excluded in trade between Mexico and Venezuela.

There were also significant exceptions in the automobile sector. For trucks weighing more than 15 tons. (Where there are no quotas or compensation agreements between Mexico and the United States in NAFTA, a two-year period of grace was fixed, to be followed by an automatic and linear tariff reduction process over the next 11 years. For other vehicles it was agreed that complete liberalization of tariff and non-tariff barriers would be achieved by year 13. Nevertheless, little is known about the concrete policies (rules of origin, counter-trade, the pattern of tariff reduction, etc.) which will be adopted in those 13 years, as this will depend on the consensus negotiations in the so-called Automobile Sector Committee.)

As well as this, there is a certain degree of asymmetry between Mexico and Colombia, at least when one takes the worldwide exports of each country as a proxy for the pattern of future trade between the two countries. Indeed, only 8 per cent of Mexican exports to Colombia are included immediately (10 per cent in 5 years' time), while 31 per cent of Colombian exports will enter Mexico tariff-free from the start. Also, Colombia can export, tariff-free to Mexico, a high proportion of goods in which it has a clear comparative advantage, such as textiles and clothes as well as paper, printing and publishing.

Quotas and Unfair Practices

Access restrictions (e.g. quotas or prior permits) will only be accepted for imports of second-hand articles, and for a list of goods which are specifically stipulated in the agreement: petroleum derivatives and many automobile sector products in Mexico's case; energy products (provided a constitutional provision requiring this exists or is created) in Colombia and Venezuela. The performance requirements maintained by Colombia and Venzuela in the automobile sector are accepted, and the Colombian Constitution is respected as regards departmental taxes on liquor purchases.[13]

The G3 allows countries to keep existing export subsidies for a four-year period, after which they should gradually be eliminated between years 5 and 10. Export and production incentive measures (such as drawback schemes) are accepted, provided they have 'minimal' effects on production and are accepted by the GATT. Export taxes are not accepted, except on certain articles of basic necessity explicitly declared in the agreement. Finally, the agreement also stipulates that goods produced in duty-free zones will enjoy full benefits provided they comply with the respective rules of origin.

4 THE G3 AND HEMISPHERIC INTEGRATION

Areas of Conflict

A few days before the signing of the G3 accords, the leadership of the National Association of Industrialists (ANDI, the most powerful trade association in Colombia), requested the president not to sign it in view of the harmful effects the agreement could have on domestic production. Their point of view was supported by most trade associations, especially in the metal manufactures and machinery sectors and petrochemicals. Not even the textile and garment industry or exporters' associations supported the agreement. On the other hand, Fedesarrollo (1994) concludes that,

Table 3.3 The Liberalization Process in the G3

Liberalization in Colombia

CIIU2		Exports from Mexico Worldwide Distribution (%)				Exports from Mexico to Colombia Distribution (%)			
		Immediate	5 years	10 years	Excluded	Immediate	5 years	10 years	Excluded
11	Agriculture and hunting	0.0	0.0	89.1	10.9	0.0	0.0	80.0	20.0
12	Forestry and wood extraction	0.0	0.0	100.0	0.0				
13	Fishing	0.0	0.0	100.0	0.0				
21	Exploitation of coal mines								
22	Petroleum and gas production	0.0	0.0	100.0	0.0	100.0	0.0	0.0	0.0
23	Metallic mineral mining	4.2	0.0	95.8	0.0	0.0	0.0	100.0	0.0
29	Other mineral mining	0.0	0.0	100.0	0.0	0.0	0.0	19.2	80.8
31	Food, beverages and tobacco	0.0	0.0	68.0	32.0	16.8	0.0	83.2	0.0
32	Textiles, clothing and leather	14.4	0.4	85.2	0.0				
33	Wood and wood products	1.0	1.0	98.0	0.0	0.0	0.0	100.0	0.0
34	Paper, printing and publishing	17.5	1.3	81.3	0.0	56.1	0.0	43.9	0.0
35	Chemical products	20.1	3.7	75.7	0.6	50.5	4.8	44.4	0.2
36	Non-metallic minerals	0.5	1.0	98.6	0.0	3.9	4.7	91.4	0.0
37	Basic metals	6.0	6.3	87.6	0.0	14.5	24.4	61.1	0.0
38	Machinery and equipment	5.5	0.8	93.7	0.0	28.6	0.3	71.1	0.0
39	Other manufacturing industry	39.5	1.7	58.8	0.0	21.0	17.0	62.0	0.0
	Total	5.7	1.1	91.3	1.9	41.7	5.3	52.3	0.8
	Total excluding petroleum	8.0	1.6	87.8	2.6	41.7	5.3	52.3	0.8

Liberalization in Mexico

CIIU2		Exports from Colombia Worldwide Distribution (%)			Exports from Colombia to Mexico Distribution (%)			
		Immediate	10 years	Excluded	Immediate	5 years	10 years	Excluded
11	Agriculture and hunting	0.0	76.1	23.9	0.0		2.2	97.8
12	Forestry and wood extraction	0.0	100.0	0.0	0.0		100.0	0.0
13	Fishing	100.0	0.0	0.0	100.0		0.0	0.0
21	Exploitation of coal mines	0.0	100.0	0.0				
22	Petroleum and gas production	0.0	100.0	0.0				
23	Metallic mineral mining	0.0	100.0	0.0	0.0		100.0	0.0
29	Other mineral mining	0.0	100.0	0.0	0.0		100.0	0.0
31	Food, beverages and tobacco	0.0	78.4	21.6	44.6		55.4	0.0
32	Textiles, clothing and leather	45.9	54.1	0.0	1.0		99.0	0.0
33	Wood and wood products	2.8	97.2	0.0	22.4		77.6	0.0
34	Paper, printing and publishing	32.4	67.6	0.0	19.8		80.2	0.0
35	Chemical products	5.3	92.4	2.2	5.6		94.4	0.0
36	Non-metallic minerals	3.8	96.2	0.0	0.0		100.0	0.0
37	Basic metals	67.0	33.0	0.0	0.0		100.0	0.0
38	Machinery and equipment	13.8	86.2	0.0	30.4		69.6	0.0
39	Other manufacturing industry	83.8	16.2	0.0	66.0		34.0	0.0
	Total	20.1	70.8	9.2	30.8		67.5	1.8
	Total excluding petroleum	30.8	67.5	1.8	30.8		67.5	1.8

Despite the criticisms that have been made of trade agreements, especially with Mexico, they have been well received by industrialists, Practically half of all businessmen support the agreement with Mexico as against 26% who see it as against their interests. The opposition is mainly among producers of tobacco, concentrated animal foods and textile manufactures. The most enthusiastic support is found in the sugar, clothing and leather manufacturing sectors. The only sector with clear reservations about the G3 is the raw materials sector (60% of entrepreneurs surveyed in this sector consider the G3 agreement as 'favourable, very favourable or indifferent', while 40% see it as 'unfavourable or very unfavourable'.

Do the losing sectors outweigh the winners, in the opinion of the trade associations? If so, what mechanisms are there to compensate the losers, or for the gainers to reveal themselves?

The chances are that some of the polemical areas of the G3 negotiation will continue to be so in the context of hemispheric integration.

Safeguard Clauses and the Fantasy of Exchange Rate Safeguards
Any trade-creating agreement should limit the use of restrictive practices such as safeguards as much as possible. Presumably, countries ought to maintain a single form of safeguard (as permitted by the GATT), in order temporarily to protect their productive sectors in the case of unexpected negative external shocks.[14] But the experience of the G3 shows that this is an extreme position and that there will be great pressure to keep safeguards when free trade areas are being negotiated, when some of the participants in the negotiations are small countries, or where there are high levels of protection for domestic producers (unlike customs unions: today it is not possible to apply safeguards among the members of Mercosur, the Andean Pact, the Central American Common Market or Caricom). The G3 tried to reach an intermediate position as regards protection: there are forms of safeguard additional to those the GATT allows to each country, but their application is relatively limited. Thus, use of the so-called bilateral safeguard[15] is permitted for 15 years (10 years in NAFTA), but this is of a tariff nature (never quotas) and it may not be invoked for more than two years (the initial year plus one year of extension). Moreover, compensation is

required when it is invoked against the threat of damage, or when it is extended to the second year. A tariff quota type of safeguard mechanism was also agreed for the agricultural sector (this only applies between Venezuela and Mexico), and another for the financial sector, with it being stipulated that each country may suspend the benefits of the services chapter in the case of severe economic and financial upheaval which cannot be solved through alternative means, or when the balance of payments is facing serious difficulties.

Colombia and Venezuela insisted on keeping an exchange rate safeguard in the G3 (which finally was not approved), reflecting the influence of 'ghosts of the past'. Indeed, it was as a result of a mistaken view of the role played by the exchange rate in different economies, and the government's capacity to affect the real exchange rate, that the so-called exchange rate safeguard was created in the Andean Pact, and which was frequently invoked by member countries.[16] Indeed, it was the discussion about the validity of the exchange rate safeguard which led Venezuela only to enter the Andean Pact in 1973, six years later than the other members. Exchange rate safeguards do not exist in any other integration agreement, but it is likely that the Andean Pact countries will again insist on this point when negotiations are held at hemisphere level. Alternative strategies should be put forward to achieve the same purpose (e.g. a greater degree of coordination in the management of fiscal and monetary policies between countries), since the exchange rate safeguard would shut out much of the continent's trade, in view of high exchange rate variability in our countries and the central role of the exchange rate as a variable of macroeconomic adjustment.

Rules of Origin
Rules of origin end up becoming a black box whose effects are unclear, which provide unknown levels of protection and which constitute an asymmetrical mechanism in favour of more developed countries. In fact, rules of origin are equivalent to 'performance requirements', prohibited in NAFTA and in the G3 for their trade-distorting effects.

According to Hufbauer and Schott (1994: 5), NAFTA's rules of origin are unsatisfactory for two reasons: first, they penalize the region's producers and and make them less efficient, by forcing them to buy expensive regional inputs; secondly, they represent an unfortunate precedent for other integration agreements, whose members may try to emulate such practices. They are even more undesirable in the G3 when one considers that present trade flows are decidedly less. Mexico insisted on the advisability of rules of origin similar to those of NAFTA, holding up the negotiations for more than six months and causing deep irritation among the Colombian and Venezuelan private sectors (despite the progress achieved).

Mechanisms were created to soften the restrictive effect of the rules. These include the so-called Regional Inputs Committee, which may temporarily classify a good as regional (despite its not fulfilling the stipulated rules of origin) when the regional inputs needed for production in this particular sector do not exist or when their quality is inadequate.

Special quotas were created for textiles and garments made with synthetic fibres, and it was accepted that Colombia could export a percentage of such products under less stringent rules of origin than those stipulated in the agreement (trade between Mexico and Venezuela in textiles and clothing was excluded from the agreement).

Certain rules of origin are not so strict in the initial period. For example, the regional content stipulated for the majority of goods is 50 per cent in the first five years and 55 per cent from the 6th year onwards. In chemicals and petrochemicals a regional content of 40 per cent was set for the first three years, 45 per cent for years 4 and 5, and 50 per cent thereafter.

Different Incentives in the Various Countries

The net benefits of hemispheric integration will be greater, *ceteris paribus*, the more total exports are destined within the hemisphere, and to the extent that manufacturing exports represent a high proportion of the total. The first factor is associated with the low probability of trade diversion,[17] and the second is related to the creation of new trade (Latin American exports of·primary products already face low or zero protection levels in the United States and Canada), as well as to more intensive economies-of-scale effects and other dynamic effects in the industrial sector (see Erzan and Yeats, 1992; Bouzas and Ros, 1994: 15).

Colombia and Venezuela accept the importance of hemispheric integration, and the G3 constitutes a key element in the process of moving towards this. The treaty was seen as a bridging agreement for the continent, and once signed it would be extremely costly to change direction. Despite the short- and medium-term traumas that Mexico may suffer as a result of its entry into NATA, its productive sector in the long run will acquire the standards of competitiveness of US and Canadian firms, and it will be able to buy inputs at low cost. In NAFTA Mexico will immediately free 44 per cent of its imports from the United States, with even higher percentages in raw materials for industry (70 per cent), in capital goods for agriculture (58 per cent) and for industry (51 per cent), and raw materials for industry (42 per cent). In five years' time, these same percentages will rise to 73, 97, 82 and 73 per cent, respectively (Echavarría, 1994).

On the other hand, the NAFTA agreement means that Colombian and Venezuelan producers will have to compete without tariff preferences in the Mexican market with producers from the United States and Canada, especially in those sectors where Mexico frees NAFTA imports immediately: coal (100 per cent) and metallic minerals (100 per cent), other minerals (99.7 per cent), agriculture and hunting (95 per cent), fishing (89 per cent) and forestry and lumber (86 per cent). In the textile, clothing and leather goods sectors where a large part of Colombia's comparative advantage lies, Mexico will free 29 per cent in NAFTA immediately, and 70 per cent in five years' time. The corresponding figures for basic publishing are 69 per cent and 83 per cent respectively. In general terms in the G3 the sectors most affected by the preferences granted to the US by Mexico will be chemicals and the publishing industry, which only become tariff-free inside the G3 in ten years' time.

4 Trade Strategy Alternatives for a Small Country: The Chilean Case

Raúl Labán and Patricio Meller

INTRODUCTION

The opening up of the Chilean economy was achieved through a far-reaching unilateral trade liberalization process, which formed one component of an overall reform package where free market prices, comparative advantage and private sector entrepreneurship all played leading roles. A sharp real devaluation of the exchange rate had an important effect on the successful expansion of Chilean exports. A brief overview of these issues is provided in section 1.

Chilean comparative advantage is mainly in natural resources. Chilean exports to industrial countries are more than 90 per cent natural resource-based: either raw materials or (first stage) processed raw materials. On the other hand, Chilean exports to Latin American countries include a significant amount of manufactures not related to its natural resource endowment. The data on revealed comparative advantage according to market destination is provided in section 2.

What are the problems related to specialization in natural resource production and trade for a developing country like Chile? And why should manufacturing exports be preferred to other types of exports? These are the issues explored in section 3.

Chile has been pursuing a unilateral trade strategy which has produced a successful expansion of exports. Why, then, should Chile change this strategy and try to become a member of preferential trade groupings? This is the subject discussed in section 4.

1 CHILEAN TRADE POLICY AND THE EXPORT BOOM

There were two separate stages in the Chilean international trade liberalization process. (1) The trade liberalization period of the 1970s, where the main feature was a great reduction of import barriers, and (2) the export expansion period of the post-external debt crisis 1980s, where the real exchange rate constituted the main, although not the only, mechanism for export promotion.

For more than three decades (1940–73) the Chilean economy had been characterized by extensive price controls and highly restricted foreign trade. The trade liberalization reform of the 1970s was intended to change the prevailing pattern of economic incentives, and so was complementary to price liberalization. In addition, it aimed at rationalizing the complex Chilean trade regime so as to eliminate the discretionary power of the bureaucracy. Tariff reduction was stated to be a clear sign of openness and a measure of equalizing incentives across all types of activity (exportables, importables and non-tradeables). During the 1970s, the exchange rate was used to offset tariff reduction, since initially the economic authorities were concerned about import competition. However, in the 1980s there was an explicit strategy to promote exports as the engine of growth: after sharp real devaluations a stable real exchange rate is maintained.

Before 1974 Chile had a highly restrictive foreign trade regime which included quotas, prior import deposits, licences, foreign exchange budgets and prohibited import lists, as well as special regimes for particular regions, particular industries and public firms, together with quite high nominal tariffs. In a five-year period, 1974–9, all non-tariff barriers were eliminated and the average (highest) nominal tariff rate was reduced from 105 per cent (750 per cent) to a flat tariff structure of 10 per cent.[1] This 10 per cent flat structure was maintained until 1982 (see Tables 4.1 and 4.2).

During the 1980s, in response to the economic situation generated by the external debt crisis, nominal tariffs were increased in stages to 35 per cent (see Table 4.2). A flat tariff structure (10 per cent) provided the authorities with an easy-to-use tool to complement the exchange rate in facing external disequilibrium; it also provided additional revenues to finance the fiscal deficit. The unilateral liberalization of the 1980s was much slower than in the 1970s; it took almost six years to reduce nominal tariffs from 20 per cent (June 1985) to 11 per cent (January 1991).[3]

Table 4.1   Chile's First Unilateral Liberalization Process, 1973–81. Average nominal tariffs (%)

1973	1975	1977	1979	1981
105	49	22	10[a]	10

Note: (a) From June onwards.
Source: Central Bank of Chile and Ffrench-Davis (1980).

Table 4.2   Second Chilean Unilateral Liberalization Process, 1982–94. Flat nominal tariffs (%)

1982	1984	1986	1988	1990	1992	1994
10	20÷35[a]	20[b]	15[c]	15	11[d]	11

Notes: (a) Tariffs were increased to 20 per cent in March 1983. (b) Tariffs were decreased to 30 per cent in March and then to 20 per cent in June 1985. (c) Tariffs were decreased to 15 per cent in January 1988. (d) Tariffs were decreased to 11 per cent in January 1991.
Source: Central Bank of Chile.

Given the balance of payments crisis of 1982, in 1982–4 real devaluations were undertaken to re-establish the level of the real exchange rate prevailing prior to 1979 (when a fixed nominal exchange rate was established). However, due to the requirements of large external debt service payments, the 1982–4 devaluations were not enough, and additional real devaluations were needed during and after 1985. These large real devaluations provided a very significant stimulus to export expansion.

In short, during the 1970s trade reforms follow the neutrality principle in equalizing incentives across goods. In a prevailing context of anti-export bias these measures were, in effect, favourable to exports, but during the 1980s there was a clear shift towards export promotion, using domestic currency depreciation as the main tool. Thus, in the last two decades, Chile has undertaken two unilateral and non-selective trade liberalizations: one radical (1974–9), and the other more moderate (1985–91). Probably the most important difference between the two episodes is that, while in the first liberalization after an initial devaluation, the peso appreciated in real terms, in the second liberalization tariff reduction was accompanied by a sharp real devaluation.

Chile's uniform tariff structure has been modified in three respects: the adoption of price bands for a number of agricultural products (wheat, sugar and oilseeds); the granting of differential tariff preferences to LAIA member countries; and, recently, the signing of bilateral free trade and economic complementarity agreements with a number of countries.

The extent to which exports have become a key sector in the Chilean economy is revealed by three indicators.

(1) The share of exports in real GDP increased significantly during the 1980s from 23 per cent (1980), to reach 34 per cent in 1990. This is associated with a more intensive use of productive factors and faster productivity growth. Another part is related to an intersectoral redistribution of income caused by the high real devaluations of the 1980s.

(2) Prior to 1970 Chile was thought of mainly as an exporter of copper and little else. As well as a big increase in copper exports there has also been significant diversification, resulting in the share of copper declining from more than 75 per cent of total exports, at the end of the 1960s, to less than 50 per cent in the 1980s (Table 4.3). In short, the present Chilean comparative advantage is structurally the same as in the past, i.e. close to 90

Table 4.3 Breakdown of Total Chilean Exports; 1970–94 (million of dollars)

Year	Mining Copper	Non-copper	Fish and Sea Products[a]	Forestry and Wood Products	Agricultural Products	Rest	Total
1970	839.8	110.6	1.4	10.2	30.1	70.8	1111.7
1980	2152.5	619.4	290.8	591.3	281.2	735.5	4670.7
1990	3910.2	729.3	862.1	869.9	899.4	1309.4	8580.3
1994	4242.0	949.5	1327.5	1623.1	1094.9	2408.1	11645.9

Note: In 1990 there was a change in the classification system; therefore intertemporal comparisons are not totally valid.
(a) Sea products are not included in 1970.
Source: Central Bank of Chile.

per cent of the export basket depends on Chile's natural resources endowment. However, there are two important differences with respect to the past: (1) There is a clear diversification among distinct natural resource-based goods in the export basket. Provided the fluctuation patterns in world prices of basic natural resource commodities do not coincide, the Chilean economy will be exposed to relatively smaller external shocks than in the past. But a more important fact is that the potential total substitution of one of the export commodities will not have the damaging effect that the appearance of synthetic nitrate had in the past. (2) Most Chilean exports are being produced by Chilean-owned enterprises; therefore, most of the surplus generated by export activities can be reinvested domestically.

(3) In our opinion, the most important indicator of Chilean export expansion is related to the increasing number of exporting firms. The number of Chilean firms (including joint-ventures and majority foreign-owned firms) exporting more than US$100 000 has increased from almost 900 (1986) to more than 1500 (1990) in only four years (Table 4.4). This is a quite different picture from the 1960s and 1970s, when the two main foreign firms (Anaconda and Kennecott) were exporting around 70 per cent of total exports.

However, it should be pointed out that the new Chilean

Table 4.4 Number of Export Firms According to Exported Volume, 1986–9

Volume of Exports	Number of Firms				
	1986	1987	1988	1989	1990
More than US$100 million	4	6	8	8	8
From US$10 million to US$100 million	38	50	66	76	87
From US$1 million to US$10 million	193	248	303	341	431
From US$100 000 to US$1 million	661	772	854	892	1034
Total	896	1076	1231	1317	1560

Source: Central Bank of Chile, unpublished data.

entrepreneurs are not Schumpeterian innovators; in this respect, they are really imitators rather than innovators. They have developed a managerial capacity, that is, the ability to coordinate and manage the distinct and complex features of modern enterprises; they are managers with organizational abilities, who select responsible and well-qualified personnel, and who are well informed about the latest technologies and developments in industrial countries. In our opinion, in semi-industrialized economies it is more important to do these things well rather than to be an innovator – incompetence and inefficiency in entrepreneurial ability are two of the main obstacles to a firm's expansion into foreign markets (Ray, 1988).

2 REVEALED COMPARATIVE ADVANTAGE

Chile's revealed comparative advantage can be examined by classifying its exports into:[4] goods comprising natural resources (NR), industrial goods based on further processing of NR exports (PNR),[5] and other industrial products (OIP),[6] and by market destination, including: United States, the European Union (EU), Japan and Latin America (LA). More than 80 per cent of Chilean exports go to these four markets (Table 4.5).

Exports to developed countries are highly intensive in NR. In 1991, NR-based exports constituted more than 61 per cent of exports going to the United States and Japan, and almost 70 per cent of exports to the EU. PNR-based exports are about 30 per cent of total exports to those markets, while OIP exports are only slightly more than 10 per cent of exports to the United States, and 5 per cent and 1 per cent in the cases of the EU and Japan, respectively. In the case of exports to Latin America, there is a more even breakdown for the three categories: PNR (38 per cent), NR (35 per cent) and OIP (27 per cent).

In the case of PNR industrial goods, the EU and Japan take 26.6 per cent and 21 per cent of total exports respectively; the United States and LA each absorb around 16 per cent. In the case of OIP, LA is the main market. NR and PNR exports together represent more than 90 per cent of total exports to developed countries, with NR mining exports going mainly to the EU and Japan, and PNR mining exports going to the United States and the EU. The United States and the EU are the main markets for NR exports of fruits, vegetables and fish, while PNR fish and forestry exports go mainly to the EU and Japan. In the OIP category, LA and the United States are the most important markets for basic metals and textile products.

Table 4.5   Sectoral Distribution of Exports According to Market
Destination, 1991 (%)

Sector	US	EU	Japan	LA	Rest	Total (%)	Total (US$ millions)
Natural Resources (NR)							
Mining[a]	9.7	38.5	24.5	8.5	18.8	100.0	4,037
Fruit and vegetables	48.2	35.7	0.7	7.2	8.3	100.0	1,081
Cattle	8.5	49.9	1.1	30.0	10.5	100.0	22
Fish	57.3	31.8	8.4	0.8	1.7	100.0	111
Forestry	0.7	6.3	30.1	1.3	61.6	100.0	67
Sub-total	18.4	37.4	19.3	8.1	16.8	100.0	5,319
Processed Natural Resources (PNR)							
Mining	39.3	31.4	6.2	13.2	10.0	100.0	451
Fruit and vegetables	25.6	16.9	9.3	33.3	15.0	100.0	505
Cattle	0.1	17.1	19.7	51.8	11.3	100.0	43
Fish	8.5	34.7	25.4	2.4	29.0	100.0	977
Forestry	8.0	21.0	30.5	22.5	18.0	100.0	872
Sub-total	16.1	26.6	21.0	16.5	19.9	100.0	2,849
Other Industrial Products (OIP)							
Chemical	15.5	18.0	4.2	29.0	33.2	100.0	507
Textiles	35.5	14.4	0.1	40.9	9.0	100.0	148
Basic Metals	11.3	10.3	0.1	68.7	9.6	100.0	181
Other	20.2	5.3	0.1	12.5	61.9	100.0	45
Sub-total	18.2	15.2	2.5	38.3	25.8	100.0	881
Total	17.6	31.8	18.2	13.7	18.7	100.0	9,049

Note: (a) This sector includes refined copper.
Source: Campero and Escobar (1992).

Examining the trend in exports to developed countries in 1986–91, Campero and Escobar (1992) found a negative association between NR exports and the corresponding industrial PNR exports to the same market destination: for example, forestry exports to the United States fall while processed forestry exports increase; a similar situation is observed for fish and cattle. This type of finding would suggest that there is some sort of substitution in the Chilean export market between NR and the corresponding PNR for a given market destination.

The present structure of Chilean exports suggests the following: Chile's comparative advantage with respect to developed countries is in NR; the observed increase of Chilean industrial exports to these markets would seem to be related to the expansion of PNR. In relation to Latin America, Chile's comparative advantage, in addition to traditional NR, seems to be in PNR and in some specific OIP (basic metals, chemicals, textiles). Chile's textile exports to the United States and to LA suggest that there is further potential for OIP exports.

This static export specialization pattern, namely strong concentration on natural resources, is consistent with: (1) Chile's static comparative advantage derived from an abundant natural resource endowment; (2) Chile's unilateral and non-selective trade liberalization of the 1970s and 1980s; (3) the instruments of export promotion that have been used in the past; and (4) the fact that trade in natural resources has traditionally been subject to lower average nominal and effective protection rates, in developed economies, than trade of goods of higher value-added. The difference in the composition of Chile's exports to Latin America vis-à-vis other regions of the world may be explained by its more similar natural resources endowment, its geographical proximity (location advantage) and the bilateral tariff preferences between LAIA member countries.

3 DYNAMIC COMPARATIVE ADVANTAGE

Specialization in Natural Resource Exports

Manufacturing exports are considered a desirable goal in the new export development strategy, but why should the export of US\$100 million of blue jeans be preferred to the export of US\$100 million of grapes? More generally, what is the disadvantage of NR exports with respect to manufacturing exports?

The current Chilean export boom has been based mainly on NR exports. The literature identifies several possible drawbacks to a development strategy based on NR exports. First, NR have low price and income elasticities of demand, so the rate of expansion of NR exports should eventually stagnate. Furthermore, following Prebisch, it could be argued that long-run terms of trade tend to move against NR. These were the basic principles used to promote the strategy of import substitution. Secondly, most NR exports go to developed countries. Given the relatively low growth rates recently observed in those countries, this further limits the growth in demand for NR. Thirdly, NR are generally subject to significant price volatility, which countries which specialize in NR exports find too costly to hedge against, thereby generating an important source of instability in the domestic economy with a consequent negative impact on investment and growth.[7] Finally, the new theories of international trade and growth stress the importance of using and developing the latest modern technology. NR exports generally use either a low-level or a very sector-specific technology, so the overall economy does not benefit from any externality from technology used in NR exports. This is an argument for promoting exports of industrial goods which require the use of modern technology.

A basic assumption of new dynamic trade growth models relates to the large positive externality generated by the technology used by the industrial sector (Krugman, 1990; Grossman and Helpman, 1991). If a country has a small comparative advantage in industry, due to the existence of a positive technology externality, then this will generate a technological advantage which will accumulate through time; the process will induce a dynamic comparative advantage for this country, while industrial production will be crowded out in the other countries (Krugman, 1981). Thus, the accumulated pattern of past production will determine the present pattern of production, and specialization becomes a self-perpetuating and self-reinforcing process because, due to the externality, there will be relatively larger increases in productivity in the specialized sector. In short, 'history matters even in the long run' because all productivity changes generated by the present situation, generate forces which preserve and reinforce the pattern of specialization (Krugman, 1987).

The 'initial conditions and hysteresis' argument leads to the same type of conclusion. A closed economy that undertakes a neutral external sector liberalization reform (low flat-rate tariff) will have a resource reallocation according to comparative advantage; in the Chilean case, this process has meant a stimulus to NR exports. These initial conditions would lead to further specialization in NR exports in future trade and production, whereas the rest of the world already has comparative advantage in manufacturing and will increase that advantage in the future.

In brief, initial conditions, history and hysteresis suggest that present Chilean NR export specialization will lead to further NR trade and production specialization in the future.

Assuming that research and development (R&D) in innovation and adaptation of new technology is concentrated in industry, then NR specialization would reduce the resources allocated to R&D. The developed countries (DCs) have a relative advantage in R&D; a less developed country (LDC) would spend resources on R&D only if its human capital had a lower wage than that prevailing in the DC, other things being equal. It is clear that LDCs cannot use many resources in R&D because of the heavy fixed costs involved. Moreover, if an LDC specializes in NR, this sector will attract all existing domestic human capital, and the few resources that the LDC spent on R&D will be crowded out by the NR sector. Thus, future LDC innovation and technology adaptation will diminish, with negative consequences for future growth; in other words, NR trade specialization could impair future LDC growth (Grossman and Helpman, 1991).

The preceding argument is similar to the one used to explain the 'Dutch Disease' phenomenon: the large inflow of foreign exchange generated by the NR sector leads to domestic currency appreciation, and thus to deindustrialization. The 'disease' aspect of the positive increase in income generated by the NR boom is in the contraction of the industrial sector. Industry and manufacturing exports are associated with the use and development of modern technology; if a country loses its industrial production capacity, it will generate a learning gap in how to use modern technology. Furthermore, the technological gap will be an increasing one; the more (the less) a country uses modern technology, the greater will be the increase (decrease) in its ability to innovate in the future. Therefore, transitory shocks could have permanent effects upon a country's growth. This is the rationale for isolating the industrial sector during an external disequilibrium adjustment process: preserving the international competitiveness of the tradeable sector is more important than keeping up the level of non-tradeables production (Krugman, 1987).

The Second Export Stage

The discussion of Chile's second export stage focuses on bringing higher value-added to current NR exports, through processing.

In other words, this second export stage is based on promoting forward NR linkages, for example by exporting apple juice, wine and canned fruit (instead of fresh grapes and apples), wood furniture and paper (instead of sawn wood), manufactured copper products, etc. The implicit assumption is that PNR goods will introduce and disseminate modern technology with, therefore, the highest domestic externality. This coincides with the above arguments.

As previously observed, there seems to be a natural sequence in the development of this type of strategy and perhaps, therefore, no special promotion measures are required. In this case, exports of certain PNR goods would naturally increase in markets to which raw NR are already being exported. Table 4.6 shows the export pattern (1970–90) of three products in the PNR category. One of the key issues is the rationale for promoting the specific

Table 4.6 Evolution of Processed Natural Resource Exports, 1970–90 (US$ million)

	1970	1980	1990
Fish meal	16	203	515
Wine	2	19	52
Paper and cardboard	15	49	82

Source: CEPAL (1992).

export of PNR goods in preference to other types of export, especially in so far as, for example, the goals of export diversification and use of modern technology have been achieved by fruit exports.

Although grapes and apples are the main items (see Tables 4.7 and 4.8), Chile has achieved a considerable diversification in its fruit exports. During the 1990s, fruit exports also include pears, peaches, plums, kiwi fruits, avocados, nectarines, apricots, cherries, berries and lemons.

Overall figures relating to the production and export of Chilean fruit show the following (Jarvis, 1991): (1) Areas planted increased by 8.1 per cent per year during the 1980s. (2) Fruit production had a 10.9 per cent annual growth rate during the 1980s as a whole, and a 12.0 per cent growth rate in the second half of the 1980s. (3) Fruit export volumes increased at 16.9 per

Table 4.7 Comparison of Export Growth Rates between Chile, Latin America and the World, for Specific Fruit, Fish and Forestry Products, 1970–90

Exports of	Growth rates[c] (1970–90)			Export level (1990) (US$ million)		
	Chile	LA	World	Chile	LA	World
Grapes	18.5	16.5	6.0	379	405	1 661
Apples	9.4	2.3	3.4	131	210	2 067
Fish capture[a]	3.0	−4.9	−3.6	6.4	17.9[b]	99.5[b]
Fish products[a]	13.3	3.9	7.1	896	3447	32 787
Raw fish[a]	26.0	14.7	8.8	207	747	13 193
Fish meal[a]	13.4	0.0	0.5	515	958	1 640
Forestry products	9.3	7.0	4.4	750	2743	94 470
Sawn wood	8.3	0.4	3.5	136	426	16 989
Wood pulp	9.6	14.0	3.5	326	962	15 817
Paper and cardboard	2.8	12.7	6.2	82	830	45 268

Notes: (a) Growth rates are for the period 1970–89 and the export level is for the year 1989. (b) Million of tons. (c) Annual growth rates shown have been calculated using the current value of exports, transformed into constant US$ (1990) using the US wholesale price index.

Source: CEPAL (1992).

Table 4.8 Trend of New Types of Fruit Exports, 1970–90 (US$ million)

	1970	1980	1985	1990	Chilean export share (1990)	
					LA %	World %
Pears	1	11	13	45	41.3	6.5
Peaches	1	7	22	55	97.2	6.9
Plums	–	3	11	40	94.1	16.6
Kiwi fruit	0	0	0	28	100.0	4.5
Avocado	0	0	1	26	61.7	14.2

Source: CEPAL (1992).

cent per year during the 1980s. (4) By the end of the 1980s fruit exports represented 43.3 per cent of total fruit production.

In short, Chile has become the main Latin American fruit-exporting country (see Tables 4.7 and 4.8). Given its relatively small share of world exports, and the advantage of the inverse season with respect to most developed countries, there is still the possibility for Chilean fruit exports to expand further. However, it is not expected that the 1980s expansion of fruit exports will be repeated during the 1990s.

Another issue related to fruit exports is that it provides a different view with respect to how to proceed in a second stage export strategy. While the expansion of PNR exports is based on forward linkages as the mechanism for introducing modern technology, the growth of fruit exports shows that the exploitation of backward linkages can also have an important effect on the application of modern technology. Exporting fresh fruit is a highly complex process requiring careful coordination and supervision of the whole chain of production, distribution, wholesale and retail trade (see CEPAL, 1990; Jarvis, 1991). The preservation of fresh quality requires a cooling system that keeps temperatures constant through the different stages of the period between production and wholesale trade. This cooling system involves the use of temperature-controlled storage places and containers, and the use of refrigerated trucks and ships. High-technology equipment and specialized human capital are required to handle large volumes of fruit which have to be kept fresh. Chilean ports have had to upgrade their systems of operation, install special, isolated, temperature-controlled storage places, and speed up the ship-loading system. To avoid rotting and pest infestation in the many different stages, fumigation has to be incorporated into the cooling system, and special modern packaging is required. Modern technology is used to produce a standard-sized high quality fruit product catering to the tastes of developed country consumers. In addition to this, due to the rapid growth of fruit exports more land has been planted, in some cases, on hillsides or in the northern part of Chile where water is scarce. This requires the introduction of a variety of technologies, such as sophisticated drip-irrigation systems. Part of this technology was imported together with human capital skills, but another part was developed locally using domestic human capital.

Backward linkages induced by fruit exports have therefore required the introduction of technological innovations. It would be very difficult to specify which type of technology has the largest external effect on the economy: the technology used in the forward processing of NR exports or the technology used in the backward linkages related to fruit exports. Mining is another

NR export sector which could have a similar backward-linkage technological effect.

In short, the production of NR could be a way to introduce modern technology in a developing country in some cases as good on the production of industrial goods.

Finally, the Asian pattern of manufactured exports demonstrates the possibility of moving into higher export-processing stages in product lines totally unrelated to the domestic availability of NR. There are a few Chilean export goods of this nature (Table 4.5). Therefore, increasing value-added to domestic NR is not the only way to expand exports.

Recent Export Trends

During the 1990s, there has been a change in the type of economies that affect Chilean export dynamism. The recession in the DCs did not have the traditional contractionary effect on total Chilean exports; the expansion of exports towards LA and Asia has more than compensated for the decline of exports to Europe (Table 4.9). In other words, the general LA trade liberalization reforms of the 1990s have helped to increase Chilean exports

Table 4.9 Chilean Export Growth by Destination Markets, 1989–93

Destination Market	Average Annual Growth Rate[a] %	Export Level 1993 US$ million
European Union	−5.9	2444
Latin America	15.2	1860
US & Canada	1.6	1716
Japan	6.1	1502
Asia (without Japan)[b]	8.0	1399
Rest	−7.5	495
Total	2.1	9416
Mercosur	11.4	1089
NAFTA	2.7	1847

Notes: (a) Growth rate is calculated for constant US$ (1993). The US-WPI has been used as deflator.
(b) Countries included are: Korea, Taiwan, China, Thailand, Indonesia, Hong Kong, Singapore, the Philippines and Malaysia.
Source: Central Bank of Chile.

within the region at an annual average rate of 15.2 per cent (1989–93), while rapid growth in Asia (excluding Japan) has generated an 8.0 per cent (1989–93) annual increase of Chilean exports to that region.

Considering manufacturing exports alone, it can be seen that LA and the United States and Canada have been very important for the expansion of OIP exports (see Table 4.10). A similar situation is observed for 'new' PNR export goods over US$10 million in 1993; in this case, some European countries and Japan appear as destination markets. Manufacturing export diversification (i.e. more items in the export basket), considering both PNR and OIP, has been more important in LA and the United States and Canada than in other world regions. Including 40 items of PNR exports and 24 items of OIP exports having a level higher than US$ 10 million in 1993, LA and United States and Canada appear more times among the three most important export destination markets.

Table 4.10 Importance of Destination Markets for 40 PNR Items and 24 OIP Items with an Export Level Higher than US$10 million, 1993

	PNR (40 items)			OIP (24 items)		
	1st Place	2nd Place	3rd Place	1st Place	2nd Place	3rd Place
Latin America	13	14	16	11	17	13
US & Canada	12	4	6	7	3	5
European Union	4	10	11	4	2	2
Japan	7	7	2	1		1
Asia (except Japan)	3	4	1		1	1

Source: Central Bank of Chile (see Appendix for list of goods).

4 ANALYSIS OF CHILEAN TRADE STRATEGY ALTERNATIVES

The main features of Chilean trade strategy up to 1993 have been the following: (1) A far-reaching unilateral trade liberalization process. (2) An export market diversification strategy meaning the absence of any 'natural trade partner' relationship.

(3) The small country assumption, or the importance of being irrelevant: Chile would always find a niche in foreign markets.

The preceding sections have shown that this strategy, in which Chile has taken its own decisions autonomously, has been very successful in expanding exports. So, if something has had positive results, why should it be changed? Why is Chile interested in entering trade agreements with different commercial partners?

Chile's Current Trade Policy Challenge

Despite the significant gains obtained in the last two decades in terms of diversifying and expanding the volume of exports (in particular since the mid-1980s), if Chile wishes to sustain a strong and stable output growth path in the future, it will have to maintain the dynamism of the export sector and diversify it more into manufacturing.

The significant changes seen recently in the domestic and external conditions that have been behind the strong expansion of Chilean exports over the past decade make it difficult to believe the country will be able to sustain export dynamism and move beyond mainly exporting natural resources, without changes in its development strategy. In particular we believe that without a change in Chile's trade policy under this new scenario, it will become more difficult to maintain the actual rates of expansion of exports, and that economic forces will tend to reinforce the existing pattern of export specialization.

Thus, the need to be able to export products with higher value-added and technological content, and the drastic change in some of the conditions that have favoured Chile's development strategy in the recent past, together with changes seen in the international context, pose a challenge for Chile to redesign its development strategy and, in particular, its export-promotion tools. This is likely to require the redesigning of education and labour-training systems, as well as public sector instruments for promoting technology and productivity. But it will also require Chile's trade policy to be remodelled, in particular so as to allow Chile to increase its manufacturing exports.

This will require, among others things, improved access conditions for such exports to foreign markets. Both developed and developing countries impose greater restrictions on products with a higher value-added; there is a significant escalation in the tariff structure according to a product's value-added content. It will certainly not be possible to obtain improved access conditions for these products by a simple unilateral tariff reduction.

Among the main conditions that have changed in recent years are: (1) a significant fall in the real exchange rate,[8] due partly to Chile's regained access to world capital markets, the overcoming of the external debt problem and the significant expansion of exports; (2) an increase in real wages at a higher rate than productivity gains;[9] (3) the difficulty of keeping the simplified 10 per cent minor export rebate (subsidy),[10] if Chile complies with GATT conditions and/or negotiates admission into NAFTA.

In the international context, there has been renewed interest in bilateral and regional trade agreements in order to promote trade, and there has been a proliferation of agreements since the late 1980s.[11] It is possible to predict that bilateral and regional trade agreements, in all their forms, will play an important role in the future. This change in international context also raises questions about the trade policy that should be followed by small open economies like Chile.

The formation of a trade bloc represents a threat for a non-member country, since the latter's ability to compete is severely damaged by the granting of preferential access (e.g. preferential tariff treatment) to potential competitors in its export markets (Krugman, 1991). Furthermore, the formation of the trade bloc may negatively affect the terms of trade of non-member countries. Thus, even though joining a trading bloc may have many problems, much worse would be to be left outside: Chile, therefore, needs to define a strategy vis-à-vis trade blocs.

In addition, much tougher competition should be expected for Chilean exports in their present destination markets in the near future, as a result of economic liberalization and export-oriented structural adjustment programmes being undertaken in various countries of the world, both in countries with significant endowments of natural resources and labour-abundant countries. This could have a negative effect on Chilean NR exports and on its ability to compete in export markets for labour-intensive manufactures. However, the expected positive impact from trends towards the opening up of new export markets, together with trends in world output and trade growth, offers new opportunities for an outward-oriented economy like Chile.

What, then, is the trade strategy to be followed by Chile in this new context? Should Chile keep on doing more of the same?

There is a broad consensus that unilateral trade liberalization seems to be a necessary ingredient of trade policy for small open economies trying to follow a medium-term development plan based on the expansion (in volume and diversification) of exports. The question is whether this policy will prove to be a sufficient condition for continued export growth, and whether or not it will allow Chile to go beyond exporting mainly NR.

Thus, the question is whether unilateral trade liberalization should be the only tool, or whether there is a role for bilateral and regional trade liberalization agreements.

Bilateralism in the Trade Strategy of a Small Open economy

It can be shown that there is a complementary role to be played by bilateral trade agreements (BTA) in the trade strategy of small open economies, since they provide benefits that cannot be obtained through unilateral tariff reduction.[12] But an initial and extensive unilateral trade liberalization (UTL) is regarded as a prerequisite for a small economy to take full advantage of the benefits of bilateralism.

Apart from the traditional justification for BTAs deriving from the potential benefits of 'trade creation' (an argument from the imports side), BTAs for small economies are usually justified on the grounds of the positive – static and dynamic – welfare implications induced by an expansion of exports to member countries, in particular, in the presence of technologies offering increasing returns to scale.

They can also be motivated by an effort to secure market access for the small country's exports – an 'insurance policy' – in particular to those markets currently receiving a significant proportion of the country's total export shipments, such as the United States, EU and Japan. This consideration provides a powerful argument for Chile to sign a BTA with Mercosur, as the latter is an important destination for Chile's manufactured goods exports. In addition, its member countries historically have tended to reverse their policies and reforms, which points to the importance of 'locking in' a preferential market access for

Chilean exports, which would probably be more costly to reverse
if it is established through a BTA.

Bilateralism may also be justified as a 'defensive' strategy. In
this regard, Butelmann and Meller (1992) argue that Mexico and
Canada are Chile's most important competitors as suppliers of
natural resources and processed natural resources to the US
market. Thus, being left out of NAFTA could have negative
effects on Chile's export potential to this market.[13] This is
probably the reason behind New Zealand's concern at the
prospect of Chile's joining this trading bloc.

Also, in a context of trade barriers in other countries and, in
particular, of a significant escalation in tariff structure according
to value-added content, a BTA could make possible a reduction
in the trade restrictions faced by Chile's exports, with a relatively
bigger impact on exports of manufactures: something that cannot
be obtained by a simple UTL.[14]

Other reasons for signing BTAs include: (1) less chance of
discretionary, and sometimes arbitrary, use of quality controls,
sanitary regulations and other forms of administrative protection
measures – for example, the case of Chilean grapes in the United
States in 1990 and Chilean apples in the EU in 1992; (2) less
chance of arbitrary anti-dumping or countervailing measures; (3)
an increase in bargaining power with third parties; and (4) the
possibility of importing stable domestic institutions. This latter
advantage is probably the most important benefit for Mexico in
joining NAFTA, by inducing it to 'import' more stable institutions, with a consequent positive impact on investment and
growth.

Nevertheless, BTAs are not free from costs and potential
pitfalls. A traditional argument against BTAs is based on the
negative welfare impact these agreements may generate, due to
'trade diversion', whereby imports from non-member countries,
with a cost advantage, are replaced by imports from trade
partners with an 'artificial' advantage created by trade preferences.

The potential distortions that BTAs can generate include: (1)
those induced in the production chain if factors have a different
tariff level than the final output. For example, if some inputs are
imported from non-member countries, resulting in an effective
disprotection to domestic producers of the final product, forcing
them to reduce output or substitute inputs with imports from

member countries, which might be of lower quality; (2) distortions associated with the political economy of trade negotiations, in which inefficient but politically influential sectors may pressure the authorities to include their products in transitory or permanent 'exception lists', or in a programme whereby tariff reductions on imports of equivalent products is implemented at a slower rate. This will induce a non-uniform tariff structure even for goods imported from member countries. Both (1) and (2) could induce domestic relative price distortions, with a negative impact on resource allocation and welfare. However, when there is already a relatively low flat tariff as in Chile, such negative effects are diminished.

In short, there are potential benefits for small open economies which can only be obtained by BTAs; furthermore, for a small economy that has made progress in unilateral trade liberalization, it is more likely that the net welfare impact of entering a BTA will be positive, since the chances of trade deviation are smaller.

As regards the choice of an integration partner, the factors most often considered from a theoretical point of view are: (1) its economic size; (2) the pre-agreement trade pattern; (3) its pre-agreement protection structure; (4) its geographical location; (5) its microeconomic and sectoral distortions; (6) its macroeconomic stability; and (7) the quality and stability of its domestic institutions.

The larger the integration partner's economic size, the larger the pre-agreement bilateral trade and the share of pre-agreement intra-industry trade over total bilateral trade, the larger the levels of protection of the integration partner(s) (of the country under consideration) with respect to the rest of the world; the smaller the sectoral distortions and more stable the integration partner(s) are, and the better and more stable its domestic institutions are, the more likely it is that a small economy will benefit from signing a BTA with this particular country or region of the world.

In the international context, the greater the proliferation of trading blocs of economic significance, the more justified will be the efforts of small economies to join some of them or to form a new one.

However, the net welfare impact of entering into a BTA will certainly depend on the specific type of agreement, ranging from a preferential trade agreement (PTA), to a free trade agreement

(FTA) (equivalent to a PTA with a 100 per cent preference), or to a customs union (CU) (an FTA with a common external tariff).

Theory does not indicate precisely which alternative dominates for a specific country. What is clear is that integration with respect to the trade partner relative to the. rest of the world is greater under a CU, if it implies a rise in the common external tariff, than in an FTA, and greater under an FTA than in a PTA. Thus, for example, in an FTA a country will take better advantage of the potential benefits of the partnership than under a PTA, but, at the same time, will be more exposed to the risks, costs and instabilities of the integration partner. Thus, which of these two alternatives of BTA to select will depend largely on the specific characteristics of the integration partners. The same is true for selecting between a CU and an FTA and between a CU and a PTA.

A Trade Strategy for Chile in the New Scenario

In the light of the analysis of the preceding sub-section we can conclude that as Chile has already implemented an extensive UTL programme, BTAs may be *potentially* beneficial and, therefore, should be used in its trade policy. However, a detailed case-by-case analysis is still needed.

Given the strong dependence of Chile's export specialization pattern on NR, and that international trade in this category of product is subject to very low tariff levels worldwide, it is difficult to believe that more extensive use of the BTA will, by itself, change Chile's present export structure to any significant degree, which we believe will continue to be biased towards NR sectors in the future.

However, not entering into BTAs will tend to diminish Chile's capacity to compete with the exports of member countries that have obtained preferential access conditions to the markets sought by Chilean products, thereby making it more difficult to sustain vigorous expansion in the export sector.

In addition to this, the liberalization and export-oriented structural adjustment programmes being undertaken by various countries throughout the world will mean, on the one hand, greater competition in current destination markets for Chilean exports (e.g. the expected surge in NR exports from Argentina and Peru similar to Chile's) and, on the other hand, greater opportunities for Chilean exports in these emerging economies. Thus, the expected net impact on Chile's export structure is ambiguous. For example, higher competition in the United States, Japan and EU markets by labour-intensive South-East Asian countries may negatively impact Chile's efforts to export a larger proportion of manufactured goods to these markets. At the same time, liberalization and better economic perspectives in these countries could have a positive impact on Chilean NR exports. Thus, the net effect is expected to be a reinforcement of Chile's present export specialization pattern.

Not engaging in bilateralism, while significant trading blocs are being formed, may also tend to reinforce Chile's present export specialization pattern. BTAs will mean a bigger market for member countries' manufacturing industries with increasing returns to scale, relative to those of non-member countries, and this trend could mean a reallocation of world production of these industries towards member countries of 'large' trading blocs. Also, there may be a reduction in tariff escalation among member economies vis-à-vis non-member countries. This will reduce the capacity of non-member countries to compete in the intra-bloc markets for goods with higher value-added.

Nevertheless, not all BTAs are expected to have the same effect on Chile's export structure. For example, a BTA with Mercosur is expected to help Chile to increase its exports of manufactures, while a BTA with South-East Asian countries or Japan is expected to have a positive impact on Chile's export volume to this region but not on its composition.

Probably, in order to diversify away from mainly exporting NR, Chile will have to complement a more aggressive use of BTAs with the redesign of other measures such as its policies towards technological innovation and adaptation as well as its labour capacitation and education policies.

Chile–Mercosur[15]

Mercosur is an attractive BTA candidate for Chile, due to its economic size,[16] its proximity, the bilateral trade pattern,[17] its still high and escalated tariff structure and large number of non-tariff barriers to trade, and the need to secure access to this important market for manufacture exports[18] – this last point may be central if the current UTL effort in these economies is reversed, as has often been the case with other reforms and policies in this region.

Furthermore, a BTA with Mercosur opens up the possibility of achieving reduction or removal of discrimination against foreign producers and investors, as well as all non-tariff barriers to trade (e.g. the statistical tax rate on imports into Argentina and the import taxes in Brazil), together with the implementation of a suitable framework for regulating bilateral trade and avoiding the use of discretionary protectionist measures. In addition, it will also increase Chile's attractiveness as an integration partner or investment target for South-East Asian economies; in other words, Chile could constitute the South American gateway to South-East Asian trade.

However, although joining Mercosur will allow Chile to take full advantage of these benefits, there are several reasons to be careful of a 'too' close partnership with this trading bloc at the present time, including the fact that the macroeconomic stabilization and structural adjustment programmes in Argentina and Brazil have still not been consolidated, the large number of sectoral distortions, a common external tariff higher and more varied than Chile's,[19] the common external trade policy requirement and, in particular, the obligation on member countries to negotiate any BTA with any country or group as a single bloc,[20] as well as some doubts about the medium-term sustainability of this CU.

Therefore, there are several problems for Chile in becoming a member of the Mercosur customs union. Indeed, this precisely has been the position of the Chilean government. But this does not imply that Chile should not try to negotiate an alternative type of BTA, which would allow it to take advantage of the benefits but, at the same time, prevent the domestic economy from becoming 'too' exposed to its sources of instability and distortion. In this respect, the preferred option would be a Preferential Trade Agreement (PTA), which would allow Chile to benefit partly from the agreement, 'lock in' preferential market access conditions for exports, and protect the domestic economy from the above-mentioned sources of instability and distortion.

However, once the instabilities and distortions in Mercosur have been resolved or significantly reduced, adequate institutional strength achieved and shown to be lasting, and the current doubts about the medium-term sustainability of Mercosur resolved, Chile should opt for an FTA.

These considerations are precisely what has motivated Chile's offer to Mercosur to consolidate and intensify the present PTA under LAIA immediately, with each member of this CU, eliminate all non-tariff barriers to trade, introduce an appropriate legal framework for regulating bilateral trade and achieve an FT area after a 10-year period for almost all goods. In addition, Chile would like to engage in formal negotiations with Mercosur on other topics, such as investment, trade in services, financial integration, etc.

In summary, Mercosur is an attractive BTA candidate for Chile, but the specific agreement to be put into force should be evaluated in detail. A key cost for Chile of not reaching an agreement with this CU is the eventual decline in its capacity to compete in its market for manufacturing exports, thereby negatively affecting its exports, both in volume and composition – that is, reinforcing Chile's present export supply structure. Mercosur also opens up the possibility for Chile to increase its exports of services and increase the expected returns from investment in its export sector, as a result of a larger export market and more secure access to it.

Chile–NAFTA

Joining NAFTA (North America Free Trade Agreement) has been the main objective of Chile's foreign trade policy since 1990. Nevertheless, this does not depend on the will of Chile's government. After Mexico, Chile has been regarded as the most likely candidate for admission into NAFTA, and, only recently, the way has been cleared for Chile to begin formal accession negotiations. However, Chile will not be able to select the type of BTA to reach with NAFTA: it will be a 'take it or leave it' negotiation.[21] A small country like Chile has negligible bargaining power, but in spite of this, Chilean negotiators should use rational arguments and general rules as their key bargaining principles.

NAFTA is an attractive integration partner for Chile given its market size, the bilateral trade pattern, the need to secure adequate access conditions to this market, the need to obtain preferential access conditions to this market vis-à-vis the rest of the world and to equal those granted by the United States to Canada and Mexico and the stability of NAFTA's macro-economy and domestic institutions.

NAFTA is also seen as important in Chile's attempt to increase its exports of manufactures, and it will increase the attractiveness of Chile as an investment alternative, since its secure access to this large market will provide a seal of approval for the country's present and future institutional reliability. However, Mexico will tend to 'crowd out' foreign investment with a NAFTA focus in other LA countries, given its geographical advantage and founder-member status.

Not joining NAFTA may tend to reinforce Chile's present export specialization pattern, making it more difficult for Chile to compete in US manufactures markets with Mexico and other economies, such as those of South-East Asia, which are undergoing a globalization process.

Chile–APEC

The Asian-Pacific region has achieved a faster rate of growth in output and trade than any other region of the world over the past three decades. The outcome has been a significant and steady increase in its participation in world trade and output, a tendency which is expected to be maintained in the near future. Within this region, APEC (Asia-Pacific Economic Cooperation Forum) in-cludes very diverse economies, including Japan, the NICs, the NAFTA countries, China, New Zealand and the region's emerg-ing economies such as Malaysia, Singapore, Thailand, the Philip-pines and Taiwan. Since November 1994, Chile has also been formally included.

The main objective of APEC is to achieve free trade in the Asian-Pacific region, through an active programme of GATT-consistent, regional trade liberalization.

Chile is expected to benefit from participation in this forum, since it will be given preferential access conditions to this market as a result of trade liberalization (which is expected to be limited and advanced at a slow rate); it may participate in the techno-logical cooperation programmes to be created to help develop infrastructure and growth in the less developed economies of the region; it will allow the countries in the Far East to have a better understanding of the Chilean economy, thereby making Chile an attractive investment target for their operations in Latin America; and it will provide a suitable framework for regulating Chile's trade with the region in a GATT-consistent way.

Growth of GDP and trade in this region will certainly have a positive impact on Chilean exports but probably not in shifting them away from mainly NR. Being a member of APEC will mainly achieve a dual marketing role: Asians will learn that there is an LA country called Chile, and Chileans will learn about a region which is set to become the world's biggest consumer market.

5 The Importance of Border Trade: The Case of Bolivia

Jorge Aseff, Justo Espejo and Juan Antonio Morales

This chapter discusses the state of Bolivian economic relations with its close neighbours, in the light of the regional trend towards economic integration.

When we began writing this chapter, our main focus was on border trade in a narrow sense. However, we soon realized that, given the current liberalization trend, border trade must evolve into economically integrated regions, i.e. regions that transcend natural boundaries but that retain locality as a central characteristic. Thus, we have devoted considerable space to exploring the scope for border trade to expand spatially.

International trade theory relies on differences between countries' factor endowments and efficiency as determinants of trade. In this chapter the approach is more empirical, giving a large weight to geographical elements and transportation costs, as well as physical infrastructure, and, to a lesser extent, economies of scale. Border trade and trade within small areas, often exhibiting low transportation and communication costs, provide extreme examples of 'natural' trading blocs and integration.[1] Regional economic integration agreements frequently require detailed policies and provisions on factor mobility. Neither of these considerations seems important in border trade, given that policy coordination is frequently irrelevant to the specific towns in contact, and labour mobility is somewhat automatic.

Bolivia has a peculiar geographical position in South America, flanked by five countries: Argentina, Brazil, Peru, Chile and Paraguay. This feature should give Bolivia's trade distinct advantages, but this has not been so, partly because of Bolivia's landlocked situation, rugged terrain and generally poor transportation infrastructure.

Bolivia's traditional exports have been mainly of high-value raw materials, such as tin and silver, and natural gas. Recently, non-traditional exports (i.e. everything else) have gained momentum. These exports are directed to a significant extent towards neighbouring states. Equally important, neighbouring countries are the most important source of Bolivia's imports. Contrary to what happens in most Latin American countries, Bolivia's neighbours are among the most important trade partners. A significant share of the trade with neighbours is deemed to be border trade, although figures are hard to come by. Difficult internal transportation and communications underscore the importance of border trade for Bolivia.

A recurrent question in the chapter is the extent to which some features of border trade can be spread to increasingly larger zones. There is also the related question of whether the economically integrated zones should be extensions of border trade or whether they should have their own distinct characteristics, many of them resulting from bilateral negotiations.

The chapter is organized as follows. In section 1 we describe Bolivian trade in the regional context, including a survey of Bolivia's regional integration agreements. In section 2 we discuss the specifics of border relations in the general international trade framework. In section 3 we explore the implications of enlarging border trade and constituting economically integrated zones. Section 4 presents some conclusions.

1 MAIN FEATURES OF BOLIVIA'S REGIONAL ECONOMIC RELATIONS

The Regional Context

Since the mid-1980s Bolivia has undertaken a very substantial unilateral trade liberalization. There are no quantitative restrictions, and there is a uniform 10 per cent tariff for all goods, except a small list of capital goods that bear a tariff of 5 per cent. There is a drawback for non-traditional exports, which, due to administrative deficiencies, can turn into a small subsidy for some goods. Apart from these features, rates of protection are essentially uniform.

Although Bolivia's liberalization policy has been undertaken unilaterally, it responds to a clear regional trend.² However, the countries are still far from a situation of free trade, for tariff rates continue to be above those of most industrial countries. Either as

Table 5.1 Bolivia's Direction of Trade, 1990–3

	1990	1993
Destination of Exports (share of total exports)		
Argentina	25.1	16.6
Brazil	8.3	2.8
Chile	3.6	2.1
Peru	5.6	9.9
Paraguay	–	–
Total to neighbour countries	42.6	31.5
Other Latin American countries	1.3	7.9
United States	19.6	22.7
Canada	0.0	0.6
European Community	28.5	35.5
Japan	0.3	0.6
Other	7.7	1.3
Total	100.0	100.0
Origin of Imports (share of total imports)		
Argentina	10.7	12.5
Brazil	17.2	10.8
Chile	12.8	7.6
Peru	3.2	4.5
Paraguay	–	–
Total from neighbour countries	43.9	35.4
Other Latin American countries	1.8	3.6
United States	22.5	24.4
Canada	0.9	0.6
European Community	14.9	18.9
Japan	10.1	10.8
Other	6.0	6.3
Total	100.0	100.0

Source: Central Bank of Bolivia, *Bulletin of the External Sector*, No. 11, 1994.

an intermediate step to free trade, or as an end in itself, Bolivia and the other countries in the region have entered since 1992 in a rush of bilateral agreements, which further reduce tariffs and quantitative restrictions. Similarity in economic policies between countries has facilitated regional arrangements and has favoured these over broader agreements, which may involve countries with different regulations.[3]

Table 5.1 shows that between 30 per cent and 40 per cent of Bolivian exports go to neighbouring countries. Exports to this trading bloc are second only to the whole European Union. It is readily seen that neighbouring countries are also by far the most important suppliers of imports to Bolivia.

The balance of trade of 1993 is indicative of the situation in recent years (Table 5.2). Bolivia has very substantial deficits with Brazil, Chile and even with Argentina, despite the sales of natural gas and the overvaluation of the Argentinian peso.[4] Only with Peru is there a small surplus.

Table 5.2 Balance of Trade with Neighbour Countries, 1993 (US$ million)

	Exports	Imports	Balance
Argentina	125.2	150.5	−25.3
Brazil	21.4	130.7	−109.3
Chile	15.7	92.2	−76.5
Peru	75.0	53.7	21.3
Paraguay	1.6	−	1.6

Source: Central Bank of Bolivia, *Bulletin of the External Sector*, No. 11, 1994.

The pattern of trade with the region is very similar to the pattern with the world as a whole. Bolivia exports mainly food products (soybeans and sugar) and raw materials (natural gas, timber, hides and metals) to its neighbours and imports manufactured goods, machinery and transportation equipment, chemical products and, to a lesser extent, food. A significant proportion of imports from neighbours is constituted by semi-processed industrial products. This is due to low transportation costs.

The data in Table 5.2 indicate only official transactions. If estimates of smuggling are added to the official figures, there are

significant changes in the trade balances and some of the conclusions above must be modified. Estimates of smuggling for each
country are obtained using partner-country data on exports to
and imports from Bolivia. The balance including unrecorded
trade appears more favourable to Bolivia in the case of trade with
Argentina. In bilateral trade with Brazil, unrecorded imports are
very large, and the deficit with unrecorded trade is significantly
greater than the deficit on recorded trade. The trade pattern with
Chile is similar, but the differences are not as high. The trade
figures with Peru are interesting. During 1991 and the first
quarter of 1992 when the sol was significantly overvalued,
Bolivia's balance with Peru was positive on both recorded and
unrecorded trade, with the latter larger than the former. From
the second quarter of 1992 through the first quarter of 1993,
Bolivia's recorded trade balance was large and larger than the
unrecorded trade balance. This was the result of higher unrecorded than recorded imports. As the sol overvaluation was
corrected to some extent, contraband imports from Peru started
to flow to Bolivia again. From the second quarter of 1993 onward
the trade balances decrease and the differences between recorded
and unrecorded trade narrow substantially.

Table 5.3 Commodity Composition of Bolivia's Imports from
Neighbour Countries, 1970–92 (US$ millions)

	1975	1985	1990	1992
From Brazil				
Machinery and transportation equipment	31.6	81.0	63.9	73.3
Manufactured articles	17.9	33.8	39.8	65.1
Chemical products	3.7	13.3	10.6	12.7
Fuels and mineral oils	1.0	1.0	0.2	8.4
Food products and live animals	4.6	0.7	1.1	2.4
Beverages and tobacco	0.2	0.7	1.1	1.1
Raw materials, except fuels	0.4	2.4	0.8	1.1
Vegetable and animal oils and fats	1.5	1.0	0.1	–
Merchandises and transactions n.i.e.*	–	0.1	–	–
From Argentina				
Manufactured articles	11.8	12.4	38.9	43.2
Machinery and transportation equipment	20.5	11.2	18.7	13.9
Food products and live animals	32.3	77.6	5.0	27.0
Chemical products	4.0	6.1	9.4	10.8
Fuels and mineral oils	0.4	0.5	0.3	4.5
Vegetable and animal oils and fats	2.1	7.0	0.4	2.4
Beverages and tobacco	0.8	–	0.4	0.5
Raw materials, except fuels	1.4	0.8	0.5	0.2
Merchandises and transactions n.i.e.*	–	0.1	–	0.1

Table 5.3 continued

From Chile				
Manufactured articles	4.2	7.8	26.9	35.1
Machinery and transportation equipment	0.5	8.8	40.8	14.0
Chemical products	0.7	2.4	9.4	11.4
Food products and live animals	5.2	3.7	7.0	8.3
Fuels and mineral oils	2.3	0.1	1.5	7.7
Raw materials, except fuels	0.2	0.3	1.9	0.7
Beverages and tobacco	–	0.1	0.1	0.2
Merchandises and transactions n.i.e.*	–	0.1	–	–
From Peru				
Raw materials, except fuels	0.4	2.9	3.6	10.2
Manufactured articles	3.4	5.0	6.3	6.9
Chemical products	2.7	3.6	6.6	5.6
Machinery and transportation equipment	1.5	11.3	4.1	0.7
Fuels and mineral oils		0.1		2.3
Food products and live animals	2.0	1.8	1.0	0.9
Beverages and tobacco	–	0.1	–	–
Vegetable and animal oils and fats	0.3		–	–
From all neighbour countries				
Manufactured articles	37.3	59.0	111.9	150.3
Machinery and transportation equipment	54.1	112.3	127.5	101.9
Chemical products	11.1	25.4	36.0	40.5
Food products and live animals	44.1	83.8	14.1	38.6
Fuels and mineral oils	3.7	1.7	2.0	22.9
Raw materials, except fuels	2.4	6.4	6.8	12.2
Beverages and tobacco	1.0	0.9	1.6	1.8
Vegetable and animal oils and fats	3.9	8.0	0.5	2.4
Merchandises and transactions n.i.e.*	–	0.3		0.1

*Not included elsewhere.

Source: Authors' elaboration with ECLA, 1984 data.

Regional Integration Agreements

Bolivia has signed several regional agreements on trade and investment, which are summarized in Table 5.4. The most important are the Andean Group and the Latin American Integration Association (LAIA), in that order. The ultimate goal of LAIA is the establishment of a free trade zone in Latin America. The integration mechanism involves bilateral negotiations, which have often been much slower than initially expected. The Andean Pact is of a larger scope than LAIA, with the aim of rapidly becoming a customs union.

The Bolivian government has stated its willingness to enter Mercosur, to which three of its neighbours belong. However, unless current Mercosur byelaws are changed, this would mean leaving the Andean Pact.

Table 5.4 Trade Balance, Including Contraband, with Neighbour
Countries, 1991–4

Quarter	Argentina		Brazil		Chile		Peru	
	Balance[a]	Balance[b]	Balance[a]	Balance[b]	Balance[a]	Balance[b]	Balance[a]	Balance[b]
91.2	25.3	28.4	−23.9	−53.9	−28.1	−25.0	3.7	4.1
91.3	36.0	37.8	−19.0	−30.2	−23.1	−20.4	3.3	3.9
91.4	25.5	29.5	−30.5	−27.0	−24.4	−21.6	2.0	3.0
92.1	38.9	38.7	−27.8	−51.4	−25.7	−22.7	3.5	4.2
92.2	14.6	16.7	−27.6	−76.2	−9.5	−32.2	10.3	5.7
92.3	16.9	19.0	−31.3	−88.0	−10.7	−36.7	11.2	6.5
92.4	17.8	19.9	−31.3	−93.0	−11.4	−38.0	11.5	6.5
93.1	14.8	17.2	−27.3	−76.3	−35.7	−32.2	11.2	5.9
93.2	−8.2	−4.7	−27.7	−98.0	−19.0	−35.8	5.1	4.0
93.3	−3.1	0.4	−26.8	−109.1	−20.1	−38.6	8.3	5.8
93.4	−1.1	2.3	−26.5	−102.8	−22.0	−41.3	9.5	6.8
94.1	−14.5	−10.5	−33.2	−118.0	−30.8	−34.8	2.8	−0.9
94.2	−8.9	−4.9	−32.3	−116.0	−37.2	−33.0	6.3	4.8

Notes: (a) Registered trade only.
(b) Registered trade plus contraband estimates.
Source: IMF, *Direction of Trade Statistics*.

Since 1992 there have been several bilateral trade agreements with neighbours, taking as a frame of reference either LAIA or the Andean Pact, but with acceleration clauses to reach mutual trade liberalization faster. It should be noted that these bilateral agreements have implications that go well beyond trade. For instance, an expected important by-product is an increase in investment. Similarly, there are political economy arguments that emphasize that FTAs enhance the credibility of other economic policies, especially those geared towards attracting foreign investment. This is because supranational arrangements reduce the room for discretionary policies and reduce the vulnerability of decision-making to interest groups.[5]

The scope of the trade agreement with Peru is very broad. In the framework of the Andean Pact, Bolivia and Peru agreed in 1992 to liberalize their bilateral trade almost completely, including: (a) zero tariffs, and (b) the dismantling of quantitative restrictions on products originating in each other's territory. The two countries also acknowledge the need to eliminate export subsidies and correct domestic trade-distorting policies. The agreement with Peru contains safeguards to cover cases of severe damage caused by imports to a given sector. There is also an annex with very detailed rules of origin.

Independent of the trade agreement but with implications for it, Peru has offered Bolivia free use of the southern port of Ilo. Bolivia would also enjoy the advantages of a duty-free zone there. The port facilities are now almost non-existent and substantial investments would have to be undertaken by Bolivia to use this sea outlet effectively. The road connecting La Paz to Ilo is also in a very poor condition. However, in the future Ilo could become a competitor to Arica, in northern Chile, as the main port serving western Bolivia.

Bolivia also has economic complementarity agreements with Argentina and Brazil, which provide for the elimination of quantitative restrictions on bilateral trade and the further development of tariff preferences for given lists of products. They also aim at the formation of industrial joint-ventures.

The agreement with Argentina is more far-reaching than the one with Brazil. It gives relevance to intra-industry trade, promoting common projects between enterprises of the two signatories, and the setting up of binational companies. Tariff reductions can reach 100 per cent, for the importation of final and intermediate goods for approved bilateral industrial integration projects. Also, goods imported in the context of this programme can be considered as of domestic origin in the calculations required to comply with rules of origin.

Interestingly, it is with Chile, the only Bolivian neighbour that does not belong to either the Andean Pact or Mercosur, that trade negotiations have been the most active. Trade between the two countries has also been increasing very rapidly, although it has produced a very large deficit in the Bolivian trade balance with Chile.

Bolivia and Chile signed an Economic Complementarity Agreement (ECA) in 1991, which falls short of establishing a free trade zone. Nevertheless, the agreement has broad scope to liberalize bilateral trade. The stated objectives of the ECA are: (1) the pursuit of growing and progressive economic integration between the two countries; (2) the facilitation of bilateral investments in the two countries; (3) the harmonious development of trade between the two countries; (4) the provision of a framework for economic cooperation of all types; and (5) the promotion of cooperation between the two countries' private sectors.

Tariff preferences are the ECA's main instrument. There is a list of items for which zero import tariffs apply for both countries, and the ECA also ratifies previous tariff concessions granted within LAIA. The list of items with tariff preferences can be enlarged by mutual agreement and the tariff concessions can be further reduced.

The ECA in many ways is more than a trade agreement. It also includes the treatment of bilateral investments and outlines procedures for cooperation in the energy field. In September 1994, Bolivia and Chile signed an Agreement for the Promotion and Reciprocal Protection of Investments, whose main objective is to improve conditions for capital movement between the two countries, including protection clauses to minimize non-commercial risk.

Regarding energy, there is already a letter of intent, signed in 1990, for the sale of Bolivian natural gas to Chile. Also, Bolivia and Chile have agreed to improve the physical infrastructure connecting the two countries. Two railroads link the countries, although the northern one is in a dire condition. A highway linking La Paz with Arica through Tambo Quemado is currently being built.

The development of Bolivian–Chilean economic relations in a very short span of time has been truly remarkable. It should not be forgotten that since the Pacific War of 1879, their relations have been very low-key most of the time, and even today the two countries do not maintain diplomatic ties. Fortunately, economic relations are erasing the old resentments on both sides of the border.

The private sectors in both countries have yet to respond to the new incentives created by the negotiations. Misgivings and preconceptions persist. In a survey of private entrepreneurs carried out by researchers of the Universidad Católica del Norte in Antofagasta, interest in trade and investment with Bolivia was shown to be very small,[6] with Bolivia's technological and economic backwardness often cited as the main reason for this. While there is not yet a similar survey in Bolivia, sceptical comments have appeared in the press. For instance, there were frequent complaints, especially by agricultural exporters, that the price bands for agricultural products in Chile act as non-tariff barriers, which annul the potential benefits of the tariff reductions in the ECA.

Bolivians feel that the results of the trade agreements mentioned above have been somewhat disappointing. Why, then, do they persist in joining FTAs and other integration schemes? There are several answers to this question.

First, Bolivia is geographically in the middle of a zone where all surrounding countries are becoming involved in free trade areas. Bolivia fears becoming isolated from international trade and capital movements should it decide to stay out. The costs of not belonging to an FTA, when all neighbours do, could be high in terms of Bolivia's present and expected trade.

Second, Bolivia is interested in enlarged markets with preferential arrangements as in an FTA, because many of its non-traditional exports, mainly agricultural commodities, face strong competition in international markets. Also they suffer from protectionist policies in industrial and developing countries outside the region.

Third, the prospect of increased trade with its neighbours provides a strong motivation to improve Bolivia's own transportation network. Linkages with foreign networks enhance the value of the domestic transportation network and the likelihood of interconnections increases with FTAs.[7] In addition, an FTA can partly compensate high transportation costs.

Fourth, the trade agreements in the region usually have special temporary clauses applying to Bolivia which lower the costs of joining. With an FTA Bolivia gains access to the potential benefits immediately, while the costs are distributed over a long period.

Lastly, membership of an FTA is seen as a way to attract foreign direct investment and financing from international lenders. In particular, loans to finance transportation projects are more forthcoming when they link two (or more) countries involved in an FTA.[8]

The neighbouring countries may be interested in Bolivia's participation in their FTA on two accounts. First, while Bolivia's market for their exports is small, it is by no means negligible. Exports, including services, to Bolivia can be especially important for certain regions within a country, such as the First Region in northern Chile. Secondly, transit trade through Bolivia may be of interest. We deal with this point later.

2 INTERNATIONAL TRADE AND BORDER TRADE

Main Characteristics of Border Trade

The single most important characteristic of border trade is that transportation costs are very low. Because of this, trade can be very active, although the overall regional development will depend on several other factors, including population density. As transportation costs fall between border towns and the main inland cities there is a natural enlargement of the border's zone of influence.

In the early stages people engaged in border trade are primarily the local population of the border posts. Such trade usually starts with goods with low transportation costs for local consumption from the nearest neighbouring country. Once the border post is endowed with government services, such as customs, the diversity of traded goods increases. Trade shifts from local traders to people from the cities inside the country. The nature of trade also changes.

The first wave of traders is usually small-time smugglers. After this initial stage, more developed forms of international trade appear, in which the border towns are mainly used as 'transit' points benefiting from the customs, warehousing and distribution services there. At this stage, the range of goods traded at the border posts does not differ markedly from the trade basket of the country as a whole. Trade first with Peru, then with Argentina and last with Brazil and Chile fits the pattern of development described above.

There are thus two kinds of border trade: (1) trade at the border points, and (2) trade as a flow through border points. Trade at border points is important in eastern towns such as Guayaramerim and, to a lesser extent, Puerto Suarez in Bolivia. These towns receive their supplies from the Brazilian towns of Guajara Mirim and Corumba respectively. Trade as a flow is characteristic of the western border towns. The clearest examples are Charaña and Tambo Quemado, on the border with Chile (see Figure 5.1).

From another point of view, border economic relationships can be seen as trade in international merchandise and non-factor services, and factor movements, especially labour. Merchandise trade is of two kinds, goods produced in Bolivia and in the

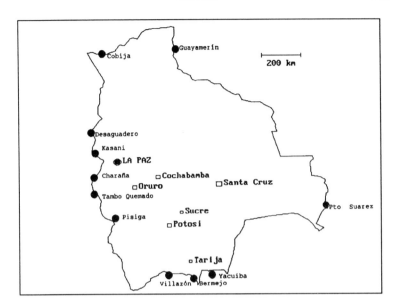

Figure 5.1 Bolivia's Border Towns and Main Cities

neighbouring countries, and goods in transit from third countries. In the latter case, trade with the neighbouring countries is in services related to the transportation and handling of merchandise in transit. For a landlocked country the amounts spent on the importation of such services can be very substantial.

Transportation costs operate like a tariff giving protection to a host of activities. In the presence of high transportation costs, the production of some goods is possible even if this is less efficient than in other countries. The tariff-like effect of high transportation costs may cause a diversified pattern of production with some industrialization, some of which exhibits increasing returns.

As transportation costs fall, the concentration of production occurs naturally, on one or other side of the national boundary, and may be impeded only by national policy measures. In addition, the government may enhance specialization by liberalizing specific economic policy constraints that block the natural development of border trade.

The examination of trade creation and trade diversion, which is fundamental in the assessment of the formation of free trade zones, should also apply to the enlarged border areas. As transportation costs fall in a given region, some trade will be diverted from other countries and regions. More importantly, intra-regional trade increases, but so does specialization in production. Border economic relationships, as stated above, are not limited to merchandise. In fact, cross-border factor movements are becoming increasingly significant. Labour moves freely, often illegally, in the border towns. Also, the profit opportunities of purchasing goods in border towns and selling them in major cities induce movements of people from locations far away from the border. This transient population can be very important.

As a result of the new laws on temporary importation of goods for re-export, there has been a rush to create duty-free zones for commercial and production purposes (Table 5.5). To date, only the commercial duty-free zones have been active.

Table 5.5 Bolivia's Outstanding Economic Integration Agreements with Neighbour Countries

Agreement	Argentina	Brazil	Chile	Peru	Paraguay
LAIA[a]	X	X	X	X	X
Andean Group				X	
River Plate Basin[b]	X	X			X
Amazonian Pact[b]		X		X	
Free Trade				X	
Economic Complementarity	X	X	X		
Investment Promotion and Protection				X	
Mercosur[c]	X	X			X

Notes: (a) Latin American Integration Association.
(b) Essentially, arrangements jointly to improve physical infrastructure.
(c) Conversations underway to adhere to this common market.

Source: Authors' compilation.

The Bolivian government has been trying to attract investment in maquila industries in towns close to its borders. Due to the absence of a border development policy, almost all duty-free zones are located close to the country's largest cities.

As is well known, maquila industries are most advantageous when producing finished products, using a well-known technological process, and for large markets that can be easily reached.

This is not so in the Bolivian border towns,[9] where the country can only offer cheap, unskilled labour. Even so, the numbers of workers in the border towns have not yet reached the critical mass required to make these towns attractive for maquila industries. While border towns cannot yet host maquilas, the city of La Paz, with its supply of services and abundant labour, has been doing so with some success, especially in the clothing and jewelry industries.

Investment from neighbours into Bolivia or vice versa is still meagre, but it is growing rapidly. Indeed, the growth is so important that Bolivia has signed bilateral investment guarantees with some countries.

It should also be mentioned that border trade is very sensitive to the general situation in the open macroeconomy. The government of Bolivia, because of lower tariffs than its neighbours and the memory of extreme exchange rate fluctuations in the recent past, strongly emphasizes exchange rate protection. In the 1980s, macroeconomic instability, which translated into exchange rate volatility (in nominal and real terms), greatly affected the direction of trade. Domestic producers frequently suffered from what they perceived as unfair competition, when Bolivia's neighbours depreciated their currency very rapidly. Bolivia could not retaliate by devaluing the Boliviano because stabilization of inflation was the top priority. While the extreme instability of the 1980s has vanished, the problem has by no means disappeared.

The effects of macroeconomic instability are felt not only in border trade, but also in factor movements, and it should be added that the border town markets for foreign exchange are very active.

Main Border Posts

Table 5.6 identifies Bolivian towns that have significant border trade or are main entrepôts, and Table 5.7 shows the populations of the main towns on the other side of the border of neigbouring countries. These tables are supported by the map in Figure 5.1.

The main trade centres with Peru, all on or close to Lake Titicaca, have very small populations, but are near La Paz, and have good road connections. Unit transport costs are moderate. The shores of Lake Titicaca are among the most densely populated areas of Bolivia and southern Peru even though they are

Table 5.6   Free Zones as of 31 July 1994

	Name	Country of Location	Type of Concession	Effective Operations
1	Zona Franca Oruro S.A.	Bolivia	Commercial & Industrial	Commercial
2	G.I.T. S.A.–La Paz	Bolivia	Commercial & Industrial	Commercial
3	G.I.T. S.A.–Santa Cruz	Bolivia	Commercial & Industrial	
4	Central Aguirre Portuaria S.A.	Bolivia	Commercial & Industrial	Commercial
5	Zone Franca Cochabamba S.A.	Bolivia	Commercial & Industrial	Commercial
6	Zona Franca Desaguadero S.A.	Bolivia	Commercial	
7	Zona Franca San Matías S.A.	Bolivia	Commercial	
8	Zona Franca Guayaramerin S.A.	Bolivia	Commercial & Industrial	
9	Zona Franca de Cobija–Pando	Bolivia		
10	Zona Franca Rosario	Argentina		
11	Zona Franca de Ilo	Peru		

Source: Bolivia's Secretaría Nacional de Industrias.

rural. The exchange of goods, services and labour from southern Peru with La Paz is very lively, involving both Bolivian and Peruvian products, as well as goods imported from third countries.

The trade points with Chile are all at very high altitudes and in areas of sparse population. They are barely transit points. The significant trade is directly between La Paz and the Chilean port-cities of Arica and Iquique. Trade, unlike that with Peru, is mostly unidirectional, with goods flowing from Chile to Bolivia, as much Chilean products as overseas products in transit through Chile. The Iquique Duty Free Zone in Chile is very important in the entrepôt trade. Most goods from the Free Zone arrive in Bolivia by truck through the Tambo Quemado border pass. Although no hard data are available, there are indications that many consumer durables of non-Latin American origin such as cars and trucks, and electric and electronic appliances pass through Iquique to western Bolivia. Unpublished data based on reliable sources estimate that trade through Iquique and Arica amounts to US$500 million.

Table 5.7 Population of Neighbour Countries in Main Towns Close
to Bolivia

Argentina Province	Town	Inhabitants
Jujuy	Sta. Catalina	3 163
	Yavi	16 641
	San Salvador de Jujuy	229 500
Salta	Salta	373 857

Source: 1991 Census.

Brazil State	Town	Inhabitants
Rondonia	Guajara Mirim	34 755
Matto Grosso	Corumba	81 145
de Sul	Porto Muritinho	11 688

Source: Anuario Estatistico do Brasil, 1985.

Chile Region	Town	Inhabitants
First	Arica	250 000
	Iquique	149 482
(Total First Region)		385 600

Source: Banco Central de Chile, 1989–93.

Peru Department	Town	Inhabitants
Puno	Puno	196 488
	Huancane	109 113

Source: Estadisticas del Peru, 1987.

Western Bolivia also trades heavily across the Argentine border. Trade is bi-directional, with the direction frequently changing according to fluctuations in the bilateral exchange rate.

In the east, of the three important trade points near the border with Brazil, the position of Puerto Suárez needs to be highlighted, as this town is next door to the medium-sized Brazilian city of Corumba. Also, Corumba is connected by rail to Santa Cruz, Bolivia's second largest city, and a highway is now being built. As with Chile, the trade flow is unidirectional with goods flowing from Brazil to Bolivia. Unlike the Chilean case, however, practically all goods are Brazilian.

As regards Paraguay, there is some trade consisting almost entirely of overseas products, but this goes through very sparsely populated areas and is mostly unrecorded.

It is worth noting that unit transport costs and distance from the border to the city of La Paz are not well correlated (Table 5.6). For example, unit transport costs from Tambo Quemado on the Chilean border are lower than from Desaguadero on the Peruvian border, despite a substantial difference in distance. Not surprisingly the highest transport costs are from towns in northern Bolivia next to the Brazilian border. The lowest costs are from Chile and Peru.

The scale of operations with Peru, through Desaguadero, with Chile through Tambo Quemado and the Arica–La Paz railroad and with Brazil through Puerto Suárez can on occasions be massive. Large-scale, well-established importers coexist with large-scale smugglers. Some border towns are progressively becoming important suppliers of services.

The border economy is still weakly integrated into the rest of the economy, but greater integration can be anticipated mainly through the services that border towns can offer to facilitate trade. These services can be especially relevant for bulky products, like semi-processed industrial inputs, which are a high proportion of Bolivian imports. Also, special border services are needed for most of Bolivia's non-traditional exports, which are also bulky.

The border zones do not, and in the next few years are not expected to, generate much income for the economy from goods-producing activities. Only when a fully integrated economic region is constituted will this occur.

As things stand now border trade is not significant enough. Domestic transportation and communications with the border towns, except those close to La Paz, are precarious and inadequate for developing high volumes of trade. Most border towns lack basic infrastructure, such as warehouses. Often, individual operations are very tiny, although they involve large numbers of people. Most of the small-scale trade is contraband.

Along the borders of Bolivia there is nothing remotely similar, not even a small-scale replica, to the cross-border economic regions formed by the northeastern United States and Ontario in Canada, or the industrial belt of Western Europe including regions of France, Belgium, Luxembourg and Germany. Except near La Paz, there is little industry: the only activity is trade.

The development of border towns is marred by two problems, which cannot be overcome by incentives to investment and production. First, none of the neighbouring countries has a large economic centre near a border town (Table 5.8). Secondly, economic instability, particularly in the 1980s, severely damaged the development prospects of the border towns.

Table 5.8 Main Entry Points to International Ground Transportation

From	Limiting Depart- ment	Entry Point	Population[a]	Distance to La Paz (km)[b]	Transportat- ion Costs (US$/qq)[b]
Argentina	Potosi	Villazon	23 670	898	2.55
Argentina	Tarija	Bermejo	21 394	1165	2.55
Argentina	Tarija	Yacuiba	30 912	1195	2.77
Brazil	Beni	Guayaramerin	27 706	1080	5.32
Brazil	Pando	Cobija	10 001	1305	5.11
Brazil	Santa Cruz	Puerto Suarez	9 860	1451	3.83
Chile	Oruro	Tambo Quemado	Rural area	250	1.06
Chile	Oruro	Pisiga	292	530	1.06
Chile	Potosi	Ollague	Rural area	901	2.13
Peru	La Paz	Puerto Acosta	5 417	194	0.85
Peru	La Paz	Desaguadero	2 755	115	1.28
Peru	La Paz	Guaqui	5 810	91	0.64
Peru	La Paz	Kasani	Rural area	165	1.28

Sources: (a) National Census of 1992.
(b) Data from the Geographic Military Institute of Bolivia.
(c) Data from the Association of Freight Carriers of Bolivia in US$ per quintal.

3 POTENTIAL BENEFITS AND COSTS IN THE EXPANSION OF BORDER TRADE

Border trade can contribute to growth in two major ways. First, by using the advantages of location, which are related to economies of scale and agglomeration, as well as externalities and increasing returns themselves. Trade as a flow through border points can indeed generate economies of scale, especially when viewed in terms of a hub-and-spoke model. 'Hubbing' in Bolivia has the potential to reduce the costs of trade significantly between the countries in the immediate vicinity.[10] However, for this

potential to become reality requires good transportation infrastructure, warehousing services and a very efficient distribution
system.[11]

Secondly, some characteristics of border trade can be extended
to increasingly wider spaces. The unique geographical situation
of La Paz needs to be highlighted in this context. It is only 500
km away from Arica, 800 km from Iquique, 250 km from Puno,
280 km from Juliaca, and 400 km from the port of Ilo. La Paz is
the largest city in the area, and Arica and Iquique are significantly further from Santiago or any other large Chilean city
than from La Paz. Similarly, Puno, Juliaca and Ilo are further
away from Lima or any other large Peruvian city than from La
Paz. Northern Chile and especially southern Peru could greatly
benefit from their proximity to La Paz. In turn, the Bolivian
capital could gain from access to the ports, transportation facilities and other services, as well as the markets these regions
provide.

Regional leaders in Chile, mainly, but also in Bolivia and Peru,
have advanced the idea of a large integrated zone to include the
First and Second Regions of Chile, the southern departments of
Peru, western Bolivia, especially the area surrounding La Paz,
and northwest Argentina. This idea would include making major
improvements to the existing port and storage facilities in Chile,
the construction of the port of Ilo in Peru, and a multinational
coordinated effort to modernize the railroad network as well as
to continue with the highway construction programme in the
integrated region. However, no plan has yet been drawn up.

Bolivia aims to become a major supplier of natural gas, in
competition with northern Argentina, which also has large deposits. Bolivia also aspires to become a regional distribution
centre for natural gas. As gas is transported via pipelines,
geography is important. The hub-and-spoke model could fully
apply to a regional market for natural gas, with a hub in the
eastern department of Santa Cruz.[12]

It is through Bolivia that a principal railway link between the
Atlantic and the Pacific can be completed. The conclusion of the
railway linking the eastern and western networks in Bolivia, of
which only one stretch is missing, could provide overland access
for Brazilian exports to the Pacific. Brazil could then export
through Bolivia to Chile, Peru and beyond, to countries in the
Asian Pacific rim. Obviously, trade in the other direction also

would be possible. One could also imagine Peru trading with Argentina through Bolivia.

As mining is a very important activity in the region, we can expect the formation of joint ventures and multinational enterprises involving firms from the four countries. This natural outcome of market forces could be given an additional impulse by coordinating reforms in each country's mining legislation, as well as public investments in infrastructure supporting mining activity.

As a prerequisite for an economically integrated zone, the current economic complementarity agreements have to develop into free trade agreements. Within an economically integrated zone, many foreign industries will find it profitable to produce in Bolivia.

The above discussion seems to lead to the conclusion that expanding border trade and, more generally, joining FTAs ought to be welfare-improving, both domestically and globally. However, international trade also generates risks. Bolivia's initial condition of significant economic backwardness vis-à-vis three of its neighbours implies the danger that its low degree of industrialization would decrease even more, production risks being confined to primary products, using location-specific factors (land and mineral resources), with little technological spillover and without the benefit of increasing returns to scale. As an outcome of the process Bolivia would be driven into a permanent situation of very low wages and incomes.[13] The core–periphery model could be replicated on a regional scale, and Bolivia could be pushed towards the outer ring. The gap in wages and incomes relative to those of the more advanced neighbours would narrow only when transportation costs fall further, when the advantages of location become less important and the mobility of industry increases.[14]

However, reversing the current liberalization programme cannot be a realistic approach to this danger. Furthermore, the enforcement of regulations restraining trade has always been very difficult and costly, although not completely ineffective, over a vast territory with low population density.[15]

The proper response to this challenge is gaining, perhaps just maintaining, high productivity in proven natural resource sectors and, ironically in view of what has been said above, in exploiting advantages in location. Some Bolivian resource-based industries (e.g. edible oils, non-ferrous metal manufactures and wood) have shown that they can compete well internationally.

4 CONCLUSIONS

In the light of our discussion, we can conclude that the importance of border trade cannot be underestimated, even if on the surface it seems remote from the main concerns of trade policy. Locally, border trade has the potential to increase production and consumption in regions that often are far from the main cities. It means economic activity in areas that otherwise would have very little, and it is a source of stable incomes.

More importantly, even if the density of population in border areas is low, they may have good prospects as transit and distribution centres for goods destined for the interior, and they have the potential to become important suppliers of services.

Border trade has been, in many ways, a precursor of current attempts at regional integration. Goods and factors have circulated freely for years within limited areas across national boundaries. As the costs of trading spatially decrease and the policy-generated barriers to international trade disappear, many (but not all) characteristics of border trade will naturally spread to the rest of the economy. Yet, geography will continue to have policy relevance: increasingly, economic policy should strive to extract the maximum benefit from location. One avenue for this is the formation of economically integrated 'regions', with the term 'region' used in a somewhat narrow sense.

Such economically integrated regions may be intensive in economic policy and international negotiations, unlike border trade. This places the problem in the context of preferential trading arrangements and joint spatial planning.

The national policy problem then is whether to have a single trade policy unilaterally pursuing further liberalization, or to have a set of bilateral agreements, on a quid pro quo basis, one with each partner country or, eventually, groups of countries. The advantages of a unilateral and non-discriminatory process should not be rejected outright, given Bolivia's economic size. The problems of timing and opportunity in liberalization, however, call for bilateral and regional arrangements, including integrated zones.

However, unfortunately, the dissimilarity in the level of Bolivia's development vis-à-vis its neighbours conditions the distribution of economic activities. Unless there is a big domestic effort Bolivia runs the risk of remaining stuck with only primary products sectors. The question of Bolivia's national advantage from preferential trade agreements with significantly larger economies, in the close vicinity, has still to reach an unambiguous answer.

Finally, Bolivia's long-term integration with other economies cannot be limited to agreements with the five neighbouring countries alone. At some point the decline in transportation costs will reduce the advantages of geographically close economically integrated zones, and Bolivia, following another Latin American trend, may find it in its interest to apply for admission into schemes with large developed countries.

6 A Small Country Perspective on Mercosur: The Case of Paraguay

Luis E. Breuer

INTRODUCTION

Paraguay entered Mercosur as its most junior partner. Its economy is small and open, and as such quite vulnerable to the external economic environment, including changes in terms of trade, international interest rates and investment flows. Its exports are undiversified by destination and especially by commodity breakdown, and prices are determined internationally.

This chapter argues that Mercosur involves both opportunities and risks for Paraguay. It is a unique opportunity because it addresses one of the main structural impediments to Paraguayan growth – the size of domestic markets which are too small to allow economies of scale. However, there are also considerable risks for the country, which cannot be ignored, including the propensity towards macroeconomic instability of the other member countries, the accelerated nature of the integration process and the lack of definition on a number of critical issues that are still being negotiated.

1 THE ECONOMY OF PARAGUAY

Paraguay is an open, export-oriented economy producing a small number of tradeable goods, mainly from the primary sector, and importing both producer and consumer goods. Openness is reflected in the high trade (import and export) coefficient which in 1990 exceeded 30 per cent.[1]

With a population of 4.2 million (1990) and an annual GDP of about US$6.7 billion (1990), Paraguay is the most junior partner of the Mercosur countries; its population represents slightly above 2 per cent of the region's total, while its output is only 1.5 per cent. Similarly, Paraguayan exports and imports represent 2.1 per cent and 4.3 per cent, respectively, of aggregate regional trade. Paraguay's population is quite young (29 per cent under the age of 10 and more than 50 per cent under 20), and is growing very rapidly (3.1 per cent per annum). Roughly half the population still live in rural areas.[2]

The structural constraints on growth in Paraguay include the small size of its domestic market, high transportation costs derived from its landlocked position, a low technological base and scarce human capital. On the other hand, the country enjoys ample natural resources in the form of abundant fertile soil and cheap electrical energy, as well as a tradition of relative macroeconomic stability together with low taxation and free movement of capital.

The Structure of the Economy

Since the completion of the Itaipú project in the early 1980s, the Paraguayan economy has not experienced much structural transformation; the share of agriculture in GDP has remained around 17 per cent since 1983. However, this figure does not truly reflect the relative importance of the agricultural sector, since it is also the main source of employment, as well as contributing 60 per cent of exports and providing most of the industrial sector's inputs. Services represent roughly half of GDP, with commerce and finance, in turn, accounting for 26 per cent. However, this ignores a significant amount of unrecorded trade, particularly with neighbouring countries.[3] The industrial sector, heavily concentrated on the processing of agricultural goods, accounts for 15 per cent of GDP.

After rapid growth in the 1970s, the economy slowed down considerably during the 1980s.[4] In fact, during the past decade, annual growth rates have been around 3.5 per cent – only slightly above demographic growth. In 1984–8, agriculture led GDP growth with an average annual expansion of 5.7 per cent. A series of bad crops reduced the growth of agriculture to 2.5 per cent during 1989–93, although this was partly offset by expansion in the service sector.

In general, Paraguay's balance of payments follows a similar pattern to those of other small, open, developing economies.[5] In the past decade, large trade deficits (around US$300 million) were financed by capital inflows, resulting from external loans to the public sector during the early 1980s and private capital flows during the late 1980s.

Recorded exports are heavily concentrated in a few, mainly primary sector products. Table 6.1 shows the composition of exports during 1991–3. Soybeans and cotton were approximately 60 per cent of total recorded exports during this period, meat and leather 13 per cent, wood 7 per cent, vegetable oils 7 per cent and other exports 15 per cent. Mercosur countries are the most important markets for Paraguayan exports (Table 6.2). In 1991–3, 37 per cent of total exports went to this region, mainly to Brazil and Argentina (28 per cent and 8 per cent of the total, respectively). Europe[6] is the second most important regional

Table 6.1 Economic Indicators of Mercosur Countries

	Argentina	Brazil	Paraguay	Uruguay	Mercosur	Paraguay as % of total Mercosur
Population (1990) (millions)	32.3	150.4	4.2	3.1	190	2.2
Urban Population (as % of total in 1990)	86	75	48	86	–	–
GDP (1990) (US$ billions)	86.4	333.2	6.7	8.5	434.8	1.5
GDP per capita (1990, US$ 000s)	2.7	2.2	1.6	2.8	–	–
Exports (goods and services 1990 US$ millions)	12.4	31.4	1.0	1.7	46.5	2.1
Imports (goods and services 1990, US$ millions)	4.1	20.7	1.2	1.3	27.3	4.3

Source: Trade figures from official sources, the rest from IDB.

market, absorbing 34 per cent of total exports, followed by the United States (7 per cent), and other countries (22 per cent).

Table 6.2 Paraguay: Composition of GDP (%)

	1983	1988	1993
Agriculture	16	17	17
Livestock	8	8	8
Forestry	2	3	3
Industry	16	16	15
Construction	7	6	5
Services	51	50	52
of which:			
Commerce/Finance	27	27	26
Electricity	2	3	4
Total	100	100	100

Source: Central Bank of Paraguay.

The breakdown of imports is shown in Table 6.3. On average during 1991–3, heavy machinery and transport equipment accounted for 40 per cent of all recorded imports, followed by petroleum products (11 per cent), tobacco and beverages (8 per cent), chemicals (7 per cent), food and textiles (7 per cent) and other goods (28 per cent). The origin of imports are similarly concentrated in the Mercosur countries, which averaged 36 per cent of the total in 1991–3. Within Mercosur, Brazil (21 per cent)

Table 6.3 Paraguay: Growth Rates by Sectors (annual averages)

	1984–8	1989–93
Agriculture	5.7	2.5
Livestock	2.9	3.8
Forestry	5.4	3.8
Industry	3.5	2.4
Construction	0.4	2.5
Services	3.4	4.2
of which:		
Commerce/Finance	3.5	3.4
Electricity	7.4	11.6
Total GDP	3.6	3.5

Source: Central Bank of Paraguay.

and Argentina (14 per cent) are the most significant. Outside Mercosur, the United States accounted for 14 per cent of imports, Europe 13 per cent and Japan 12 per cent (Table 6.4).

Table 6.4 Paraguay: Balance of Payments

	1980	1985	1993
Current Account	(373)	(132)	(607)
Exports	564	552	725
Imports	864	660	1478
Trade Balance	(300)	(108)	(753)
Services, Net	(78)	(32)	104
Transfers	5	8	42
Capital Account	331	52	206
Errors/Omissions	(30)	33	487
Reserves	1	47	(86)

Source: Central Bank of Paraguay.

Entrepôt Trade

Ever since colonial times, unrecorded trade has flourished in the region as a reaction to government regulations aimed at controlling commerce. Between the 1940s and the late 1970s, Argentina and Brazil maintained high external tariffs and used other non-tariff barriers to promote domestic industrial production.[7]

Such policies led to a number of distortions, including the channelling of considerable unrecorded trade through Paraguay, where tariffs were lower or less rigorously enforced. The expansion of this trade was enhanced by the construction of road transportation to Brazil in the late 1960s and the Itaipú hydroelectric dam in the 1970s and early 1980s.

Today, the city of Ciudad del Este (population 150 000), which borders Argentina and Brazil, enjoys a flourishing entrepôt trade and tourist industry. Prices of certain luxury goods are not very different from those in other open and much larger markets (e.g. Miami). In addition, increasing links have been developed with informal urban labour markets in the Brazilian cities of São Paulo and Rio de Janeiro.

Reliable statistics on the volume of this trade are not available, but selected indicators show that Paraguay is one of the world's highest per capita importers of cigarettes and alcoholic beverages, with average imports exceeding US$112 million during the early 1990s – equivalent to 80 per cent of total petroleum imports in a country that purchases all of its oil abroad!

Investigation of Mercosur countries' official trade statistics in 1993 shows total recorded trade with Paraguay of US$1.7 billion, twice the amount recorded by Paraguayan statistics. Studies on the links between entrepôt trade and the rest of the Paraguayan economy are not available, but casual information suggests that it is an important source of employment, particularly in selected regions of the country, as well as a significant source of foreign exchange.

Itaipú and Yacyretá

During the early 1970s, Paraguay signed an agreement to build two large hydroelectric dams, Itaipú and Yacyretá, with Brazil and Argentina, respectively. Construction took place between 1975 and 1982 at a total cost of US$18 billion.

Today, the two projects have a considerable influence on the Paraguayan economy through purchases of Paraguayan goods

Table 6.5 Paraguay: Composition of Exports (US$ millions) and Distribution (%)

	Exports				Distribution			
	1991	1992	1993	1991–3 Average	1991	1992	1993	1991–3 Average
Soybeans	157	137	224	173	21.30	20.85	30.90	25
Cotton	319	209	165	231	43.28	31.81	22.76	33
Vegetable Oil	44	57	49	50	5.97	8.68	6.79	7
Wood	44	53	64	54	5.97	8.07	8.83	7
Meat	55	48	47	50	7.46	7.31	6.48	7
Leather	28	38	54	40	3.80	5.78	7.45	6
Other	90	115	122	109	12.21	17.50	16.83	15
Total	737	657	725	707	100.00	100.00	100.00	100

Source: Central Bank of Paraguay.

Table 6.6 Paraguay: Destination of Exports (US$ million) and Distribution (%)

	Destination				Distribution			
	1991	1992	1993	1991–3 Average	1991	1992	1993	1991–3 Average
Brazil	203	171	215	196	27.54	26.03	29.66	28
Argentina	45	64	65	58	6.11	9.74	8.97	8
Uruguay	11	11	7	10	1.49	1.67	0.97	1
Mercosur	259	246	287	264	35.14	37.44	39.59	37
Europe[a]	252	220	258	243	34.19	33.49	35.59	34
United States	34	34	53	40	4.61	5.18	7.31	6
Japan	4	2	1	2	0.54	0.30	0.14	–
Other	188	155	126	156	25.51	23.59	17.38	22
Total	737	657	725	705	100.00	100.00	100.00	100[b]

Notes: (a) Includes Germany, Belgium, Spain, France, Holland, Italy, Switzerland.
(b) Numbers do not add up due to rounding.
Source: Central Bank of Paraguay.

Table 6.7 Paraguay: Composition of Imports (US$ million) and Distribution (%)

	Imports				Distribution			
	1991	1992	1993	1991–3 Average	1991	1992	1993	1991–3 Average
Heavy Machinery	427	269	339	345	33.49	21.75	22.95	26
Transport Equipment	153	175	207	178	12.00	14.15	14.01	13
Petroleum Products	130	145	147	141	10.20	11.72	9.95	11
Tobacco Products and Beverages	111	112	112	112	8.71	9.05	7.58	8
Food Production	38	58	66	54	2.98	4.69	4.47	4
Chemical Production	79	84	100	88	6.20	6.79	6.77	7
Textiles	32	27	44	34	2.51	2.18	2.98	3
Other	305	367	462	378	23.92	29.67	31.28	28
Total	1275	1237	1477	1330	100	100	100	100

Source: Central Bank of Paraguay.

and services and transfers to central government from the sale of electricity to Brazil. Total resource flows to the Paraguayan

Table 6.8 Paraguay: Origin of Imports (US$ million) and Distribution (%)

	Imports				Distribution			
	1991	1992	1993	1991–3 Average	1991	1992	1993	1991–3 Average
Argentina	152	201	211	188	11.92	16.25	14.28	14
Brazil	234	263	340	279	18.35	21.26	23.00	21
Uruguay	10	11	19	13	0.78	0.89	1.29	1
Mercosur	396	475	570	480	31.06	38.40	38.57	36
United States	186	169	203	186	14.59	13.66	13.73	14
Europe[a]	181	173	164	173	14.20	13.99	11.10	13
Japan	165	142	171	159	12.94	11.48	11.57	12
Other	347	278	370	332	27.22	22.47	25.03	25
Total	1275	1237	1478	1330	100.00	100.00	100.00	100.00

Note: (a) Includes Germany, Spain, France, United Kingdom, Italy, Switzerland
Source: Central Bank of Paraguay.

Table 6.9 Paraguay: Receipts from Binational Electric EN (US$ million)

	1989	1990	1991	1992	1993	1989–93
Itaipu	141.4	254.3	266.5	325.2	360.0	1347.4
Purchase of Goods	90.0	141.0	162.9	170.5	170.5	734.9
Transfers to	51.4	113.3	103.6	154.7	189.5	612.5
Yacyreta	108.0	48.0	43.9	35.6	37.8	273.3
Total	249.4	302.3	310.4	360.9	397.8	1620.8

Source: Central Bank of Paraguay.

economy from the two projects during 1989–93 amounted to over US$1.6 billion, roughly a quarter of 1993 GDP (Table 6.5). Of this amount, US$1 billion went directly to the private sector and US$612.5 million to central government.[8]

Paraguay's Economic Relations with Argentina and Brazil

Paraguay's economic relations with Argentina and Brazil, are deep and far-reaching:

1. Trade: Brazil and Argentina are Paraguay's main trading partners both in terms of destination of exports and origin of imports.
2. Itaipú and Yacyretá: Joint administration with the respective governments.
3. Export corridors for Paraguayan goods: The vast majority of Paraguayan exports go through either Argentinian or Brazilian territory. River transport, and to a lesser extent rail and road, connect the country to the port of Buenos Aires and access to foreign markets, while goods also travel the Brazilian highway system to the port of Paranaguá where the country enjoys port privileges.
4. Immigration: Despite unreliable statistics, there are many Paraguayan immigrants and migrant workers in Argentina, where labour markets have traditionally provided an important escape valve for demographic pressures in Paraguay. Moreover, remittances from Paraguayan workers in Argentina are presumably an important source of foreign exchange. On the other hand, many Brazilian farmers migrated to eastern Paraguay in the early 1970s, contributing to the sharp expansion of commercial agriculture during that period.
5. Foreign investment: Brazil and Argentina are important sources of foreign investment in Paraguay, particularly in the commercial agricultural and agroindustrial sectors and, in the case of Brazil, the financial sector.

2 THE PARAGUAYAN VIEW OF MERCOSUR

Substantial progress has been achieved since 1991, in spite of enormous obstacles arising from the different economic structures and macroeconomic conditions of the member countries. The agreement on common external tariffs was the most difficult issue to tackle, given the divergent views of the member countries. Of the four countries, Brazil had the highest external tariff levels, while Paraguay had the lowest and, in general, the most open external regime. Argentina and Paraguay both favoured low external tariffs, in contrast to Brazil, while Uruguay adopted a position in between.

The set of common external tariffs was a compromise agreement. Brazil and Argentina (including the 10 per cent statistical tax) will have to reduce their tariffs; there is little change for Uruguay; while Paraguay will have to increase its tariffs.

Despite advances on the external front, little progress has been achieved in policy coordination, especially macroeconomic policy. The lack of coordination is reflected in wide differentials in economic indicators such as inflation rates, and sharp swings in real exchange rates between member countries. Greater convergence through the coordination of policies is perhaps the single most important challenge to be met, as this provides a solid foundation upon which to build the integration process.

From an economic perspective, countries may aim for economies of scale, as well as market access and foreign investment. Politically, regional integration might be used to ensure the sustainability of domestic policy reforms, or as a result of demonstration effects from well-publicized initiatives (such as the European Union and NAFTA).[9]

In Paraguay's case, the Rodríguez administration took the country into Mercosur, mostly for political reasons. A democratic political reform process led to a series of market-friendly economic reforms including the liberalization of financial and exchange markets, and comprehensive fiscal and trade reforms.[10] Integration with other democracies in the region provided the chance to anchor these reforms and gather international support by breaking the country's external isolation.

Yet, given the economic linkages described above, Paraguay's access to Mercosur was not only desirable on economic grounds, but it was unavoidable. Locking in market access to Argentina and Brazil was simply essential. Moreover, moving into a rules-based trading arrangement with its larger neighbours was clearly to Paraguay's benefit, as were the opportunities in terms of attracting foreign investment.

Most business and intellectual groups in Paraguay approved of entry into Mercosur, as it was seen as an insurance to the democratic process, as well as an opportunity to expand domestic markets and remedy the informalization of the economy.[11]

Initial misgivings, however, were expressed by the commercial sectors of Ciudad del Este, since the adoption of the common external tariff would greatly reduce their possibilities for engaging in commercial arbitrage. Similarly, peasant (*campesino*) and labour organizations have consistently opposed the country's participation in Mercosur.

Benefits of Mercosur

The main benefit for Paraguay clearly lies in the elimination of tariffs by its main trading partners, Brazil and Argentina, which, in essence, expands the market for Paraguayan goods, from 4.2 million to over 190 million people.

Thus, Mercosur provides economies of scale which have been absent throughout Paraguay's economic history, and provides a competitive position for their meat, cotton and soybeans, particularly in the Brazilian market, on top of the cost advantage of supplying to nearby markets. In addition, the transportation sector should benefit, given Paraguay's geographical location, by being able to link a number of prosperous Brazilian states to Argentina.

Mercosur may also serve as a catalyst for foreign investment aimed at the regional market or resulting from a perceived improvement in investment opportunities. In turn, these investments could play an important role in the modernization of the Paraguayan economy. Information transfer, through the incorporation of improved technology by foreign firms and through demonstration effects on local producers, could play a very positive role in the growth prospects of the Paraguayan economy. Increased competition from foreign firms could also be a powerful force for improving domestic producers' efficiency in an economy which has been traditionally isolated from intense foreign competition.

While it is still too early to identify clear trends, there has been a moderate increase in foreign direct investment from Mercosur participants in raw materials processing industries, while non-regional investors are creating a large industrial park in the city of Ciudad del Este.

The implementation of a rules-based commercial arrangement with larger neighbours, as well as with third countries or regions, is obviously an important benefit to Paraguay.

The Risks of Mercosur

The main risk faced by Paraguay is that of integration with larger and more sophisticated economies. Moreover, the transition periods for both the free trade area and the customs union are brief, and there are no redistributive mechanisms similar to those of the European Union to allow for the levelling of the playing field.

Thus, it is quite possible that market penetration by products from Argentina and Brazil could lead to a sharp rise in structural unemployment and to an experience similar to that of Spain when it joined the European Community.[12] Paraguay, however, cannot afford a social safety net like Europe's. In the absence of agreements on free movement of labour, this situation may lead to social problems which could call into question the political sustainability of the integration process.

Moreover, the lack of progress in the areas of economic convergence and macroeconomic policy coordination creates additional uncertainty, as it exposes Paraguay to sharp changes in its terms of trade. Indeed, the Convertibility Plan (1991) in Argentina and, most recently, the Real Plan in Brazil (1994) have led to sudden real appreciations of the Argentinian peso and Brazilian real, respectively, vis-à-vis the Paraguayan Guaraní.

In addition, the establishment of common external tariffs, higher than those of Paraguay, could divert trade towards less efficient producers in the region due to preferential tariff treatment. However, transportation costs already give neighbouring countries a competitive advantage over nonregional suppliers, and this might limit the amount of trade diversion that takes place.[13]

3 CONCLUSION

When Paraguay joined Mercosur, it did so more for political than economic reasons, but at present, the main challenge facing the country is to adapt an ongoing process, which began as a collaborative effort between Argentina and Brazil, to its own needs. The negotiating process has already provided Paraguay with some advantages, including a longer list of exceptions to the common external tariff, a longer adaptation period, a smaller domestic-content ratio during the transition period and veto power over decisions. In addition, the establishment of a free trade zone in the area of Ciudad del Este has also been accepted by the partners.

However, other demands such as the establishment of a redistributive mechanism to finance infrastructure projects, like the one in the European Union, have not prospered. Nor has there been any compensation for the fact that the country has had to raise tariffs with third party countries or regions.

Despite the limitations, it is clear that Paraguay has no short-term viable alternative to Mercosur: economic links with the region are simply too strong to allow otherwise, with the prospect of becoming isolated from its main economic partners. Furthermore, the opportunities that arise from this regional integration might well be the driving force for the modernization of the economy in the next decade, despite the considerable risks involved.

7 The North American Free Trade Agreement: Policy- or Investment-led?

Maureen Appel Molot

1 INTRODUCTION: AN APPROACH TO FREE TRADE AGREEMENTS

For both Canada and Mexico, the decision to negotiate free trade with their most important trading partner was a dramatic change in policy direction. Canada, which had long eschewed a free trade arrangement with the United States, negotiated the Canada–US Free Trade Agreement (FTA), which came into effect on 1 January 1989. Then, just as Canadians were beginning to adjust to their new relationship with the United States, Mexican President Carlos Salinas and US President George Bush announced (in June 1990) that their two countries would begin discussions on a bilateral free trade pact. For Mexicans, the decision to seek a free trade agreement with the United States was the culmination of a concerted effort to liberalize their economy since the mid-1980s. For Canada, it had the potential to erode some of the gains of the FTA.

In reality, the North American trade and investment regime (NATIR) had been evolving for some time. This is not to diminish the significance of the recently signed formal trade agreements, but to understand the decisions to negotiate the free trade agreements one needs to pay attention to what preceded them, both in terms of state policies and in terms of the behaviour of multinational enterprises (MNEs).

The World Investment Report 1992 distinguishes between policy- and investment-(FDI-) led integration. Policy-led integration is exemplified by the European Union: states initiate policies that reduce the trade barriers between them (UNCTC, 1992: 35). FDI-led integration occurs when the behaviour of firms acts as 'the principal driver of regional integration' (UNCTC, 1992: 36);

according to this Report, regional integration between Canada and the United States has been 'primarily' FDI-led (UNCTC, 1992: 40). In reality, the line between policy-led and FDI-led integration is less clear (UNCTC, 1992: 36). The dynamics of regional integration are shaped by the ongoing relationships between states and multinational firms, especially when economic links across countries participating in a new regional arrangement are deep and pre-date the negotiation of the agreement.

The World Investment Report 1994 contrasts 'shallow' and 'deep' integration. 'Shallow' integration results from trade and related financial flows between economies (UNCTC, 1994: 129). 'Deep' integration ensues from the decisions of MNEs to organize the production and distribution of goods and services across a number of economies using the new information and production technologies (UNCTC, 1994: 138). State policy decisions are integral to the evolution process; as states reduce the barriers to the movement of goods, capital and services, i.e. to deeper integration, firms take 'advantage of the possibilities of cross-border interactions . . . [to] strengthen . . . international governance at the production level' (UNCTC, 1994: 145). Busch and Milner's conception of a 'domestic political theory of regionalism' suggests that as competition for international markets becomes more intense, 'internationally oriented sectors will increasingly *demand* and states will be more willing to *supply* regional trade arrangements' (1994: 260). MNEs press for regional trading agreements because they anticipate that these will protect investment and facilitate the organization of production in accordance with efficiency-seeking rather than market-seeking objectives (Gestrin and Rugman, 1994: 583–4).

The *demand* for a regional trade arrangement must be seen as both a reflection of the structure of a domestic economy and as an evolving phenomenon. What the North American experience demonstrates is that states can be ahead of MNEs in their assessment of the importance of regional trading arrangements. States may determine that participation in a free trade agreement is the best guarantor of economic growth regardless of whether there is much domestic demand. What then unfolds, whether economic ties move in the direction of 'deep' integration, is the result of corporate decisions about the attractiveness of the new strategies of production.

This chapter will demonstrate the interaction between policy-led and FDI-led integration. It begins with an overview of the economic linkages that have evolved across the three countries and that demonstrate the 'deepening' of economic integration in North America.[1] It will then examine the Canadian, American and Mexican decisions to negotiate free trade. The chapter concludes with some discussion of the implications of the process of integration in North America for the rest of Latin America.

2 TRADE AND INVESTMENT LINKAGES IN NORTH AMERICA

Writing in 1960 about Canada–US economic ties, Hugh Aitken suggested that 'the relatively unrestricted mobility of capital' between the two countries 'has done more to integrate . . . [their] economies than any single factor except geography' (1961: 19). A similar sentiment with respect to Mexico has been captured by Sidney Weintraub's assertion that 'silent integration' between Mexico and the United States has been fostered through foreign direct investment (FDI) and intra-firm trade (1990: 122). In this section we shall use trade and investment data to illustrate the nature of economic linkages across North America.

Trade

The United States has long been Canada's most important trading partner. In 1960, only 56 per cent of Canadian exports went to the United States: by 1994 the percentage had climbed to 82 per cent (Table 7.1). Canada's export dependence on the United States has intensified since the implementation of the FTA in January 1989, despite the downturn in the US economy in the early 1990s, with its exports to the United States across a number of categories outperforming those to the rest of the world (Schwanen, 1993).[2] In 1993, Canada's Cdn $145 billion in exports to the United States represented slightly more than 20 per cent of the country's GDP; moreover, the 1992–3 increase in Canadian merchandise exports to the United States exceeded Canada's total exports to all other OECD countries in the same year.[3]

Table 7.1(a) Canadian Exports to and Imports from the United
States (% of total exports and imports)

	1975	1980	1985	1989	1991	1993	1994
Exports	62%	61%	75%	71%	76%	81%	82%
Imports	66%	68%	69%	64%	62%	65%	68%

Table 7.1(b) Mexican Exports to and Imports from the United
States (% of total exports and imports)

	1975	1980	1985	1989	1991	1993
Exports	57%	65%	60%	70%	74%	79%
Imports	62%	62%	67%	68%	70%	70%

Source: All figures were taken from the IMF's *Directory of Trade Statistics*
(various years).

The United States is also the most important source of Canadian imports, although the percentage of Canadian imports
emanating from the United States has fluctuated over the last two
decades. Mexico too has become increasingly dependent on the
US market for both its exports and imports in recent years. On
the other hand, Mexico and Canada have a much more limited
trading relationship. In 1992 Canada was Mexico's second export
market (up from sixth a few years ago) and Mexico was 15th
among Canada's export destinations. Mexico's exports to Canada
have grown more significantly than the reverse in the last five
years, primarily as a result of auto parts sales, and Canada
currently has an unfavourable balance of trade with Mexico (of
some Cdn $2 billion).[4]

NAFTA has made a difference to trade patterns in North
America. In 1994, NAFTA's first year, Canada's trade increased
with both the United States and Mexico: from January to August
1994, Canada's exports to the United States increased by 20 per
cent; exports from the United States to Canada grew by 18 per
cent; those from Canada to Mexico by 33 per cent and from
Mexico to Canada by 31 per cent.

More revealing than gross trade figures are those that demonstrate the composition of intra-North American trade. Table 7.2
reveals the high concentration of Mexican exports in a few

Table 7.2 Structure of Intra-North American Trade, 1989–93
(percentage distribution)

	Year	From Canada to Mexico	From Mexico to Canada	From Canada to USA	From USA to Canada	From Mexico to USA	From USA to Mexico
1. Mineral fuels,	1989	0.0%	2.9%	8.8%	2.1%	15.8%	2.9%
lubricants and	1990	0.8%	3.3%	10.8%	2.6%	17.5%	2.9%
related	1991	3.2%	3.8%	11.3%	1.5%	15.0%	2.7%
products	1992	4.7%	7.0%	10.7%	1.5%	13.4%	3.1%
	1993	3.3%	6.1%	10.6%	1.3%	12.2%	2.5%
2. Agricultural	1989	25.5%	9.8%	4.7%	3.0%	9.8%	8.8%
products	1990	19.5%	10.6%	4.9%	5.6%	9.6%	7.4%
	1991	14.8%	5.8%	5.3%	6.1%	9.0%	7.0%
	1992	28.3%	5.3%	5.7%	6.0%	7.5%	7.3%
	1993	29.4%	5.0%	5.6%	5.8%	7.6%	6.8%
3. Chemicals	1989	0.6%	0.8%	4.5%	5.5%	2.1%	8.9%
and related	1990	1.8%	0.7%	4.7%	7.4%	2.2%	8.2%
products	1991	1.0%	0.6%	4.8%	7.8%	2.3%	8.0%
	1992	0.9%	0.6%	5.0%	8.2%	2.3%	7.8%
	1993	2.1%	0.7%	4.9%	8.4%	1.9%	8.3%
4. Crude	1989	7.2%	1.3%	9.0%	3.0%	2.3%	6.0%
materials	1990	7.7%	1.2%	8.2%	3.6%	2.5%	5.0%
other than	1991	6.2%	0.7%	7.0%	3.3%	2.3%	4.9%
fuels	1992	4.1%	0.4%	7.3%	3.2%	2.0%	4.5%
	1993	4.6%	0.4%	7.6%	3.1%	1.6%	4.3%
5. Machinery	1989	34.5%	64.2%	44.4%	45.3%	44.8%	45.4%
and trans-	1990	37.6%	73.8%	44.6%	54.6%	45.4%	47.8%
portation	1991	41.2%	80.8%	44.5%	54.1%	48.0%	47.2%
equipment	1992	37.7%	75.1%	43.9%	53.7%	50.5%	46.9%
	1993	40.3%	72.7%	44.2%	54.2%	51.9%	47.4%
6. Manufac-	1989	27.2%	20.9%	23.0%	13.6%	20.1%	22.5%
tured goods	1990	26.0%	9.7%	21.2%	21.7%	18.4%	23.1%
	1991	27.4%	7.9%	20.8%	22.6%	19.0%	24.9%
	1992	22.8%	10.7%	21.0%	23.0%	19.8%	25.6%
	1993	19.9%	14.8%	20.8%	22.8%	20.4%	26.2%
7. Commodities	1989	3.8%	0.6%	5.5%	27.4%	5.0%	5.4%
and transac-	1990	6.1%	0.6%	5.6%	4.4%	4.4%	5.6%
tions not	1991	1.6%	0.4%	6.4%	4.6%	4.5%	5.3%
elsewhere	1992	0.6%	0.4%	6.3%	4.3%	4.3%	4.8%
classified	1993	0.4%	0.3%	6.3%	4.4%	4.3%	4.5%

Table 7.2 Continued

Total (billion	1989	0.525	1.447	88.20	78.27	27.18	24.97
US$)	1990	0.508	1.477	91.36	82.97	30.18	28.37
	1991	0.48x	2.24	91.14	85.14	31.18	33.22
	1992	0.63x	2.27	98.48	90.16	35.18	40.60
	1993	0.613	2.79	110.93	100.20	39.93	41.63

Sources: US International Trade Administration, National Trade Data Bank; and Statistics Canada, *Exports by Country and Imports by Country*, various years. The 1993 Canada–US trade figures are from the US Department of Commerce, *U.S. Foreign Trade Highlights 1993* (Washington: US Department of Commerce, July 1994). The 1993 Canada–Mexico trade data are from Statistics Canada, *Imports by Country: January–December 1993* and *Exports by Country: January–December 1993* (Ottawa: Statistics Canada International Trade Division, 1994).

products, (Unger, 1994: 345), the significance of intra-North American trade in machinery and transportation equipment and the importance of Mexico as a market for Canadian and US manufactured goods. Mexico's exports to the United States are accounted for by a small number of MNEs: estimates suggest that, in 1991, 76 per cent of total Mexican exports, including oil, came from 30 firms (Unger, 1994: 345).

Investment

The pattern of foreign direct investment within North America resembles that of trade flows. In 1991, 64 per cent of the stock of foreign investment in Canada was from the United States while 58 per cent of Canadian direct investment abroad was in the United States (Knubley et al., 1994: 151). Sixty-three per cent of FDI in Mexico emanates from the United States, while Canadian FDI in Mexico historically has been very small, accounting for about 1.5 per cent of total FDI in that country. Mexican investment in Canada is minuscule.

The high levels of US FDI in Canada and Mexico have their origins in historical state import-substitution industrialization policies (what Gestrin and Rugman (1994) refer to as market-seeking activities). The 1965 Mexican legislation permitting the establishment of maquiladora factories (see below) encouraged many US MNEs to invest in offshore plants for the production and re-export of goods to the United States.

Both Canada and Mexico have used a variety of policies to restrict FDI, though both countries have liberalized their investment regimes over the last decade.[5] This liberalization, together with steady Canadian and Mexican tariff reductions (whether due to GATT[6] or unilateral state decisions), has meant that MNEs in North America have increasingly structured their production for efficiency purposes along continental lines.[7] Canadian tariffs declined substantially after the Tokyo Round and as a result many MNEs moved to rationalize their production between Canada and the United States either by closing their Canadian subsidiaries or, in some cases, allocating them specific product mandates (Litvak, 1991). This continental organization of production accelerated with the implementation of the FTA.

The link between trade and investment within North America is evident when we examine the importance of MNEs as traders. Statistics on intra-firm or inter-affiliate trade are difficult to determine. However, it is clear that this kind of trade is increasing as a proportion of total trade within North America and will increase further, as investment restrictions in Mexico are removed and more US (and a few Canadian) multinationals locate in Mexico. Using 1989 US data, Vernon notes that exports from US-based MNEs to Canada accounted for 69 per cent of total US exports to Canada and that of these exports, 65 per cent were non-arm's length (i.e. they were sent to affiliates of the exporter). The comparable statistics for Mexico were 46 per cent and 52 per cent (Vernon, 1994: 31). Eden cites statistics which indicate that in 1990 43 per cent of Canadian goods imports from the United States and 45 per cent of Canadian merchandise exports to the United States were intra-firm (Eden, 1994: 7). Since machinery and transportation equipment, primarily autos and auto parts, comprise the overwhelming proportion of Mexican exports to Canada (75 per cent in 1992), and about half that in the reverse direction (37.7 per cent)[8] we can assume that the bulk of this trade too is intra-firm.

The deep economic ties that have evolved within North America are largely the result of firms' decisions regarding the most efficient organization of production, while state policies have facilitated the rationalization of production across the three countries. It is also evident that the US economy dominates that of its trading partners and that each is heavily dependent on it.

3   THE EVOLUTION OF THE NORTH AMERICAN TRADE AND INVESTMENT REGIME

This section examines the evolution of the NATIR as it has developed between 1961 (the change in US Tariff Items 806/807) and the end of 1993 (the NAFTA Agreement). The interaction between state policies and the views and pressures of major economic interests is emphasized, demonstrating a change in attitude on the part of all three countries in North America towards negotiated free trade agreements. What is also clear is that this change in perspective was the result of new assessments of the global economy on the part of important domestic actors in Canada and Mexico. In both countries firms were becoming more export-dependent and intra-firm trade was growing in significance.

Canada

Canada's economic ties with the United States have been long and close: concerns about creeping economic integration with the United States and the implications of this for Canadian sovereignty have considerable history. For most of the postwar period Canada relied on multilateral negotiations to manage its relationship with the United States, but more recently direct bilateral pacts have been prominent. Three Canadian policies have facilitated these economic linkages – the Auto Pact, the FTA and the NAFTA.

The Auto Pact
This agreement essentially allowed free trade in finished vehicles and parts between Canada and the United States,[9] and was negotiated to overcome the problems of an inefficient and high-cost Canadian auto industry. The pact was a sectoral free trade agreement under which auto production by the Big Three (Chrysler, Ford and General Motors) in Canada and the United States was integrated to allow longer production runs and the benefits of economies of scale. This in turn would ensure continued vehicle assembly in Canada and the viability of the Canadian auto parts industry. The automotive MNEs recognized the benefits of an agreement which would allow them to rationalize vehicle production across the two countries. In many respects, the

Auto Pact and the rationalization of production it facilitated anticipated what would transpire in other industries as tariffs fell.

The Canada–US Free Trade Agreement

The decision to negotiate the FTA was a sea change in the way Canada chose to structure its relationship with its major trading partner. The Conservative Party under Brian Mulroney came to power (in September 1984) opposed to free trade with the United States,[10] but committed to creating jobs and to making Canada attractive to foreign investors. This was part of a larger Conservative government strategy for economic renewal, an important component of which was improved relations with the United States.

One year later, in September 1985, the prime minister announced that Canada was going to seek a free trade agreement with the United States. Free trade was hardly a new issue in Canada. Indeed, a possible FTA had been one of the constants on the post-war Canadian agenda. What was different in 1985 was a change in the understanding of the global environment by leading groups of Canadians, which led to a recognition that a new strategy had to be found to govern the intense Canada–US economic relationship.

On the bureaucratic side, a handful of officials in the Departments of Foreign Affairs and Finance became convinced that Canada's future economic well-being required secure access to its largest market, and they worked assiduously over nearly three years, to convince their political masters of this view. They began with a publication on Canadian trade policy which, after detailing Canada's trade dependence, concluded that sectoral free trade[11] with the United States was the appropriate course to follow (Department of External Affairs, 1983). They then persuaded the Liberal government to pursue the sectoral option, in other words, to replicate the Auto Pact in other areas.

Although the US response to the sectoral initiative was favourable, finding sectors on which both countries could agree proved difficult. A sectoral strategy vitiated the kind of larger trade-offs possible in a broader negotiation (Hart, 1994: 57–62) and therefore reduced the political attractiveness of this option. Through the autumn of 1984 these same officials started to manoeuvre the new Conservative government in the direction of full bilateral free trade. The Tories' predisposition to liberalize investment restrictions and their desire to ensure that a future government could not reverse their initiatives reinforced their receptiveness to this point of view.

Officials had support for free trade from a variety of important domestic constituencies. A number of provincial premiers – most significantly, those from Alberta and Quebec – were strong advocates of Canada–US free trade.

Most significantly, attitudes in the Canadian private sector were changing, though MNEs' support for free trade was initially more cautious than the Busch and Milner formulation suggests. The Business Council on National Issues (BCNI), comprising the major corporations in Canada (both domestic and foreign-owned), moved toward free trade with the United States in stages.[12] It first proposed a 'trade enhancement agreement', which a BCNI publication described as 'complementary to' sectoral free trade and which included a commitment by 'the two governments, as well as the respective private sectors to an examination of the advantages and disadvantages of liberalized Canada–US trade', but 'not a proposition to create a free trade area with the US' (BCNI, 1984: 3 cited in Lipsey and Smith, 1985: 74; emphasis in original). BCNI wanted a forum that would depoliticize Canada–US trade disputes, but they took some time to recognize that the establishment of such a mechanism could come only in the context of a comprehensive free trade agreement.[13] By 1985 BCNI had adopted a free trade stance, and this helped to push the government towards an FTA.

More critical in the domestic Canadian context was the reversal of the Canadian Manufacturers Association's historical opposition to free trade with the United States.[14] Larger numbers of Canadian companies were becoming active in international trade and more Canadian exporters were experiencing the threat or reality of US contingency protection. Moreover, the recession of the early 1980s and growing competition from European and Japanese firms persuaded the CMA and its members that they had to adopt a new strategy. The result was a message to the Canadian government that the CMA was prepared to accept free trade (Doern and Tomlin, 1991: 46–50). All corporations, regardless of ownership, saw bilateral free trade as promoting the restructuring of the Canadian economy as well as restricting the opportunity for state intervention (Leyton-Brown, 1994: 358).

Canada and NAFTA

The Canadian state did not anticipate Mexico's interest in free trade with the United States and was caught off guard by President Bush's positive response to President Salinas's June 1990 proposal. The Conservative government was uneasy about yet another debate in Canada over free trade. However, after considerable internal discussion, they decided to participate in the NAFTA talks.

Canada's decision was more defensive than offensive. Canada could not afford to sit on the sidelines when the rules governing trade and investment in North America were being negotiated. A bilateral US–Mexico free trade agreement might endanger many of the gains won under the FTA and make Canada a less attractive investment site; in a scenario of two bilateral free trade agreements in North America, the United States would be the common party and thus the investment site of choice.[15] On the positive side, Canadian firms would gain from access to a growing Mexican market, and the negotiations would allow Canada to resolve a number of irritants with the United States that had arisen under the FTA.

Canadian economic agents were less enthusiastic about NAFTA than about the FTA. As noted above, Canada's economic ties with Mexico were, and remain, limited. For Canadian firms adjusting to the FTA, particularly those that were labour-intensive, the prospect of another free trade agreement, particularly one with a low-wage partner, was of great concern. There was also concern about competition with Mexican producers for the US market.[16] None the less the business associations which supported the FTA all argued that Canada had to participate in the NAFTA talks because it could not allow others to define the North American trade and investment regime. Most of the provincial governments that had supported the FTA took a similar stance on NAFTA.

United States

Trade policy formulation in the United States is a tug-of-war both between branches of the state and between different perspectives on the appropriate direction for US trade policy. Although multilateralism continues to be the ultimate objective, US domestic responses to a changing global economy and increasing competition have tarnished its credibility.

Special US Tariff Provisions
Silent integration between the US and Mexican economies began
with the passage by the United States, in 1961, of an outward
processing programme under Tariff Items 806 and 807 (Hart,
1990: 64). Large MNEs were the major US beneficiaries of this
initiative. The programme allowed the re-import into the United
States of goods manufactured in Mexico with US inputs, with
duty imposed only on the value-added abroad. Combined with
the Mexican maquiladora programme (described below), US
MNEs began to locate offshore in Mexico and import consumer
electronic goods, transportation equipment and textiles, apparel
and footwear into the United States (Weintraub, 1990a: 78). With
Mexico, as with Canada, US policy decisions permitted MNEs to
organize their production increasingly on efficiency criteria.

The Canada–US Free Trade Agreement
The United States responded positively to Canada's free trade
overtures for two reasons, one international and one bilateral. At
the international level there was considerable US frustration with
the lack of progress of the Uruguay Round. Bilateralism offered
another avenue to promote continued trade liberalization as well
as an opportunity to make progress on some of the newer trade
concerns such as investment, services and intellectual property
(Aho and Ostry, 1990: 155). If multilateral negotiations were
problematic, an FTA would demonstrate to the EU and Japan
that the United States was prepared to utilize other means to
attain its goals.[17]
     At the bilateral level the US officials, particularly those in the
Office of the US Trade Representative (USTR), saw free trade
with Canada as a way to codify the more liberal investment
posture of the Mulroney government.[18] The Reagan administration had a number of other objectives in the free trade talks; these
included issues of intellectual property, services, government
procurement, subsidies and the resolution of outstanding bilateral
trade disputes (Leyton-Brown, 1994: 359).
     The US administration was kept apprised of the evolution in
Canadian thinking on free trade. There were many meetings
between officials of USTR and their Canadian counterparts over
sectoral and, subsequently, bilateral free trade. As views were
exchanged, members of the USTR made clear what kind of deal
might be acceptable in Washington (Doern and Tomlin, 1991:

20–9; Hart, 1994: chapters 4 and 6). These discussions notwithstanding, when the bilateral talks began, the US administration
had difficulty formulating its negotiating position across a host of
issues (Hart, 1994).

American firms initially exhibited little interest in free trade with
Canada, as the Canadian organization of major MNEs, BCNI,
discovered when it met its US counterpart, the American Business
Roundtable in 1983 (Doern and Tomlin, 1991: 48). This corporate
attitude changed little even as negotiations were underway in 1986
and 1987. Doern and Tomlin suggest that this lack of business
pressure on the US administration to conclude an agreement might
have been one of the factors contributing to the inability of the US
administration to focus on the FTA talks (1991: 105–6).

This US corporate stance can partly be explained by the
traditional lack of attention to Canada–US issues in the United
States. More significant was the diversity of corporate views on
trade issues. In the mid-1980s many American firms were more
concerned with fair, rather than with free, trade. Support for free
trade was centred in the service sector, which had become
sensitive to the new issues on the trade agenda, such as intellectual property, and less in manufacturing. A third reason was that
tariff reductions under the Tokyo Round had already facilitated
considerable corporate rationalization of production between
Canada and the United States. Only in July 1987, after the FTA
talks had been underway for more than a year, did a US
corporate coalition in support of free trade emerge.[19]

Opposition to an FTA in the United States came primarily from
natural resource and agricultural interests, which frequently complained about what they deemed unfair Canadian trade practices.
Organized labour in the United States also opposed an FTA.

The Reagan administration did not anticipate any difficulty in
getting congressional approval to negotiate free trade with Canada. The House of Representatives Ways and Means Committee
indicated that it would neither hold hearings on the topic nor
raise objections to the negotiation of free trade with Canada
(Hart, 1994: 143; Leyton-Brown, 1987: 152).

The situation in the Senate was different. There, the Chairman
of the Senate Finance Committee, Robert Packwood, and a
number of his colleagues used the fast-track debate to attack the
administration's trade policy and the president's desire for fast-
track authority. Their complaints were only secondarily against

Canada, although senators from lumber-producing states expressed considerable hostility about Canadian lumber exports to the United States. On the last possible date, fast-track authority was granted, although on a negative vote.[20]

The US and NAFTA

Three agreements signed between the United States and Mexico from 1985 to 1989 established a closer working relationship between the two countries on economic issues and built confidence, particularly in Mexico, about its ability to negotiate with the United States. These comprised a trade agreement in 1985, a framework agreement establishing new consultation and dispute settlement procedures in 1987, and a 1989 'Understanding', which committed the two parties to continued efforts to improve their economic ties (see below).[21]

The US administration applauded NAFTA as a means to strengthen and stabilize the Mexican economy and to reinforce the liberalization of trade and investment regulations begun by President Salinas. As with Canada, the conclusion of a free trade agreement with Mexico would make the reintroduction of more restrictive economic policies more difficult. Uncertainty over the outcome of the 1988 Mexican presidential election and fears of Mexican political instability heightened US receptivity to the Salinas initiative.

In contrast to the limited debate in the United States over the FTA, the NAFTA proposal generated considerably more controversy. Interests on both sides of the debate made their positions very clear during the debates over fast-track and the implementing legislation.

US MNEs that had rationalized at least some their production, under the auspices of US Tariff Items 806 and 807, supported NAFTA as a means to opening the Mexican economy further. These firms, which had already committed the resources necessary to alter the character of their operations in Mexico from market- to efficiency-seeking (Gestrin and Rugman, 1994: 583), lobbied hard for strong investment provisions in the NAFTA agreement. Some industries (for example, autos) pressed the US administration to negotiate NAFTA clauses to protect their interests.[22] Smaller US corporations that supply inputs to the MNEs and those that would face domestic competition from Mexican goods were more uncertain about NAFTA; many of these corporations also demanded special treatment under the agreement. US glass- and steelmakers expressed concern about their ability to compete with Mexican products. Growers of fresh produce, already facing competition from Mexico, opposed NAFTA because they anticipated an additional deterioration in their position. US labour was vehemently opposed to NAFTA,[23] as were a variety of environmental and religious groups.

Domestic opposition notwithstanding, President Bush received fast-track authority to negotiate the NAFTA. In the interval between the completion of the NAFTA negotiations and the introduction of the enabling legislation those opposed to the agreement had an opportunity to regroup and again press their views. With a Congress more receptive to some of their concerns, the coalition of labour, environmental and religious groups was able to force President Clinton to agree to the negotiation of side-agreements on labour and the environment in return for support of the NAFTA legislation. Passage of NAFTA through the House of Representatives was uncertain until the end, when the legislation passed by a larger margin than had been anticipated.

Mexico

Like Canada, Mexico's economic linkages with the United States evolved through a combination of state policies and the investment decisions of MNEs. Similarly, the decision to pursue bilateral free trade was taken at the top by a coterie of technocrats, rather than as the result of corporate demand. Both countries worried about growing US protectionism. There were also major differences between the two, both in the quality of their economic linkages with the United States and in the degree to which there was broad societal debate over free trade.

Maquiladora Programme

Of the various economic policies adopted by the Mexican state, the maquiladora programme was the most important in terms of tying the Mexican economy to that of the United States. Established in 1965 to provide employment for Mexicans living in the northern border region of the country, the programme allows firms to import materials into Mexico duty free for assembly purposes on the basis that they will be re-exported. US Tariff Items 806 and 807 were the US complement to the maquila legislation. With the requisite legislation in place on both sides of the border, the number of maquila firms grew rapidly. By January 1992, there were close to 2000 such operations employing close to 500 000 people; these plants accounted for nearly half of Mexico's exports to the United States and a significant percentage of Mexican imports (Weintraub, 1990: 79).[24] The majority of the maquila plants are owned by US corporations, both MNEs and medium-sized companies. Many of the largest US MNEs, including the Big Three auto producers and the major consumer electronics firms, have maquila plants. Economic integration is deepening between the United States and Mexico, but remains more shallow than that between the United States and Canada.

Mexico and NAFTA

For many years the Mexican economy imposed restrictions on FDI and domestic content provisions on foreign firms operating in the Mexican market. Mexico took advantage of high oil prices in the 1970s to borrow in order to finance economic development and sustain its policy of import-substitution industrialization. With the fall in oil prices and the recession of the early 1980s, Mexico faced a serious debt burden. Capital fled and the value of the peso fell. President de la Madrid (1983–8) introduced a number of economic reforms, among them a reduction of restrictions on FDI, and applied for Mexican membership of the GATT. His successor, President Salinas de Gortari, continued the liberalization of the Mexican economy, a critical component of which was his approach to the United States to negotiate NAFTA.

There was a number of parallels between the Mexican and Canadian free trade decisions. Like Canadian Prime Minister Brian Mulroney, President Salinas did not enter office intent upon free trade with the United States. His first important bilateral foray was the conclusion of a series of agreements in October 1989 under which Mexico and the United States agreed to sectoral trade talks, the specification of sectors for co-investment, the liberalization of trade in steel and the maintenance of the existing framework for consultation and dispute resolution (Hart, 1990: 63). As with Canada, sectoral free trade foundered because of the difficulty in identifying sectors where gains could be balanced. Salinas's decision to pursue bilateral free trade came after an early 1990 visit to Europe to promote trade and investment. Disappointed with the European response, Salinas recognized that Mexico's future lay in closer economic ties within North America (Cameron et al., 1992: 182).

President Salinas had a number of goals in his pursuit of free trade with the United States. Mexico had also experienced growing US protectionism. The Mexican president worried about the potential loss of US market share to Canadian goods with the implementation of the FTA. Furthermore, Salinas was sensitive to the need for continued inflows of FDI, if the Mexican economy was to create much needed jobs, and of the potential for competition for investment dollars from Eastern Europe. A free trade agreement would strengthen investor confidence both by improving market access for exports and by committing Mexico to lasting economic liberalization (Helleiner, 1993: 48). Political debate in Mexico over NAFTA was far more constrained than that in either Canada or the United States. A strong state with a strong president meant that President Salinas and his advisers (many of whom, like him, were US-trained) were able to impose their own free trade preferences. Bureaucrats recruited to the Secretariat of Trade and Industrial Development (SECOFI) had clear free trade convictions (Pastor and Wise, 1994: 478). The Mexican state adopted a secretive stance on NAFTA, revealing very little information on the negotiations other than what it wanted the populace to hear (Aguilar Zinser, 1993: 207). Although there were intra-state debates on the impact of NAFTA, state-commissioned research was not made public (Pastor and Wise, 1994: 480).[25]

The Mexican state could also control the legislature. Early in the process the Salinas administration decided that because the Mexican Constitution requires only Senate ratification of treaties, the Chamber of Deputies would not have the opportunity to debate NAFTA. Aguilar Zinser suggests that the reason for this decision lies in the size of the opposition representation (45 per cent) in the Chamber in contrast to the overwhelming PRI control of the Senate (1993: 208). Media discussion was also dominated by pro-NAFTA forces (Weintraub, 1994: 4).

The formulation of corporate positions on NAFTA was a function of the degree of international orientation of firms as well

as perceptions of the potential impact of free trade on particular
sectors and companies. Large corporations had long supported
liberalization of the Mexican economy. National associations
such as the Confederation of Chambers of Industry (CON-
CAMIN), which represents the major manufacturers, COMPAR-
MEX (the Employers' Confederation of the Mexican Republic)
which had strong ties to exporters located in northern Mexico,
and the Confederation of National Chambers of Commerce
(CONCANACO) all advocated Mexico's entry into the GATT in
the late 1970s. By the time Mexico joined the GATT in 1986
many large Mexican firms had increased their international
economic activity (Pastor and Wise, 1994: 464–5) and a small
number were, as Unger indicates, accounting for a disproportion-
ate share of Mexico's exports to the US (1994: 345).

Although the state's free trade perspective was shared by
Mexican MNEs, the state none the less, undertook to organize
corporate support for its initiative. Its vehicle was a state-
sponsored forum or 'peak association' on free trade, COECE (the
Mexican Business Coordinating Council for Free Trade), whose
role was to bring together various business associations to develop
a common strategy for the negotiations. Groups wanting input
into the formulation of a Mexican position on NAFTA had to
belong to COECE. There was no other association with any
legitimacy.

Through their associations and COECE, major Mexican firms
enjoyed a close working relationship with the state during the
NAFTA talks, and also had the capacity to anticipate the impact
of NAFTA on their sectors.

The situation of the small and medium-sized firms during the
NAFTA talks was somewhat different. Most of these firms
belonged to CANACINTRA (the National Chamber of Manufacturing Industry), which had historically been more protectionist. Although many CANACINTRA members believed
that NAFTA would benefit only large Mexican firms, the association continued to participate in COECE and eventually
supported the agreement. Some CANACINTRA members
broke ranks with the organization, asserting that COECE did
not adequately represent their views (Pastor and Wise, 1994:
481). These producers had far less information on the negotiations and on the merits of a free trade option. One study on
small and medium-sized manufacturing companies suggests some

confusion about free trade on the part of these generally more domestically-oriented firms; it revealed virtually equal support for sectoral and free trade agreements as the preferred strategy to increase access to US and Canadian markets (del Castillo and Vega, 1991: 5). What was attractive to this segment of Mexican business was the continuing opening of the Mexican economy, although they recognized that how this opening occurred would dictate future success or failure.

Not all sectors supported freer trade. Those industries which saw themselves as vulnerable under NAFTA – textiles and trucking, for example – sought a longer phase-in period and complained about inadequate financing to ease adjustment (Pastor and Wise, 1994: 481). The traditional base of the ruling PRI, the smaller-scale entrepreneurs, peasants and labour, was largely ignored in the NAFTA process (Pastor and Wise, 1994: 464–5, 480).

CONCLUSIONS

The discussion of the Canadian, US and Mexican experiences demonstrates the difficulty of separating policy-led and invest-ment-led integration. There is a continuing interaction between the two, one that has been enhanced by the globalization of production and the increasing importance of intra-firm trade. What is interesting about the North American example is that the participating governments did not anticipate, indeed perhaps could not have anticipated, the way in which their pre-free trade policies would promote the evolution of close bilateral economic relationships.

The North American experience also illustrates the importance of ideology and of changes in ideology; in both Canada and Mexico political leaders radically altered their views on the appropriate national relationship with the United States. Both states led their corporate sectors into support for free trade.

In terms of wider hemispheric integration, the FTA and NAFTA negotiations demonstrate that whether regional trading arrangements evolve and deepen depends on the investment decisions of firms. The experience in all three NAFTA countries illustrates that the motivation for corporate support for free trade lies in a desire to protect investments. It is also clear from the

FTA and NAFTA processes that firms are more likely to support state-free trade initiatives than to demand them.

In terms of the expansion of NAFTA, states are again ahead of MNEs. The United States was the first of the NAFTA signatories to contemplate the inclusion of Chile, though interest in NAFTA expansion has waned in the United States. By early December 1995 it was clear that Congress was not prepared to grant President Clinton fast-track authority, with the result that negotiations on Chile's entry into NAFTA will probably not resume again until late 1997.

The uncertainty over US capacity to continue NAFTA expansion talks has prompted Canada and Mexico to consider extending parts of the agreement to Chile without US participation. The Canadian state has been a strong supporter of Chile's accession to NAFTA, in part because of the old Canadian tradition of a search for counterweights to the United States and in part because of Canada's new advocacy of free trade. Canada's trade with Chile is modest, as Raúl E. Sáez's paper in this volume illustrates, although Canadian exporters have expressed interest in gaining easier access to a number of specific Chilean sectors. The real impetus for Canadian interest in Chilean accession is investment. Because Canada is one of the biggest foreign investors in Chile, Canada is anxious to conclude a foreign investment protection agreement similar to that in NAFTA.

Mexico and Chile have had free trade since 1991. They are currently exploring the feasibility of upgrading their relationship to include such areas as services and technical barriers to trade, as well as a dispute settlement mechanism. Whether the three states are able to conclude a 'bridging' arrangement, which would be less comprehensive than full Chilean access to NAFTA, remains to be seen. Whatever the outcome, what is significant is state interest in the enlargement of NAFTA, that is policy-led integration. Integration between Chile and NAFTA is 'shallow' and will remain so. MNEs will support the extension of NAFTA to Chile, particularly if it includes investment protection, though they may be less interested in expansion beyond Chile.[26] Distance and investment patterns mitigate against the quick evolution of 'deep' integration between NAFTA and the economies of Latin America.

8 Social Issues and Labour Adjustment Policies: The Canada–US FTA Experience
Ann Weston

1 INTRODUCTION: SOCIAL POLICIES AND HEMISPHERIC ECONOMIC INTEGRATION

There is now growing recognition of the need to address social policies in the course of economic integration. While for a long time social standards have typically been viewed as a domestic issue – the result of national preferences with regard to the allocation of fiscal resources, national legislative history, etc. – increasing international economic linkages, resulting from a surge in trade and especially investment flows, have brought with them concern about social standards.

In principle, and often in practice, increased trade should bring welfare gains through a reallocation of resources, greater specialization and increased output. But there has been mounting concern about short-term adjustment problems, especially in Canada at the end of the 1980s when trade liberalization coincided with global recession, a domestic fiscal crisis and an appreciating Canadian dollar, on top of the restructuring caused by new technologies and changing demand patterns. In Canada and many other developed countries, unemployment rates increased, especially in labour-intensive, low-skilled manufacturing industries. Work by Wood (1994) and others has shown in particular that these trends are likely to be exacerbated by increased trade with developing countries. Others, however, point to the restructuring caused by new technologies, changing patterns of demand, and increasing competition with the rest of the world for trade and investment.

The question, then, is what should be the appropriate response. There are two types of approach advocated to varying degrees. Wood and many others (e.g. Howse, 1993) have argued for increased adjustment assistance in the form of training and, given the lag before this translates into increased employment, income support. Others, while agreeing that changes are needed in the social programmes, feel that the emphasis should not be on the 'right' to adjustment support so much as the 'responsibility' to adjust. (The criticism being that past programmes have created disincentives to retrain and seek employment in other industries; see below.) They are also more optimistic about the capacity of the Canadian economy to adjust without intervention.

Others have called for mechanisms going beyond the present safeguard clauses or trade remedy laws of the GATT/WTO – for example, to include social standards, allowing the use of duties to offset social dumping, etc. (Stanford et al., 1993; Campbell, 1994). Even well-known advocates of trade liberalization within the Canadian government have argued that as economies become more integrated discussion is needed about positive norms for behaviour in the area of social policy as well as competition policy and environmental standards.[1]

Distributional problems associated with economic restructuring are also prevalent in Latin America, with considerable evidence that income inequalities have worsened in many countries (see for example, work by Berry and Stewart, forthcoming; McKinley and Alarcon, 1994; amongst others). In some cases, increasing trade deficits suggest that the problem is the time-lag for export industries to expand, whereas imports have grown rapidly. Another explanation is that in middle-income countries specialization has tended to promote relatively more skill-intensive industries. Other factors include the unequal distribution of land, capital, technology and information, skewing the gains from trade.

In many countries secondary income has not been able to offset the inequitable distribution of primary income, often because social safety nets, labour legislation and redistributive fiscal policies, though minimal, have been weakened. (Cuts in trade taxes can exacerbate fiscal pressures and require larger cuts in social spending; labour legislation is often related to lower labour costs, allowing employers greater flexibility in hiring/firing, and thus attractive to foreign investment.) As Berry and Stewart (forthcoming) note: 'liberalisation policies often involve modifying or eliminating these institutions. Where they do, this adds to inequality – as in Chile [and] Argentina . . . but where they remain in place, they can help offset some inegalitarian tendencies, as . . . in Costa Rica.'

There is growing consensus, therefore, that for economic integration to be socially (and politically) sustainable, there must be greater attention paid to its social impact. This may lead to the conclusion that the process of trade liberalization should be modified (in terms of its speed and scope as well as the underlying rules of the game) and/or that complementary amendments be made to social policies.

In Latin America, national governments are addressing these issues, with most emphasizing and strengthening social programmes rather than reforming their trade agendas. The regional development bank – the Inter-American Development Bank – is providing financial resources and technical expertise (with as much as 50 per cent of lending in the future to be allocated for social purposes compared to 25 per cent on average in the past).

This chapter focuses primarily on Canadian experiences – and experiments – with social policies in the context of trade liberalization, as well as fiscal reform, new technologies and changing demand. In the first part of the following section, the fiscal pressures are outlined. This is followed by a review of recent developments in unemployment and unemployment insurance policies. There is also a short comparison with adjustment assistance policies in the United States. The third section examines the various mechanisms being used by the three NAFTA countries to address labour standards, as well as a number of other proposals for integrating social standards more broadly with trade. The chapter ends with a brief set of conclusions.

2 KEY ELEMENTS IN THE CANADIAN SOCIAL POLICY DEBATE

The ongoing debate about the future of Canadian social policies is being driven by three concerns: the fiscal deficit, unemployment and poverty. All three are closely interconnected. They appear to have been exacerbated by the restructuring of the

Canadian economy. Interestingly, and in sharp contrast to earlier debates, little of the discussion in Canada is questioning whether our openness, as a result of the Canada–US Free Trade Agreement (FTA), the North American Free Trade Agreement (NAFTA), the Uruguay Round and a possible Americas Free Trade Agreement (AFTA) should be reviewed: whether the social problems we confront could be alleviated by changing the nature of these agreements. Rather, these are increasingly accepted as 'givens'; the discussion has focused instead on what types of social programmes Canada both needs and can afford given its increasingly open economy.

The Deficit

Government debt now stands at $700 billion, or more than 60 per cent of Canadian GDP,[2] and debt servicing, which cost some $38 billion in 1994, is absorbing an increasing share of expenditure. In fact, the government's annual deficit is due primarily to the debt service associated with *compounding* debt.

The federal government would like to reduce the deficit from 6 per cent to 3 per cent of GDP, but it is generally argued that Canada cannot afford to raise taxes from the present level of more than 40 per cent of GDP, as the NAFTA and the FTA, by increasing the mobility of capital, goods and labour between the two countries, have made it increasingly difficult to maintain a large differential in corporate, sales and even personal income taxes.

Thus, most emphasis has been on reduction of government expenditures, with the focus mainly on social programmes, which cost the federal government about $39 billion in 1993, coincidentally roughly equal to Canada's $40 billion annual federal deficit.

Unemployment and Unemployment Insurance

Another important factor behind the review is the perception that Canada's social programmes have been unable to deal with 1990s-style unemployment, including the adjustments resulting from the FTA and the NAFTA. As in many Western European countries, there has been a long-term growth in structural unemployment, and some suggest this may have been exacerbated, rather than alleviated, by unemployment insurance (UI) and the rest of the social safety net, to the extent that they distort incentives to retrain and return to work.

Unemployment was in double digits from February 1991 – peaking at 11.8 per cent, in November 1993 – until November 1994, when it fell to 9.6 per cent. The length of unemployment has increased: the number of people unemployed for more than a year trebled to 13 per cent between 1976 and 1993. In September 1994 this number reached 214 000 or 16 per cent, compared to 57 000 or 5.4 per cent in September 1990. Structural unemployment in Canada has grown by 2.5 percentage points in the past 25 years to 8.5 per cent.

Unemployment is considerably higher than this in certain industries. Employment in manufacturing fell by 338 000 or 16 per cent from 1989 to 1992; it then rose in 1993–4, but still remained 12 per cent below the level in 1992. The share of total non-agricultural employment in manufacturing has dropped from 21 per cent in 1980 to 15 per cent since 1992. This has been matched by a steady increase in the share of services from 61 per cent in 1980 to 69 per cent in 1994.

Unemployment rates are also considerably higher in certain regions and provinces. In the case of Atlantic provinces, poor job market prospects caused by the closure of the fisheries have even discouraged many people from registering as unemployed. There is also a significant difference in the labour market experiences of native groups and young people. In 1994 as many as 18.5 per cent of men less than 25 years old were unemployed compared to 14.3 per cent of young women, while for aboriginals unemployment has been twice the national average (Government of Canada, 1994a: 17). On the other hand, the gender differential has narrowed.

There has been considerable debate about the extent to which these various changes in the pattern of employment and unemployment have been due to the FTA and NAFTA. Most would concur that the agreements have accelerated the expansion of some industries and the decline of others. Goods and service industries able to take advantage of liberalized access under the FTA to increase their exports to the US market include office and telecommunications equipment, precision instruments, various equipment and tools, and business services. Canadian industries facing increased competition from US goods include clothing, furniture and furnishings, other household goods, meat and processed foods (Schwanen, 1993).

But disagreement focuses on the net effects – one study found that overall unemployment in 1991 would have been higher (by 0.1 of a percentage point) in the absence of the FTA (Pauly, 1991). Another estimated that the tariff phase-out led to the loss of 53 000 jobs, or some 15 per cent of manufacturing unemployment (Waverman, 1993), while overall employment may fall by 3.3 per cent once the FTA tariff cuts are fully phased in (Gaston and Trefler, 1994).

In general, it is expected that the NAFTA will also expand demand for high value-added production, but increase competition for industries with a predominantly low-wage, low-skilled workforce, thereby adding to existing pressures for greater wage inequality: 'Wage losses can be substantial for many workers as they are displaced to their next best alternative job. This is especially the case for workers who are older, less educated, blue-collar, unionized, and who have considerable seniority and industry specific human capital' (Gunderson, 1993).

In response, there has been growing concern with the adequacy of existing adjustment mechanisms. In the past, Canada has operated a number of sector-specific programmes, though generally they were little used partly because of strict eligibility criteria and partly because there was less labour displacement than expected (e.g. the Transitional Assistance Benefits programme for the auto industry, to deal with adjustments caused by the Canada–US Auto Pact, only provided relief to 3100 workers in total during its operation from 1965 to 1976). These put more emphasis on income support than adjustment. Some 65 per cent of workers receiving assistance under the CIRP (Canadian Industrial Renewal Plan, 1981–6, for displaced workers in the clothing, textile, footwear and tanning industries) and the ILAP (the Industry and Labour Adjustment Programme, 1981–3, for designated industries and communities) returned to their former employers compared to the average 40 per cent for workers in all industries (Trebilcock et al., 1990: 142).

By far the largest single labour market programme in Canada is unemployment insurance (UI). It has come under increasing scrutiny in recent years for a variety of reasons, related in particular to efficiency and equity, though the extent to which it should promote adjustment rather than being primarily a redistributive tool is a matter of some debate. Originally conceived to provide short-term support to workers in between jobs, it now appears to support workers facing long-term or recurring unemployment. This is reflected in the fact that many workers and firms, and even some provincial governments, have been long-term, repeat-users of UI.

Neither UI contributions nor benefits vary with frequency of use; both are a function of wage levels, while benefits also depend on the number of claimants and the duration of unemployment. Until recently only ten weeks' contributions were needed to qualify for 42 weeks of benefits. In most cases, cross-subsidized industries (i.e. those that received more than they contributed) are those with both higher than average claim rates and lower than average wages (Corakand Pyper, 1994, p. 3.9). Also, in most cases, the layoffs are temporary (i.e. where the worker had earnings from the same firm within a year of being laid off) rather than permanent.

An important question, then, is whether access to UI has deterred firms in these industries from responding to lower demand by undertaking structural changes in their production (such as lowering wages or other costs). It would appear to have encouraged them instead to lay off workers, if only temporarily, in the knowledge that these workers will be able to receive UI until they are needed again. There are several examples of workers being hired for the minimum UI qualifying period before being laid off again, such as the fish processing industry. Even some provincial governments have organized public works schemes on this basis to reduce the number of workers on welfare, to which provinces contribute. (It should be noted, however, that in every cross-subsidized industry, including construction, there is a significant number of firms which do not make use of UI in this way.) Another concern is whether the resulting relatively high UI rates and wage rates are constraining the growth of employment in other firms or industries (e.g. services) with better long-term growth prospects.

Similarly, has UI deterred workers in provinces like Newfoundland moving to other parts of Canada where there are employment opportunities? To what extent have high UI costs imposed a drag on employment in these other provinces? A number of authors have questioned whether net-contributing provinces like Ontario will be prepared to tolerate their continued cross-subsidization of employment in other provinces, on the grounds, for instance, that it may constrain their capacity to compete internationally. In particular, Courchene argues that with the decline of east–west trade links, there may be less tolerance for interprovincial transfers on this scale (1994: 43).

One feature of UI that has been challenged is that it is unconditional. There is no obligation on the part of recipients to participate in training which by strengthening their skills might increase both the probability and length of their re-employment as well as their future wages (and thus their UI contributions). In sharp contrast to many West European countries, the bulk (over 70 per cent) of Canadian income support has been in so-called passive programmes. The need to shift from passive income support to more active or 'trampoline' training and re-employment measures has been a constant theme in debates about Canadian labour market policies in the last ten years (see, for example, the MacDonald Commission Report of 1985 on the development prospects for Canada), if not longer.

Another problem is the high and punitive marginal tax rates acting as a disincentive for income-earning activities. Finally, there has been concern with UI's impact on income distribution. Some studies have indicated that 60 per cent of UI payments go to the top three income quartiles (Trebilcock et al., 1990: 140).

Cost reduction in the case of UI (to achieve both lower rates for employers and employees, and to reduce government exposure to cost overruns) has been achieved by reducing overall coverage. Reforms introduced since 1990 have lengthened the qualifying period and shortened the length of benefits, though with some variations according to the level of local unemployment. For example, pre-1990 maximum benefits throughout Canada were 50 weeks. From April 1994 they have varied from a maximum of 36 weeks in an area with less than 6 per cent unemployment to 50 weeks in an area with 12 per cent or more unemployment (Government of Canada, 1994b: 95). Likewise, minimum qualifying periods and lengths of benefits also vary. A person who had only worked for 19 weeks in the first area would not be eligible for any UI benefits, whereas in the second area she would qualify for 35 weeks of benefits. Benefit rates have also been reduced to 55 per cent of previous earnings (to a ceiling of $780 weekly income) for most claimants, though low-income claimants with dependants may still receive 60 per cent. Finally, people quitting jobs without due cause or fired for misconduct are ineligible for benefits. Overall these modifications have had the effect of cutting the numbers on UI. The number of claimants fell by 38 per cent from the peak in July 1992 to August 1994, to the lowest level since September 1989. The decline in UI coverage, from 73 per cent to 61 per cent of all unemployed people from July 1992 to August 1994, has produced annual savings to the federal government of $3 billion. Some people have been encouraged to stay in employment; but others have not had the choice and as a result the numbers on welfare have risen, increasing the costs for provincial governments.

Also under discussion now are contribution rates which would rise with UI use, both by employer and/or employee. Alternatively, it has been suggested that frequent users could be given lower, means-tested benefits. This 'adjustment insurance' would be coupled with a package of employment development services, such as community service or training and employment programmes (Government of Canada, 1994b: 31). If defined as those with more than three claims in the previous five years, about 38 per cent of UI claimants in 1991 would have received lower benefits, and more than two-thirds of claimants in Newfoundland and PEI (ibid.: 33). Changes in UI rules along these lines could have a major economic and social impact in the Atlantic provinces if not phased in gradually.

The government is also considering how best to increase insurance for non-standard workers i.e. part-time, multiple job and self-employed workers, 20 per cent of whom are not presently covered. This is important as non-standard jobs account for a growing share of the labour market – as much as 30 per cent of all employment in 1993. UI is presently not available for people working less than 15 hours or earning less than $156 a week, i.e. mainly women and youths. But UI extension could lead to workers not being hired or being given fewer hours, for example, if the threshold is lowered from 15 to 10 hours (Government of Canada, 1994a: 60).

A major innovation since 1990 has been the dedication of up to 15 per cent of UI funds for so-called 'Developmental Uses' programmes. In 1994 some $2 billion or 11 per cent of projected UI funds were to be spent on training costs, allowances, mobility assistance and self-employment measures for 400 000 UI claimants.

In short, Canadian social policy – and especially the set of programmes dealing with unemployment, income support and training – is in a state of flux as a result of many pressures, including the fiscal crisis as well as the economic restructuring caused by technological change and Canadian trade liberalization. Some of the social policy changes are overdue, such as removing the punitive tax rates on additional income for UI or welfare claimants. But others, such as the shift from the federally-funded universal approach of the past with a strong emphasis on redistribution, to a much more regionally differentiated and conditional approach, are controversial. The right to income support will increasingly depend on individuals' willingness to participate in various training or other schemes, while the levels of support are being reduced. There is scepticism about the outcome, whether the training programmes will prove effective in assisting adjustment, reducing structural unemployment or raising wages, and whether the lower UI and welfare benefits will merely increase poverty especially in Atlantic Canada.

Comparisons with the United States

Comparisons of Canadian social policy with policies in the United States were common during the debate over the FTA for various reasons (see Weston, 1994). As already mentioned, one concern was the associated differential in production costs and the impact on investment decisions. Would the mobility of investment and trade following the FTA put pressure on Canada to reduce its social programme costs? Could Canadian producers argue that the lower fiscal costs of US social programmes give US producers an unfair advantage? On the other hand, could US firms complain about the cross-regional and industrial subsidies implicit in the Canadian UI system? There is also interest in the economic and social lessons from US experience with workfare.

One reason that US experience has attracted Canadian interest is that it has maintained relatively low, single-digit unemployment rates – in November 1994, unemployment fell to 5.6 per cent, the lowest level for four years. But there is considerable questioning of the social sustainability of existing policies, given widening inequalities between different income and racial groups, reflected in the growing number of low-skilled, low-wage workers.

UI is the major labour market support policy in the United States, though it covers less than 40 per cent of unemployed workers (or 2.5 million people in 1990; Hufbauer and Schott, 1992: 114). Compared to the Canadian scheme, its wage replacement rate is lower (35–40 per cent of the previous year's wages) and of shorter duration (6–9 months). As in Canada, however, the United States has tended to place greater emphasis on income maintenance (over 70 per cent of all labour market spending) than on employment promotion.

Besides UI, the United States has operated a special trade adjustment assistance (TAA) programme for workers and firms displaced by trade. Since 1962 TAA has been attached to most key Trade Bills in order to win political support for trade liberalization. The terms of access (less rigid eligibility and speedier delivery) and level of benefits have been expanded over the years. Even so many requests for assistance have been rejected partly because of the difficulty in establishing whether trade was in fact the major cause of labour displacement (Mitchell, 1976).

The US TAA programme shares some characteristics with Canada's UI programme in the sense that one study found as much as 75 per cent of workers receiving TAA were on temporary lay-off and returned to their old jobs (Trebilcock et al., 1990: 123). TAA was liberalized in the 1974 Trade Act, leading to a sharp increase in its use – as many as 1.2 million workers received benefits from 1977 to 1981, compared to 54 000 altogether from 1962 to 1974. A further change introduced in the 1988 Trade Act was to extend eligibility to workers in supplier and service firms, indirectly affected by imports, but no money has been allocated to make this provision effective (OTA, 1993: 33). From 1987 to end-1992, only 315 000 workers were covered by TAA (Shelburne, 1993: 12) (and according to OTA (1993: 33), in 1991 only 25 000 workers or 1 per cent of people unemployed for longer than six months). Nearly a third of assisted workers were in the clothing industry, a further 15 per cent in transport equipment and 13 per cent in electronics/electrical products.

At one point the US administration proposed merging the TAA with another labour placement and training assistance programme (known as JTPA) for fiscal and other reasons, as the former was costing on average US$7000 per worker (Hufbauer and Schott, 1994: 116). Another suggestion was that Congress enact a new labour adjustment programme to improve job opportunities for all workers in the lower end of the labour market, not just those affected by the NAFTA (OTA, 1993). This more comprehensive approach would have involved the integration of various programmes such as Economic Dislocation and Worker Adjustment Assistance (EDWAA) – a programme involving some training, related income support and job advice – TAA and UI. In the United States, UI has typically had much lower coverage than in Canada, with only 40 per cent of all unemployed workers covered in 1990, for only 37 per cent of previous earnings, and for only 26 weeks (OTA, 1993: 33).

Instead, as part of its NAFTA implementing legislation, the United States introduced a special NAFTA Transitional Adjustment Assistance (NAFTA–TAA) programme. This goes further than the traditional TAA in that it offers assistance to workers displaced by production shifting offshore to Mexico (or Canada), as well as workers displaced either directly or indirectly by imports. In addition, farm workers or family farmers not covered by UI are eligible. In the first nine months of the scheme's operation some 30 000 workers had filed claims for assistance of which a third, or 10 345, had been certified by the Department of Labor. As much as a half of these were related to relocation of production. These numbers probably understate the extent of worker displacement, however, some workers may have chosen to submit claims for the regular TAA which has less rigid deadlines (Anderson, 1994). Recent reports suggest NAFTA–TAA may be relaxed to allow for greater flexibility, e.g. in the time limits for training eligibility (Inside NAFTA, 5 October 1994, p. 7).

3 OPTIONS FOR INTEGRATING SOCIAL POLICY INTO THE HEMISPHERIC ECONOMIC INITIATIVE

To date, the chief supranational instrument for addressing social policy concerns in the NAFTA has been the North American Agreement on Labour Cooperation (otherwise known as the NAFTA Labour Side-Agreement) or NAALC. The NAALC came into effect in January 1994, at the same time as the NAFTA. It is still too early to determine whether it has lived up to expectations about its strengths or its weaknesses (see, for example, Stanford et al., 1994). While each country has designated its National Administrative Office (the main body responsible for handling national requests for consultations), the trinational, coordinating Secretariat to be based in Dallas, Texas, was unlikely to be fully staffed and functioning before January 1995.

To recap briefly, the labour side-agreement provides a framework for increasing discussion and understanding about labour policies and standards in the three countries, and for some technical cooperation. It also provides a framework for handling disputes about persistent non-enforcement of certain domestic standards, where trade is involved. All listed standards may be the subject of ministerial consultations. For a slightly longer list there may be investigations by a panel. Only disputes in three areas (child labour, minimum wages and occupational health and safety), if they are not resolved, may lead to penalties – fines in the first instance (to be used in addressing the problem under investigation) and in the second trade penalties for Mexico and the United States – but fines for Canada (see Weston, 1994). It does not set out to prevent countries from lowering their standards (through legislation), let alone to create new continental standards.

Canada has been preoccupied with seeking agreement from the provinces – a necessary process given the provinces – jurisdiction over a number of labour standards in the side-agreement. A model agreement has been prepared in consultation with the provinces, which is now being presented to the provincial cabinets (and legislatures) for approval. There is no indication as yet that any legislature will reject the agreement, though some provincial governments have expressed strong concerns about the NAFTA (notably Ontario and British Columbia). Should they reject the side-agreement, it will limit Canada's capacity to request consultations (as the rules require that for a general issue, provinces accounting for at least 35 per cent of Canada's labour force must have signed on, or in the case of an industry-specific issue, provinces with 55 per cent of the labour force in that industry).

There have been several technical cooperation meetings. Some have focused on health and safety – the exchange of information by representatives of industry (labour and management) and government on 'best practices' in the electronics, construction and petrochemicals industries. Others have examined the collection of statistics on accidents and productivity (comparing measurement methods, etc.). Information materials on child labour have also been exchanged. Some intergovernmental sessions on pay and employment equity and other issues, which had been planned for the autumn of 1994, were postponed to allow for the change of government in Mexico.

There has also been a conference on labour–management cooperation (with 70 Canadian participants, including government officials, labour relations experts and labour lawyers) with case-studies on industrial relations. Besides information-sharing, an objective is to build mutual understanding and strengthen trilateral professional networks. For example, in November 1994, the US Bar Association decided to hold a two-day meeting in Montreal on labour and employment law, and the two NAFTA side-agreements.

Finally, there has been some transfer of technology, for example, the export of surplus (but not redundant) air sampling equipment from Canada to Mexico to be used in high-hazard industries.

In addition, there have been four claims filed with the US National Administrative Office, of which two have been dealt with. Both were registered by US unions and involved complaints about freedom of association, the right to organize and occupational health and safety standards in Mexico – and the failure of the Mexican government to enforce its laws in two plants, one in Chihuahua and one in Ciudad Juarez, where workers were dismissed following organizing activities and complaints about work practices. After investigation and a hearing in each case, the NAO found that most of the workers had been able to reach financial settlement with their employer, pre-empting investigation by the Mexican authorities, while the safety issue had not been raised with the relevant Mexican authorities. So it did not recommend either matter be taken to ministerial consultation. Instead, it suggested the three countries undertake cooperative programmes for government officials, business and labour, to learn more about each other's domestic labour laws and union rights, as well as the scope and purpose of the NAALC (US NAO, 1994). These results disappointed US and Mexican labour groups on the grounds that some workers had only accepted severance pay after the NAO had rejected their cases, while others had done so because of financial need. Another two cases concerning union rights, both at plants in Nuevo Laredo, are under investigation (*Naftathoughts*, December 1994).

Areas for further discussion include extending the scope of the agreement both to new areas and to new member countries, and funding. The labour movement, especially in the United States, would like to extend the number of processes for addressing basic labour rights such as the right to organize. The Mexican government might wish to include undocumented workers and their lack of rights to minimum wages in the United States, especially in the light of the recent vote in California on Proposition 187 denying undocumented workers and their families the right to public services (notably health and education). But both such initiatives will be constrained by the Republican-dominated US Congress. It may also oppose extension of the NAALC to other countries in the hemisphere, as they accede to the NAFTA (or AFTA), though this is supported by the US and Canadian governments.

Besides the resources of any fines, there is no financial mechanism in the NAFTA for addressing labour adjustment or social policy issues in the three countries. Despite its name, the North American Development Bank is a bilateral, US–Mexican mechanism for addressing border environmental problems – not a trinational development bank analogous to the Inter-American Development Bank (IDB), as its name suggests. With an expanded hemispheric membership, however, it would be appropriate for greater linkages with the IDB. For example, the IDB could help to fund social programmes to help countries adjust to economic integration and to strengthen labour standards covered by the agreement.

Finally, it is likely that some of these linkages between trade, labour standards and social policies will be addressed in a broader, multilateral context. Alternative approaches such as voluntary codes of conduct (e.g. Reebok) and fair trade labels are already being adopted by transnational corporations and alternative trade organizations – but their impact and credibility are limited as they are often minimalist and self-regulating. The International Labour Organization (ILO) has proposed a system of social labelling, which it would manage. It seems inevitable that the relationship between trade and labour standards will be raised at an early stage in the World Trade Organization (WTO) despite initial resistance to the idea. Discussions of norms and/or sanctions could build on the NAALC model, especially the Canadian version.

4 CONCLUSIONS

Canada's social policy reforms are partly driven by the government's attempts to reduce the fiscal deficit. Another concern is the capacity of the workforce to adjust – to move from industries facing declining demand as a result of changing technology and demand, as well as increased import competition from the United States, Mexico and elsewhere, into expanding industries. The Canadian government is adopting a more hard-line approach – reducing benefits and making them more conditional – for instance, placing increased emphasis on training, instead of the previous, more passive approach in both unemployment insurance and welfare. But it remains to be seen whether this is sufficient to reduce the structural unemployment which has emerged as the economy has become more open.

The NAFTA labour side-agreement has not addressed these issues, being more focused on labour standards. Several meetings have been held, for example, on industry-specific health and safety issues, and labour–management cooperation practices, suggesting it is having some success as a vehicle for technical cooperation. But the capacity of the agreement to resolve disputes about labour standards is limited. For this reason, there will continue to be pressure within other international fora to consider ways to enforce labour standards. Within the hemisphere, unless there are major changes to the architecture of the NAFTA as it expands into an AFTA, external assistance with the design and delivery of social policies will remain with the Inter-American Development Bank.

9 Trade Disputes and Settlement Mechanisms under the Canada–US Free Trade Agreement

Richard G. Dearden

1 INTRODUCTION[1]

The Canada–US Free Trade Agreement created a general dispute resolution mechanism for government-to-government disputes and a unique binational panel system to review final anti-dumping and countervailing duty determinations rendered by agencies in Canada and the United States. The parties[2] to the Agreement also provided for binational panel review of statutory amendments to trade statutes and binational review of actual safeguard actions.

During the operation of the FTA, binational panels established under the general dispute resolution mechanisms rendered five decisions; more than 40 decisions were rendered by binational panels reviewing final anti-dumping and countervailing duty determinations and three Extraordinary Challenge Committee decisions were issued. No binational panels were established to review statutory amendments of trade statutes, nor was there any binational review of actual safeguard actions.

In addition to the various panel systems created by the FTA, the Agreement encouraged the avoidance and resolution of disputes through its institutional bureaucracy in the form of the Canada–United States Trade Commission and the numerous committees and working groups established to anticipate and resolve trade frictions through consultations.

In the light of the enormous volume of two-way trade of goods and services during the operation of the FTA, the actual number of trade disputes between Canada and the United States was relatively very low. Nevertheless, disputes were immediate. Within days of the implementation of the Canada–US FTA, Canada triggered the general dispute resolution mechanism with respect to disputes involving plywood (standards required to be fulfilled for use in Canadian housing) and wool (the percentage content of wool by weight in a garment for the garment to be considered woollen). Disputes were also eclectic involving many chapters of the Agreement (e.g. rules of origin, agriculture, energy, cultural industries exemptions, nullification and impairment issues, export restrictions, import restrictions, procurement and non-tariff barriers).

The Canada–US FTA's dispute resolution mechanisms have been responsive and workable, providing a way of enforcing the FTA's structure of rules and obligations that have imposed a positive discipline on the enormous trading relationship between Canada and the United States. This paper highlights the operation of the FTA's dispute resolution mechanisms, discusses some of the panel decisions rendered under the FTA and concludes with an analysis of the effectiveness of the FTA's dispute settlement system in the resolution of trade disputes between Canada and the United States during the past five years.

2 OVERVIEW OF THE TRADE DISPUTE SETTLEMENT MECHANISMS UNDER THE CANADA–US FREE TRADE AGREEMENT

The Canada–US FTA created binational panels to resolve disputes in three areas: (1) government-to-government disputes or general trade disputes regarding the interpretation or application of any provision of the Agreement; (2) anti-dumping and countervailing duties: (a) review of amendments to anti-dumping or countervailing duty statutes for consistency with the Agreement and the GATT; and (b) review of final anti-dumping or countervail determinations; and (3) disputes regarding actual safeguard actions taken pursuant to Chapter 11 of the FTA.

Government-to-Government Disputes – Chapter 18

Chapter 18 Panel Cases
Binational panels established pursuant to Chapter 18 of the FTA dealt with five trade disputes during the operation of the FTA:

(1) Canada's landing requirement for Pacific coast salmon and herring; (2) lobsters from Canada; (3) article 304 and the direct cost of processing; (4) durum wheat; and (5) Puerto Rico UHT milk. The first three will be reviewed here.

Canada's Landing Requirements for Pacific Coast Salmon and Herring

Background
A 1987 GATT panel found that a Canadian export prohibition on unprocessed Pacific salmon and herring was a violation of GATT article XI:1 and that it was not exempted under article XX(g) as a conservation measure. Canada then implemented a landing requirement for Pacific coast salmon and herring in April 1989 requiring that all salmon and roe herring caught in Canada's Pacific coast fisheries be landed at a licensed landing station in Canada for the purpose of gathering statistical and biological sampling information.

The panel was required to rule on whether Canada's landing requirement amounted to an export restriction within the meaning of GATT article XI:1 (incorporated by reference into article 407 of the FTA) and, if so, whether the landing requirement was a conservation measure exempted by GATT article XX(g) (incorporated by reference into article 1201 of the FTA).

Decision
Export Restriction. The Chapter 18 panel concluded that the new landing requirement was a restriction on 'sale for export' within the meaning of GATT article XI:1 and was therefore contrary to FTA article 407. The panel rejected the argument that GATT article XI:1 required proof of actual negative trade impact. Rather, the panel was of the view that in order to establish an export restriction contrary to article XI:1, it must be shown that the measure in question has altered the competitive relationship between foreign and export buyers. Although the Canadian landing requirement appeared neutral, in that it applied equally to fish destined for domestic and export markets, the panel found that it imposed significant additional costs on those export buyers who would otherwise have chosen to ship salmon and herring directly from the fishing grounds to landing sites in the United States.

Conservation of Natural Resources. GATT article XX(g) provides
an exemption for measures relating to the conservation of exhaustible natural resources. Both Canada and the United States
agreed that the 1987 GATT panel, which considered Canada's
earlier export prohibition, correctly interpreted article XX(g) in
deciding that a measure must be 'primarily aimed at the conservation of an exhaustible natural resource in order to be
considered as relating to conservation'.

The Chapter 18 panel recognized that article XX(g) was
intended to allow governments sufficient latitude to implement
their conservation policies and that its purpose was not to
promote trade interests at the expense of legitimate environmental concerns. However, the panel noted that some measures
might achieve both a conservation-promoting effect and a trade-
restricting effect. In such circumstances, the correct test to be
applied under article XX(g) was, in the panel's view, whether the
measure would have been adopted for conservation reasons
alone.

In the case of measures such as Canada's landing requirement
which impose greater burdens on foreign buyers than on domestic
buyers, the panel concluded that the genuineness of a measure's
conservation purpose could only be determined by deciding
whether a government would have adopted the measure if its own
nationals would have had to bear the cost of the measure. In order
to answer this question, the panel examined the objective conservation benefits of the landing requirement from the standpoint of
its contribution to data quality and its administrative advantages.
The panel then compared these benefits to alternative trade-neu-
tral methods of attaining the same ends.

Summary of Final Reports. Following a detailed consideration of
the issues, the panel concluded that the conservation benefits of
the landing requirement would depend on the volume of un-
landed exports which would be expected to occur in the absence
of a landing requirement. In the case of the salmon and herring
fisheries at issue, the panel was of the opinion that Canada's
landing requirement applicable to 100 per cent of the catch could
not be said to be 'primarily aimed at' conservation within the
meaning of GATT article XX(g) and was therefore not exempt
pursuant to FTA article 1201. The panel was, however, of the
view that a landing requirement could be considered to be

primarily aimed at conservation if provision were made to exempt from landing such proportion of the catch which would not impede the data collection process. The panel indicated that the precise proportion would depend on the data and management needs of each fishery but that a range of 10–20 per cent of the catch would provide appropriate guidance.

Resolution
Canada finally accepted the panel's Final Report in February 1990. Differing interpretations of the Final Report led to the prolonged negotiations on how to remedy the violations. Under the new arrangement, 20 per cent of salmon and herring caught in British Columbia fishing grounds was permitted to be transported directly to the United States in 1990, increasing to 25 per cent from 1991 through 1993. The remainder of British Columbia salmon and herring would remain subject to Canadian landing requirements.[3]

Lobsters

The panel's terms of reference required that it determine whether the 1989 amendments to the United States' Magnuson Fishery Conservation and Management Act (the 'Magnuson Act'), prohibiting the sale or transport in or from the United States of whole live lobsters smaller than the minimum possession size in effect under US federal law, amounted to an import restriction within the meaning of GATT article XI:1. If the answer to this question was in the affirmative, the panel was also to decide whether the 1989 amendments were exempted by GATT article XX.

The effect of the Magnuson Act amendments was that lobsters from foreign countries with minimum size requirements smaller than the US federal minimum were, henceforth, prohibited from entering into interstate or foreign commerce within or from the United States. Prior to the 1989 amendments, lobsters harvested in US federal waters could not be sold in interstate commerce if they failed to meet federal minimum size requirements. Persons found selling undersized lobsters could, however, avoid conviction by establishing that the lobsters had been purchased in a jurisdiction, such as Canada, which imposed smaller minimum size requirements.

Canada argued that the 1989 Magnuson Act amendments violated the prohibition against import restrictions in GATT article XI. In Canada's view, since the effect of the measure was to prevent Canadian undersized lobsters from entering into US commerce, the 1989 amendments amounted to a border restriction of the kind prohibited by GATT article XI. Moreover, in Canada's view, the measure could not be justified under GATT article XX(g) as being 'primarily aimed at' the conservation of US lobsters.

The United States argued that the Magnuson Act amendments were an 'internal measure' covered by the 'national treatment' provisions of GATT article III, rather than a 'border measure' governed by GATT article XI. Pursuant to article III, measures affecting the 'internal sale, offering for sale, purchase, transportation, distribution or use of' products must not discriminate unfavourably against imported products so as to afford protection to domestic production. Since the amendments applied equally to US lobsters as well as to Canadian lobsters, in the United States' view, GATT article XI had no application to the 1989 Magnuson Act amendments.

The panel issued a split decision, with the three American members ruling in favour of the United States' contention that article XI did not apply to the measure. The two Canadian panelists dissented.

In the majority's opinion, the Magnuson Act amendments were internal measures of the kind governed by GATT article III. The majority was of the view that articles III and XI were mutually exclusive in that measures could fall under one or the other article but not under both. Article XI, therefore, had no application to the US measure.

The two Canadian members of the panel were of the opposite view. In the minority's opinion, the Magnuson Act amendments were clearly a border measure subject to article XI. The minority noted that, since the Magnuson Act amendments prevented Canadian undersized lobsters from entering the United States in the first place, the measure could only be viewed as affecting imported products.

Having decided that the Magnuson Act amendments violated article XI, the minority examined the issue of whether the measure was saved by GATT article XX(g) which provides an exemption for measures relating to the conservation of exhaustible natural resources. Noting that the burden was on the United States to prove that the measure was 'primarily aimed at' conservation, the minority concluded that the United States failed to discharge this onus.

Article 304 and the Direct Cost of Processing

Canada requested a Chapter 18 panel as a result of an administrative decision by the US Customs Service dealing with the treatment of interest as a direct cost of processing. The US Customs Service found that

> interest expense which is not covered by a mortgage, i.e., unsecured loans, inter-company loans and lines of credit, will not be considered allowable as a direct cost of processing or direct cost of assembling for origin determination purposes. Interest expenses relating to loans for general and administrative purposes are specifically excluded as a direct cost of processing or direct cost of assembling under the Agreement.

This finding was subsequently incorporated in the United States Customs Regulations.

Article 304 of the Canada–US FTA states in part:

> Direct cost of processing . . . means the costs directly incurred in, or that can reasonably be allocated to, the production of goods, including: rent, mortgage interest, depreciation on buildings, property insurance premiums, maintenance, taxes and the cost of utilities for real property used in the production of goods.

The Panel was asked to determine whether the definition of 'direct cost of processing' or 'direct cost of assembling' set forth in article 304 includes interest payments on a debt of any form, secured or unsecured, undertaken to finance the acquisition of fixed assets such as: (1) real property, (2) a plant, and/or (3) equipment, used in the production of goods in the territory of a party.

The Meaning of Article 304

The panel concluded that the wording of article 304 indicates that a two-pronged test exists due to the use of the disjunctive 'or'. The first element of the test 'the costs directly incurred in

... the production of goods' refers to costs which are directly incurred in relation to the production of goods. The second element of the test 'the costs . . . that can reasonably be allocated to the production of goods' does not rely on the concept of 'directness'. Consequently, the traceability of the costs seems to form the basis of the two-pronged test. The second element of the test does not refer to costs which arise directly from the production of goods. Therefore, the panel concluded that this second prong is intended to enlarge the meaning of the defined terms. However, the second element of the test is restricted by the use of the term 'reasonably'. Therefore, an allocation of the costs which are not necessarily direct but which are reasonable would be within the objectives and purposes of the FTA.

Interpretation of 'Interest'
The panel held that the term 'interest' should be read to mean 'bona fide interest incurred under a loan agreement entered into on arms' length terms in the ordinary course of business'.

The Treatment of Mortgage Interest
The panel stated that it would be 'reasonable' to include industrial and manufacturing plants within the meaning of 'real property' based on the usual interpretation of the terms 'real property' and 'machinery and equipment' in both Canada and the United States. Therefore, machinery and equipment may be included as part of 'real property' when it is 'permanent and essential to the purpose for which the building is employed'. In addition, the panel concluded that the term 'real property' would include 'not only the land, but plant and equipment sufficiently annexed to the land to become "fixtures"', since the FTA expressly provides that interest paid on the whole of the debt so secured may reasonably be included as an allowable cost.

The panel rejected the US argument that accounting principles provide a basis for differentiating non-mortgage interest from mortgage interest in respect of real property.

The Treatment of Non-mortgage Interest
The panel reiterated that the inclusion of any cost in the value content calculation is constrained by the concept of 'reasonableness'. The panel expressed the view that if a cost is 'analogous to a direct cost', and is 'readily and objectively assignable to the

acquired asset' which is closely associated with the production of goods, then it may reasonably be included. The panel emphasized the underlying requirement that the interest be 'readily and objectively' assignable to the acquisition of a production asset.

The panel rejected the US argument that the provision of credit is a 'financial service', as understood in article 304(g) (which excludes such costs from the definition).

The Form of the Loan Transaction
The panel was not convinced that the parties had intended to single out mortgage financing to the exclusion of other forms of financing, arguing that the same features of a mortgage applied equally to a chattel mortgage of personal property. The panel also stressed that the ordinary meaning of the term should be given based on the Vienna Convention Law of Treaties. Consequently, the 'difficulties of proof in particular cases should not artificially restrict the meaning to be applied to the general words of article 304'. Finally, the panel suggested that there were no reasons offered in the FTA to conclude that producers should be required to finance the acquisition of their means of production by mortgages 'rather than other methods of financing which may, in particular circumstances, be more commercially appropriate'. In the panel's view, the potential abuse of this section is to be restricted by the requirement that the interest cost be 'reasonably allocated' to the production of those goods. Consequently, for a cost to be included in the content value calculation it should meet the following requirements that: (1) the interest is bona fide; (2) the transaction is at arm's length; and (3) the borrowing was in the ordinary course of business to finance the production of the goods.

The panel concluded that it would be reasonable to include non-mortgage interest which is related to the acquisition costs of the real property.

Interest on Machinery and Equipment
The panel rejected the US position, which required it to draw a negative inference that interest on machinery and equipment should be excluded 'despite the existence of circumstances that would call for their inclusion under the two-pronged definition in the opening words of article 304'.

Object and Purpose of the FTA
The panel stressed that the objectives and scope of the FTA clearly seek to create a trading arrangement which benefits the producers of goods of the parties, as well as increases the employment and income opportunities to persons living within Canada and the United States. Consequently, the inclusion of non-mortgage interest would not be inconsistent with the larger objectives and purposes of the FTA. The panel further indicated that it does not believe that 'the form of security (if any) securing the debt in respect of which interest is payable is determinative'. Accordingly, unsecured debt to acquire fixed production assets should also be included in the calculation. The panel, therefore, concluded that the form of the debt is not a controlling circumstance which should lead to the exclusion of unsecured debt to acquire fixed production assets in the value content calculation.

Determination and Recommendations
The panel determined that:

1. bona fide interest payments on debts of any form, secured or unsecured, undertaken, on arm's length terms in the ordinary course of business, to finance the acquisition of fixed assets such as real property, a plant and/or equipment used in the production of goods in the territory of a party, are includable in the 'direct costs of processing' or 'direct costs of assembling' set forth in article 304; and
2. the US interpretation of article 304 was inconsistent with the provisions of the FTA.

The panel recommended that the parties resolve the dispute by implementing new regulations and internal administrative procedures which would be necessary to be consistent with the panel's determination. This recommendation was adopted.

Anti-dumping and Countervailing Duties – Chapter 19

Anti-dumping and countervailing duty disputes were affected in two significant ways[4] by Chapter 19 of the Canada–US Free Trade Agreement: (1) no amendments could be made to existing anti-dumping and countervailing duty laws without notification and consultation with the other party; (2) binational panels were created to review final anti-dumping and countervailing duty determinations rendered by the various governmental agencies relating to international trade.

Statutory Amendments to Anti-Dumping and Countervailing Duty Laws
The FTA did not alter the substance of existing anti-dumping and countervailing duty laws, and the fact that neither the FTA nor the North American Free Trade Agreement did not eliminate the use of anti-dumping and countervail actions has been described by Canada's International Trade Minister Roy MacLaren as the 'black hole' of those Agreements.

Each party reserved the right to apply its anti-dumping law and countervailing duty law to goods imported from the territory of the other party. The parties also reserved the right to change or modify their anti-dumping law and countervailing duty law. However, if a party proposed to amend an anti-dumping or countervailing duty 'statute',[5] notification and consultation requirements arise and a binational panel review could be invoked.

A binational panel could be established to declare whether: (1) the amendment was inconsistent with GATT, the GATT Revised Anti-Dumping Code and the GATT Subsidies Code; (2) the amendment was inconsistent with the object and purpose of the FTA and Chapter 19; or (3) the amendment has the function and effect of overturning a prior decision of a panel that has reviewed a final anti-dumping or countervailing duty determination and does not conform to (1) and (2) above.

No binational panels were established to render declaratory opinions about statutory amendments during the operation of the Canada–US Free Trade Agreement.

Binational Panel Review of Final Anti-dumping and Countervailing Duty Determinations
Introduction. One of the most original aspects of the FTA was the creation of binational panels to resolve disputes involving final anti-dumping and countervailing duty determinations. A binational panel review could be requested to determine whether a final anti-dumping or countervail determination was in accordance with the anti-dumping or countervailing duty law of the importing party. A decision of a panel was binding on the parties with respect to the particular matter before the panel, unless the

panel decision was challenged before an Extraordinary Challenge Committee.

Grounds for Review – Canada. The three grounds available to a binational panel to set aside a decision or order of the Canadian International Trade Tribunal or the deputy minister were that these agencies: (1) failed to observe a principle of natural justice or otherwise acted beyond or refused to exercise jurisdiction; (2) erred in law in making the decision or order; (3) based the decision or order on an erroneous finding of fact made in a perverse or capricious manner or without regard for the material before it.

Grounds for Review – United States. Two standards of review of anti-dumping and countervailing duty determinations in the United States are articulated for different categories of administrative determinations:
1. Determinations of US international trade agencies not to initiate investigations, as to whether there is a reasonable indication of material injury, or material retardation of the establishment of an industry, will be held unlawful if they are arbitrary, capricious, an abuse of discretion, or otherwise are not in accordance with law.
2. Final anti-dumping and countervailing duty determinations of either the Department of Commerce or the United States International Trade Commission will be held unlawful if they are unsupported by substantial evidence on the record or otherwise are not in accordance with law.

The 'arbitrary and capricious' standard applied to determinations not to take action or, in the case of the USITC, to terminate an investigation after only a preliminary investigation. The 'substantial evidence' standard applied to determinations made after an investigation has been conducted and a record has been made.

Request for Review. Either party to the FTA could request a binational panel review. However, it was not only the parties to the FTA that were entitled to make such a request. Any person who would otherwise be entitled under the law of the importing party to commence domestic procedures for judicial review of a final determination could request such a review and this request had to be granted. Thus, importers, exporters and Canadian producers involved in an anti-dumping or countervail action before the Canadian International Trade Tribunal were entitled to trigger a binational panel review.

Remedies. The panel could uphold the Final Determination or remand it for action not inconsistent with the panel's decision. Where the panel remanded a Final Determination, it had to establish as brief a time as was reasonable for compliance with the remand, taking into account the complexity of the facts and legal issues involved and the nature of the panel's decision.

Extraordinary Challenges Committee. Although decisions of the panel are final and are not subject to an appeal to domestic courts, the Agreement provided for an extraordinary challenge of decisions of a panel in three situations. Where a party alleged: (a) a member of the panel was guilty of gross misconduct, bias or a serious conflict of interest or otherwise materially violated the rules of conduct; (b) the panel seriously departed from a fundamental rule of procedure; or (c) the panel manifestly exceeded its powers, authority or jurisdiction, and any of these actions materially affected the panel's decision and threatened the integrity of the binational panel review process, that party could avail itself of the extraordinary challenge procedure set out in Annex 1904.13 if the allegation was made within a reasonable time after the panel decision was issued.

A three-member Extraordinary Challenge Committee (ECC) had to be established within 15 days of a request, and Committee decisions were binding on the parties with respect to the particular matter between the parties that was before the panel.

In the event that one of the grounds for the extraordinary challenge was established, the Committee had to vacate the original panel decision or remand it to the original panel for action not inconsistent with the Committee's decision. If the original decision were vacated, a new panel had to be established. In the event that the extraordinary challenge grounds were not established, it affirmed the original panel decision.

There were three ECCs established during the operation of the FTA (all at the request of the United States). In all three cases the ECC upheld the binational panel decisions in issue.

Fresh, Chilled and Frozen Pork

The US Extraordinary Challenge to a binational panel decision on Canadian-subsidized *Fresh, Chilled and Frozen Pork* was unanimously dismissed. The ECC dismissed the request for extraordinary challenge for failure to meet the standards for extraordinary challenge under the FTA.

The United States had alleged that the panel in its second remand decision 'seriously departed from a fundamental rule of procedure or manifestly exceeded its powers, authority or jurisdiction' in five instances: (1) the panel created a due process principle independent of US law; (2) the panel improperly considered non-record evidence; (3) the panel improperly applied a procedural rule of finality; (4) the panel effectively applied a *de novo* standard of 'substantial evidence on the record'; and (5) the panel re-weighed evidence in a manner contrary to US law by requiring that the ITC find 'price underselling' in order to find a likelihood of negative impact on US pork prices.

The ECC, before examining the merits of the US allegations, addressed its role. The ECC pointed out that 'as its name suggests, the extraordinary challenge procedure is not intended to function as a routine appeal. Rather, the decision of a binational panel may be challenged and reviewed only in "extraordinary" circumstances. It is clear that the extraordinary challenge procedure is intended solely as a safeguard against an impropriety or gross panel error that could threaten the integrity of [binational panel review] process.'

The Committee held that its only function is to ascertain whether each of the three requirements set forth in article 1904.13 has been established, namely: (1) the Committee must find that a panel or a panel member is guilty of one of the actions set forth in paragraph 1904.12(a); (2) the Committee must find that such action 'materially affected the panel's decision'; and (3) the Committee must determine that the action 'threatens the integrity of the binational panel review process'.

After examining each of the US arguments, the ECC concluded that 'none of the allegations provides a basis for jurisdiction for an extraordinary challenge under [the] FTA . . . and that none of the alleged errors materially affected the Panel decision or threaten the integrity of the Panel review process under the FTA', and therefore decided that the US request for an extraordinary challenge failed to meet the standards set forth under the FTA.

Safeguards

The Canada–US Free Trade Agreement's counterpart to article XIX of the General Agreement on Tariffs and Trade is found in Chapter 11 of the FTA. The 'safeguard' or 'escape clause' of the FTA permitted the temporary imposition of import restrictions to remedy serious injury caused by increased imports. Two tracks are set forth in Chapter 11, the 'bilateral' track allowing the parties to escape temporarily from the tariff-reduction commitments of the FTA itself, and the 'global' track setting forth the terms under which the parties will treat each other in the event either invoked the provisions of GATT article XIX.

The 'bilateral' track set out in FTA article 1101, permitted a party to suspend the FTA's scheduled customs duty reductions and, with limits, to increase duties during the FTA's 10-year transition period, if imports from the other party increased absolutely, and if they alone were a substantial cause of serious injury to a domestic industry producing like or directly competitive goods.

The 'global' track set out in FTA article 1102 required the parties to exclude each other under certain circumstances from actions taken under GATT article XIX against fairly traded imports (i.e. non-dumped and non-subsidized imports). During the FTA negotiations and prior to the implementation of article 1102, the US president took safeguard action against Canadian shakes and shingles.

One of the main objects behind the global safeguard measures set out in the FTA is to prevent a party from being 'sideswiped' by an emergency action aimed primarily at exporters from other countries. For instance, Canada claimed that it was sideswiped by the US safeguard action against specialty steel. The requirements that exports be excluded unless they are 'substantial' and 'contribute importantly' to the serious injury, or threat thereof, reduces the possibility of 'sideswipe' cases.

In a significant step in the field of international trade dispute settlement procedures, article 1103 of the FTA provided for binding arbitration, under article 1806, with respect to disputes concerning actual actions[6] not resolved by consultations. Any dispute regarding the bilateral track, the global track or compensation were subject to binding arbitration after the action was taken.

The FTA was the first international trade agreement wherein a contracting party to the GATT agreed to allow an international panel to make a binding decision about the use of safeguard measures imposed within GATT article XIX. During the operation of the Canada–US FTA there were no actual safeguard actions taken by Canada and the United States and as a result binding arbitration panels were never established.[7]

NORTH AMERICA FREE TRADE AGREEMENT

The topic of this chapter is 'Trade Disputes and Settlement under the Canada–US Free Trade Agreement'. However, because the Agreement has been suspended and replaced by the North American Free Trade Agreement, the following are highlights of the dispute settlement provisions of NAFTA and the investor-state arbitration mechanism established by Chapter 11 of NAFTA. NAFTA creates mechanisms to settle disputes and also contains requirements that lead to the avoidance of disputes.

Avoidance of Disputes Transparency and Due Process

NAFTA's institutional bureaucracy assists the parties in managing the operation of the Agreement, anticipating disputes and working out differences through meetings and consultations. Two principles reflected throughout the NAFTA that greatly assist in the avoidance of disputes are transparency and due process.

In essence, transparency is 'openness'. Transparency requirements allow exporters/importers of goods, service providers and investors to know and understand the rules that must be complied with in order to do business in the territory of another party.

Due process is in essence 'fair play'. It is in the interest of an exporter/importer, service provider or investor to require that the laws and the rules of another party be applied fairly. Due process comes in many forms, including notification, expeditious processes, an opportunity to respond or be heard, prompt and sufficient provision of information, prompt decision-making, independent and impartial review of administrative rulings and reasons for a decision.

The Preamble to NAFTA states in part that the parties resolve to establish clear and mutually advantageous rules governing their trade and to ensure a predictable commercial framework for business planning and investment.

The Objectives of the NAFTA state in part:

> The objectives of this *Agreement*, as elaborated more specifically through its principles and rules, including . . . transparency, are to: (a) eliminate barriers to trade in, and facilitate the cross-border movement of goods and services between the territories of the Parties; (b) promote conditions of fair competition in the free trade area; (c) create effective procedures for the implementation and application of this *Agreement*, for its joint administration and for the resolution of disputes . . .

Dispute Settlement

The NAFTA contains three major regimes to deal with trade disputes: (1) settlement of disputes between governments (Chapter 20); (2) binational panel review of final anti-dumping and countervail determinations (Chapter 19); and (3) investor-state arbitration for the enforcement of obligations under the Investment Chapter (Chapter 11).

In the event that consultations fail, dispute settlement before panels becomes very litigation-oriented. That is to say, lawyers must be engaged, briefs must be filed, evidence must be marshalled and arguments must be made. Clearly, the dispute resolution mechanisms are responsive and workable, they provide a much needed way of enforcing NAFTA's structure of rules and obligations that give discipline to the Parties' trading relationships.

Chapter 20 Dispute Resolution
The NAFTA provides detailed procedures governing government-to-government disputes. These disputes involve three

stages: (1) consultations (including in some instances expert consultations, e.g. border measures affecting agricultural products such as meat or potato inspections; (2) a meeting of the Free Trade Commission; and (3) panel proceedings.

Before the adversarial Chapter 20 panel proceedings are invoked, the NAFTA requires the parties to engage in formal consultations and alternative dispute resolution within the framework of the Free Trade Commission. Under article 2007.5, the Commission may: (1) call on technical advisers or create working groups, (2) use good offices, conciliation, mediation or such other dispute solution procedures, or (3) make recommendations, to assist the parties to resolve their dispute before resorting to a panel proceeding.

Should consultation and alternative dispute resolution fail to resolve government-to-government disputes, Chapter 20 panels proceedings are initiated. The panels resolve disputes between the NAFTA parties regarding: (1) the interpretation or application of a provision of NAFTA; (2) an actual or proposed measure of another party that a party considers is or would be inconsistent with the obligations of NAFTA; (3) an actual or proposed measure (although not inconsistent with NAFTA) that would nullify or impair a benefit that a party considered it could have reasonably expected to accrue to it under NAFTA.[8]

The Chapter 20 NAFTA panel proceedings are broadly similar to Chapter 18 Canada–US Free Trade Agreement panel proceedings.

The dispute resolution mechanism under Chapter 20 of the NAFTA is not mandated to deal with all trade-related disputes.

Binational panel reviews of anti-dumping and countervailing duty determinations and investment dispute resolution are reserved for Chapters 19 and 11 respectively. Domestic judicial review and appeal mechanisms of origin determinations and advance customs rulings are provided for under Chapter 5.

Unlike the FTA Chapter 18 panel decisions, the NAFTA requires that panel members remain anonymous should separate opinions be issued.

Similar to the FTA, the NAFTA requires the disputing parties, on receipt of the final report from the Chapter 20 panel, to agree on the resolution of the dispute, by not implementing, or removing, the measure not conforming with the Agreement or causing nullification or impairment in the sense of Annex 2004. A new remedy added to the NAFTA, is the entitlement of the aggrieved party to compensation under certain circumstances.

In the event that resolution is not reached between the parties, Article 2019 allows suspension of benefits by the complaining party. One major difference in NAFTA is the requirement that the suspension must first only apply to the particular sector affected by the measure before a suspension covering other sectors can occur.

Chapter 19 Panels
The provisions of Chapter 19 of the NAFTA are similar to those of Chapter 19 of Canada–U.S. Free Trade Agreement which provide *inter alia* for binational panel review of final anti-dumping and countervailing duty determinations. Chapter 19 panels under NAFTA are permanent. Binational panels have also been created to provide declaratory opinions about the consistency of statutory amendments of anti-dumping and countervailing duty laws with NAFTA and the GATT.[9] The decisions of the Chapter 19 binational panels are final unless a party requests the establishment of an Extraordinary Challenge Committee. The decisions rendered by the Chapter 19 panels and Extraordinary Challenge Committees under the Canada–US Free Trade Agreement will serve as useful guides for NAFTA Chapter 19 panels and NAFTA Extraordinary Challenge Committees.

A new feature found in NAFTA Chapter 19 is the creation of a special committee review process to safeguard the binational panel process, where the application of a country's domestic law undermines the functioning of the panel process.

To date there have been no hearings held by a NAFTA Chapter 19 panel involving Mexico. Thus, it is far too early to make any assessment about panels involving Mexican administering authorities and Mexican panelists. The dissenting minority in the *Softwood Lumber* Extraordinary Challenge Committee decision expressed serious concerns about Mexican panelists being able to understand US administrative law because they are trained in a civil law system rather than a common law system. It is highly doubtful that this will be problematic – Quebec lawyers trained in civil law have sat as Canadian Chapter 19 panelists without any problem understanding US administrative law principles. One issue to monitor will be the fact that there is a shortage of bilingual people willing to serve as Chapter 19 panelists. The hearings of the Chapter 19 panels involving Mexico will be simultaneously translated, but the record will not be translated – it remains to be seen whether the monolingual panelist will be disadvantaged. It is to be noted that federal proceedings in Canada such as Canadian International Trade Tribunal cases are often simultaneously translated and have operated quite effectively. A solution to this issue is to appoint permanent bilingual panelists.

Investor-State Arbitration

One of NAFTA's objectives is to increase substantially investment opportunities in Canada, Mexico and the United States and to ensure a predictable commercial framework for business planning and investment. The obligations and principles set out in the Investment Chapter seek to fulfil these objectives by governing how a government must treat 'investors of a party' and 'investments' in its territory.

The arbitration mechanism for the settlement of investment disputes is built on the pillars of equal treatment of investors of the parties and due process before an impartial tribunal. Each party agrees to submit investment disputes to arbitration in accordance with a specific set of procedures. This agreement by the parties is without prejudice to the rights and obligations of the parties under Chapter 20's government to government dispute settlement procedures

A Chapter 11 investor-state arbitration must be conducted in accordance with one of the following three sets of rules: (1) the ICSID Convention, provided that both the disputing party and the party of the investor are parties to it; (2) the Additional Facility Rules of ICSID, provided that either the disputing party or the party of the investor, but not both, is a party to the ICSID Convention; or (3) the UNCITRAL Arbitration Rules.

A disputing investor who submits a claim to arbitration must: (1) consent to arbitration under the NAFTA procedures, and (2) waive the right to initiate or continue domestic law proceedings with respect to the alleged offending measure, except those for 'injunctive, declaratory or other extraordinary relief, not involving the payment of damages'. Almost identical conditions precedent apply to claims by an investor of a party on behalf of an enterprise.

As a final award against a party, the Tribunal may order, separately or in combination, only monetary damages and any applicable interest and/or restitution of property. Where restitution is ordered, the disputing party is entitled to pay monetary damages and any applicable interest in lieu of restitution. The Tribunal may not grant punitive damages.

A Tribunal award is not binding, except between the disputing investor and the disputing party and in respect of the particular case. Each NAFTA party is required to enforce a final award in its territory. Where a disputing party fails to abide by or comply with a final award, the NAFTA Commission may (on delivery of a request by the winning party) establish an arbitral panel under article 2008. The panel will determine whether the failure to comply is inconsistent with the NAFTA obligations and, in the event of inconsistency finding, recommend that the party so comply. Additionally, the disputing investor may seek enforcement of a NAFTA arbitration award under the ICSID Convention, the New York Convention, or the Inter-American Convention regardless of whether the Commission is requested to establish an arbitral panel.

An investment obligation under NAFTA that warrants note is the expropriation and compensation article 1110 because it is expected to be the focus of investor-state arbitration disputes.

A NAFTA party may not directly or indirectly nationalize or expropriate an investment of an investor of another party in its territory or take a measure tantamount to nationalization or expropriation of such an investment ('expropriation'), except: (1) for a public purpose; (2) on a non-discriminatory basis; (3) in accordance with due process of law and certain minimum standards of treatment; and (4) on payment of compensation.

Recent experience in Canada would suggest that a NAFTA party's expropriation powers are clearly not unfettered under the NAFTA regime. In Canada, investors have claimed that the Canadian government must pay compensation to US cigarette manufacturers if it mandates the plain packaging of cigarettes, thus expropriating the intellectual property rights of those US investors. A US aerospace company may claim compensation from the Canadian government if the Canadian government terminates a long-term lease agreement it has entered into to redevelop two terminals at Toronto International Airport. Provincial and state governments may be restricted in implementing measures that prohibit foreign companies from extracting natural resources even if the restriction is for environmental purposes. A provincial government that proposes to create a state-run automobile insurance system to displace foreign insurance companies must also have an eye on the expropriation and compensation obligation.

The scope of the concepts of direct and indirect 'expropriation' and 'tantamount to expropriation' will not be known with certainty for some time. It is clear, however, that the expropriation and compensation obligation will have an impact upon the type of measures a NAFTA party can implement domestically and has already had such an impact. For instance, the Canadian House of Commons Standing Committee on Health issued a Report 'Towards Zero Consumption-Generic Packaging of Tobacco Products' wherein the majority commented that any plain cigarette packaging proposal requires that 'special attention must be paid to Canada's international obligations'; the minority members of the Committee concluded that 'plain cigarette packaging may well violate Canada's international trade obligations'. Although an arbitral panel was not established in the first year of NAFTA's operation to deal with expropriation issues, it is quite likely that such panels will be established with frequency during the next few years.

Advisory Committee on Private Commercial Disputes Regarding Agricultural Goods

NAFTA establishes an Advisory Committee on Private Commercial Disputes Regarding Agricultural Goods. The Advisory Committee reports and recommends to the Committee on Agricultural Trade for the purpose of developing systems in each NAFTA country 'to achieve the prompt and effective resolution of private commercial disputes in agricultural products, taking into account any special circumstance, including the perishability of certain agricultural goods'.

Agricultural goods are different from other goods; they are prone to perish within a short timespan. Any disputes in their trade requires immediate attention for a prompt solution. In Canada, this requirement for fast processing of disputes is addressed by a statutory regime of 'licensing and arbitration requirements', while the United States has a similar system for settling domestic agricultural product disputes. These statutes are seen to have provided a useful basis to address trans-NAFTA territory trade in agricultural products on a timely basis.

Currently, Mexico resolves its domestic agricultural disputes through its court system, which presumably takes longer time. In the event of a dispute in agricultural products occurring in Mexico, North American traders cannot expect speedy resolution before their products lose their marketable value. One of the major tasks of the article 707 will be the harmonization of dispute resolution mechanisms so that private commercial disputes involving trans-NAFTA territory, can be resolved in each NAFTA territory on a timely and equitably basis.

4 CONCLUSION

How effective were the binational panels that were established under the Canada–US Free Trade Agreement in resolving trade disputes? If effectiveness is measured against the goal of ensuring a predictable commercial environment for business planning and investment, the answer is that the FTA's dispute resolution mechanisms improved predictability, but in no way guaranteed security of access for Canadian exporters to the US marketplace. The experience during the past five years reveals that domestic interests in both countries were very aggressive in using trade remedies and in defending the use of non-tariff barriers to restrict access of foreign goods and services.

One of the major shortcomings of the Canada–US Free Trade Agreement and NAFTA is that neither treaty eliminated the use of anti-dumping or countervail actions in the free trade area. As a result, the NAFTA parties have established a trilateral working group on dumping and anti-dumping duties and another trilateral working group on subsidies and countervailing duties. In the light of the political climate in Washington today, it is highly unlikely that any substantive achievement will occur prior to the next US presidential election to eliminate the use of anti-dumping and countervail actions. While the goal is laudable, the political reality is grim.

Some observations can also be made about the effectiveness of the binational panels that were established during the operation of the Canada–US Free Trade Agreement. As a general comment, Canadian exporters should be quite pleased with the outcome of panel results under Chapters 18 and 19. This assessment is not based upon a win–lose record. In the case of general disputes, Canada could rely upon rules with time-limits to seek to resolve disputes with the United States. As the weaker economic partner, a rules-based approach to dispute resolution is desirable in managing the trading relationship. With respect to the Chapter 19 panel process, Canadian exporters continued to bear the brunt of US trade remedy laws, but clearly witnessed panel after panel remanding issues back to the Department of Commerce and the International Trade Commission. In short, Chapter 19 panels did have an impact on the practices of the agencies administering the trade remedy laws in the United States and Canada.

Throughout the duration of the Canada–US Free Trade Agreement there were only five panel decisions under the government-to-government dispute resolution mechanism created by Chapter 18. The parties clearly preferred to resolve disputes through consultation and negotiation. Experience under NAFTA is the same, with Canada and the United States seeking negotiated settlements of trade issues in two very politically contentious sectors – softwood lumber and wheat.

The lack of use of Chapter 18 panels may also be due in part to the fact that the parties wanted certainty in the outcome of the resolution of a dispute which can occur when you negotiate the solution, but not when the decision is left in the hands of a panel of five experts. In the first Chapter 18 Panel decision in *Pacific Salmon & Herring* the panel provided the parties with its solution to the problem although its terms of reference did not ask for this advice. This proposed solution reportedly surprised the parties. The parties subsequently negotiated a solution that was close to the one recommended by the panel. In the *Lobsters* case, the terms of reference were tightly drafted so that the panel only answered the questions it was asked. The *Lobsters* panel, however, split on national lines – the three American panelists agreeing with the US position, the two Canadian panelists agreeing with the Canadian position. There was thus some concern in the early stages of the FTA that panels would split along national lines; in the light of subsequent Chapter 18 panel findings, this concern proved to be unfounded.

The Chapter 18 FTA panels' reasons, and effectiveness in general, suffered as a result of a lack of resources. The panels should be given technical support such as that provided to GATT panels by the Secretariat.

Many commentators have pointed to a need to develop more specialized rosters of panelists which, in the case of disputes focused upon the GATT, include only those panelists having in-depth knowledge of the GATT and its Codes.

However, the parties must also address the issue of compensation for panelists. Although 'qualified' panelists may agree to serve on one panel for $400 per day to enjoy the 'experience', the pool of qualified panelists is reduced by paying them so little.

In *Durum Wheat*, the panel made an unsolicited recommendation to the parties that panels of a more permanent nature, rather that *ad hoc* panels, would be very beneficial in developing expertise and consistent interpretation of the Agreement.

Chapter 18 panels are extremely secretive and the parties definitely want it this way. As a result, private parties do not know what representations their government made to the panel on their behalf behind closed doors. Issues would be better understood by interested persons if the proceedings were conducted in the open.

10 Trade and Investment Between Canada and the LAIA Countries*

Raúl E. Sáez

This chapter gives a quantitative overview of the economic relations between Canada and Latin America, with analysis restricted to the relatively larger countries of the Western Hemisphere.[1] It is organized as follows. Aggregate trade flows between Canada and the LAIA (Latin American Integration Association) countries are reported and described in the first section. Section 2 looks at the goods traded between Canada and individual LAIA countries. In section 3, Canadian direct investment in Latin America is analysed. Finally, some short concluding remarks are made.

1 AGGREGATE TRADE BETWEEN CANADA AND THE LAIA COUNTRIES

Latin America in Canada's Foreign Trade

This section reviews the size of Canada's trade with the Western Hemisphere[2] and with the member countries of LAIA by looking at aggregate exports and imports.[3]

Canadian exports to the Western Hemisphere have grown from just under US\$2 billion in 1986 to US\$2.5 billion in 1993, with exports to the LAIA countries rising from US\$1.5 billion to US\$2.1 billion (Table 10.1). The most dynamic export market for Canadian products in the region has been Mexico, which has replaced Brazil as Canada's largest market, with exports doubling between 1986 and 1993. However, exports to Brazil have remained stagnant. The third market in the region is Venezuela, with exports of US\$394 million in 1993 up from US\$291 million in 1986. Exports to the other LAIA countries are much smaller,

Table 10.1 Exports of Canada, 1986–93 (millions of US$)

Destination	1986		1990		1993	
World	89 706	100.0%	126 447	100.0%	140 748	100.0%
Western Hemisphere	1 979	2.2%	2 067	1.6%	2 560	1.8%
LAIA	1 549	1.7%	1 602	1.3%	2 141	1.5%
LAIA		100.0%		100.0%		100.0%
Argentina	49	3.2%	40	2.5%	103	4.8%
Bolivia	7	0.5%	4	0.3%	6	0.3%
Brazil	566	36.5%	411	25.7%	575	26.9%
Chile	63	4.1%	163	10.2%	152	7.1%
Colombia	134	8.7%	177	11.0%	179	8.4%
Ecuador	61	3.9%	31	1.9%	42	2.0%
Mexico	288	18.6%	488	30.5%	599	28.0%
Paraguay	2	0.1%	2	0.1%	6	0.3%
Peru	79	5.1%	49	3.1%	65	3.0%
Uruguay	9	0.6%	16	1.0%	20	0.9%
Venezuela	291	18.8%	221	13.8%	394	18.4%

Source: IMF, *Direction of Trade Statistics Yearbook* (1993 and 1994).

although those to Chile and, to a lesser extent, Argentina have grown in the last seven years. More than half the growth in exports can be explained by the expansion of exports to Mexico.

Canadian imports from the Western Hemisphere grew from US$2.6 billion in 1986 to US$5.1 billion in 1993, while those from the LAIA countries rose from US$2.1 to US$4.5 billion (Table 10.2). Imports from Mexico are by far the largest from the region, rising from US$849 million in 1986 to US$1.6 billion in 1990, then jumping to US$2.9 billion in 1993. As with exports, most of the increase in imports from the Western Hemisphere and LAIA can be explained by imports from this country. The other LAIA countries are much smaller suppliers of products, although imports from Argentina, Chile, Colombia and Ecuador were higher in 1992–3 than in 1986–7. What is striking is that the value of imports from Ecuador is similar to that of much larger economies such as Argentina, Chile and Colombia.

Canada has been running a growing trade deficit both with the Western Hemisphere and LAIA every year from 1986 to 1993: its explosive increase is due to the trade deficit with Mexico (over

Table 10.2   Imports of Canada, 1986–93 (millions of US$)

Origin	1986		1990		1993	
World	83 308	100.0%	119 673	100.0%	134 914	100.0%
Western	2 635	3.2%	4 191	3.5%	51 251	3.8%
Hemisphere						
LAIA	2 146	2.6%	3 656	3.1%	4 516	3.3%
LAIA		100.0%		100.0%		100.0%
Argentina	63	2.9%	132	3.6%	98	2.2%
Bolivia	7	0.3%	22	0.6%	8	0.2%
Brazil	592	27.6%	744	20.4%	668	14.8%
Chile	92	4.3%	170	4.7%	179	4.0%
Colombia	89	4.1%	125	3.4%	147	3.3%
Ecuador	26	1.2%	139	3.8%	110	2.4%
Mexico	849	39.6%	1 631	44.6%	2 931	64.9%
Paraguay	5	0.2%	1	0.0%	1	0.0%
Peru	46	2.1%	119	3.3%	54	1.2%
Uruguay	11	0.5%	43	1.2%	21	0.5%
Venezuela	366	17.1%	530	14.5%	299	6.6%

Source: IMF, Direction of Trade Statistics Yearbook (1993 and 1994).

US$2.3 billion in 1993). The only country with which Canada has regularly maintained a trade surplus is Colombia.

Thus, trade with the Western Hemisphere and, within this, the LAIA countries has increased in the last seven years. Total trade (exports plus imports) with the Western Hemisphere went from US$4.6 billion in 1986 to US$7.7 billion in 1993 and with LAIA from US$3.7 billion to US$6.7 billion in the same period, with most of the rise explained by trade with Mexico. However, as can be seen in Tables 10.1 and 10.2, the Western Hemisphere and LAIA are relatively small trade partners for Canada.

The region is still a relatively small market for Canadian exports and, furthermore, its share of total Canadian exports has tended to decrease since 1986. The share of LAIA countries also decreased between 1986 and 1993, but it has slightly recovered since 1990. Among LAIA countries, Mexico's share has risen sharply since 1993, while Brazil's has fallen. The individual share of Chile has been higher in the 1990s than in the 1980s, while the reverse has been the case in Colombia, and Venezuela's has fluctuated.

The Western Hemisphere's share in Canada's imports has remained low, even though there is rising trend, as shown in

Table 10.1. That is also the case of LAIA countries, with a share exceeding 3 per cent of Canada's total imports. What is striking is how imports from LAIA have become more geographically concentrated: in 1993, 65 per cent of them originated in Mexico. This has occurred at the expense of Brazil and Venezuela, whose shares have fallen. The shares of other countries, such as Argentina, Colombia, Chile and Peru, also show slight reductions in the 1990s compared to the late 1980s.

To summarize, the Western Hemisphere, including LAIA, is not yet a significant trade partner for Canada. About 2 per cent of Canadian exports go to countries in the Western Hemisphere, other than the United States and about 3 per cent of imports come from these same countries. If exports to the United States are excluded for 1993, the Western Hemisphere's and LAIA's shares of Canadian exports rise to 10 per cent and 8 per cent, respectively. In the case of imports, the shares are 11 per cent and 10 per cent, respectively. What is important to note is the significant increase in trade between Mexico and Canada, even before NAFTA.

Canada in Latin America's Foreign Trade

If one looks at the trade figures from the point of view of the countries of the Western Hemisphere, one also finds a large increase in exports to and imports from Canada in value terms.

Exports from the Western Hemisphere increased from US$1.4 billion in 1986 to US$4.3 billion in 1993. In the case of LAIA countries, in the same period exports to Canada rose from US$1.1 billion to US$3.8 billion. Although the figures in Table 10.3 are different from those of Canadian imports from Latin America in Table 10.2,[4] the main conclusions from the Canadian statistics are verified.

Canada's share of total Western Hemisphere and LAIA exports is relatively small and seemed to be declining until 1990. The rise from 1990 to 1993 is explained by the Mexican figures, and may be due to the change in data source (see note 4). Among individual countries in Mexico and apparently also Peru, there is an increase in the share of exports going to Canada. For the other countries, even Brazil and Venezuela, the share of exports to Canada seems to be declining.

The trade data in Table 10.4 show that imports from Canada grew between 1986 and 1993 both in the Western Hemisphere

Table 10.3 Latin American Exports to Canada,[a] 1986–93 (millions of US$)

Origin	1986	Share in Total Exports	1990	Share in Total Exports	1993	Share in Total Exports
Western Hemisphere	1449.0	1.8%	1920.0	1.5%	4340.0	2.7%
LAIA	1148.4	1.6%	1493.3	1.3%	3804.0	2.7%
Argentina	53.8	0.8%	81.2	0.7%	90.0	0.7%
Bolivia	0.1	0.0%	0.2	0.0%	2.0	0.2%
Brazil	437.0	2.0%	522.0	1.7%	455.0	1.2%
Chile	58.4	1.4%	56.2	0.7%	61.0	0.6%
Colombia	73.1	1.4%	69.9	1.0%	60.0	0.8%
Ecuador	4.9	0.2%	7.3	0.2%	100.0	2.9%
Mexico	224.0	1.4%	226.0	0.8%	2665.0	5.6%
Paraguay	0.2	0.1%	0.7	0.1%	na	na
Peru	18.2	0.7%	27.9	0.9%	88.0	2.5%
Uruguay	6.7	0.6%	25.9	1.5%	11.0	0.7%
Venezuela	272.0	3.2%	476.0	2.6%	272.0	1.6%

Note: (a) The data in this table differ from those in the previous one because in this case it is reported by Latin American countries. However the 1993 trade data with Canada of Argentina, Ecuador, Mexico and Venezuela in the IMF publication are taken from Canadian records. na: Not available.

Source: IMF, Direction of Trade Statistics Yearbook (1993 and 1994).

and LAIA. The increase is mostly explained by larger imports of Canadian products by Mexico, but the value of imports by smaller countries such as Venzuela, Colombia, Chile, Ecuador and Peru also increased. Brazil is the second largest importer of Canadian products.

In contrast to the figures in absolute values, Canada's share in total Western Hemisphere and LAIA imports declined between 1986 and 1993 (see Table 10.4). The share of imports in individual countries such as Brazil, Colombia and Peru also fell, but increased in Venezuela.

To summarize, from the perspective of Latin American countries, Canada is still a relatively small trade partner. In spite of the increase in both exports to and imports from Canada, the

Table 10.4 Latin American Imports from Canada,[a] 1986–93
(millions of US$)

Destination	1986	Share in Total Imports	1990	Share in Total Imports	1993	Share in Total Imports
Western Hemisphere	1659.0	2.3%	2204.0	2.0%	2413.0	1.4%
LAIA	1209.8	2.3%	1585.5	1.9%	2328.0	1.6%
Argentina	49.5	1.0%	24.6	0.6%	113.0	0.6%
Bolivia	4.7	0.7%	6.4	0.9%	7.0	0.6%
Brazil	486.0	3.1%	486.0	2.1%	655.0	2.6%
Chile	54.3	1.7%	224.3	3.1%	203.0	1.8%
Colombia	116.3	3.0%	196.8	3.5%	207.0	2.1%
Ecuador	31.6	1.7%	41.0	2.2%	46.0	1.4%
Mexico	214.0	1.9%	391.0	1.3%	599.0	1.0%
Paraguay	0.7	0.1%	2.5	0.2%	4.0	0.2%
Peru	51.2	2.9%	22.9	0.8%	60.0	1.5%
Uruguay	7.5	0.9%	13.0	1.0%	40.0	1.7%
Venezuela	194.0	2.5%	177.0	2.9%	394.0	3.5%

Note: (a) See note in Table 10.3.

Source: IMF, *Direction of Trade Statistics Yearbook* (1993 and 1994).

share of Canada as a market for exports and as a source of imports is not rising. Both from a Canadian perspective and a Latin American one, trade with the rest of the world is, in general, growing faster than between the two. Reversing this trend should be the goal of economic relations between Canada and the Americas in the future.

2 GOODS TRADE BETWEEN CANADA AND INDIVIDUAL LAIA COUNTRIES

In this section I look at trade between Canada and individual LAIA countries at the product level. In the case of the larger traders with Canada (Argentina, Brazil, Chile, Colombia, Ecuador, Mexico, Peru and Venezuela) the ten major exports and imports at the 8- or 10-digit level of Canada's tariff schedule were chosen, while only the five major products were chosen for the smaller trade partners (Bolivia, Paraguay and Uruguay).[5]

Canadian Exports to Latin America

Table 10.5   Major Exports of Canada to LAIA

Products	Exports in Cdn $ 000s	Share in Exports to LAIA	Share in Total Exports of Product
Wheat and meslin	488 643	18.7%	20.1%
News print, in rolls or sheets	260 863	10.0%	4.3%
Parts of electrical apparatus for line telephone or line telegraphy	90 868	3.5%	7.1%
Bituminous coal	78 993	3.0%	4.3%
Parts and accessories of bodies for motor vehicles	66 863	2.6%	6.4%
Potassium chloride	64 404	2.5%	5.4%
Other parts and accessories for motor vehicles	58 120	2.2%	1.3%
Durum wheat	55 074	2.1%	12.3%
Chemical wood pulp	47 431	1.8%	1.6%
Diesel oil	41 261	1.6%	8.9%
Total ten major	1 252 520	47.9%	

Source: Statistics Canada.

I begin by looking at the major products exported by Canada to each of the eleven members of LAIA in 1993. Table 10.5 shows that the ten major products exported to these countries are mostly natural resource-based products: wheat, news print, wood pulp, potassium chloride, etc. Only three are manufactured goods not based on natural resources: parts of electrical equipment for telecommunications, parts of bodies for motor vehicles and parts of motor vehicles. However, the basket of goods varies from country to country (see below). Canadian exports to LAIA countries are not very diversified: the ten major goods account for 48 per cent of the total. At the level of disaggregation used here, LAIA countries appear to be an important market for specific Canadian exports, but not in general. For those goods exported to several countries the share of LAIA as a group in Canadian exports varies from 20 per cent (wheat) to 1.3 per cent (parts of motor vehicles). Latin America is a significant market for most of these products as shown in Table 10.5.

The ten main exports to Argentina accounted for half Canadian exports to that country in 1993, and include capital goods[5] and intermediate goods. Among the latter, some are directly based on natural resources. For some products the Argentinian market seems very important: for example, hydraulic turbines, machinery for the extraction and preparation of animal fats, and heavy water. However, it should be kept in mind that we are looking at exports in one year only and at a very disaggregated level.

Exports to Bolivia were much more concentrated than those to Argentina. The five major products accounted for 71 per cent of the total, with two of them (parts of electrical apparatus for telephony, and wheat) accounting for more than 55 per cent of the total. Again, we have mostly capital goods and intermediate products based on natural resources, with one good for final consumption (mackerel). Except for the latter, exports to Bolivia do not appear to be very important for any of these five products, a not surprising finding given the small size of the Bolivian economy.

For the same reason, one might expect that exports to Brazil would be very diversified. But this is not the case. The ten main products represented 77 per cent of exports in 1993 and two of them (wheat and news print) together represented more than 44 per cent. As with exports to Argentina and to Bolivia, these ten products can be classified as capital goods or natural resource-based intermediate goods. Although for no product is the Brazilian market as significant as Argentina is in some cases, Brazil receives more than 2.5 per cent of Canadian exports of these goods, with several of them in the range 9–12 per cent.

In what appears to be an emerging pattern reflecting Canada's comparative advantage vis-à-vis Latin America, the ten major exports to Chile are also a combination of capital goods and intermediate goods based on natural resources. Although 96 per cent of Canadian molybdenum exports went to Chile, for all other products the share of this country is relatively small. The importance of Canadian foreign investment in Chile is shown in the fact that one of the main exports is contractors equipment, which will be returned to Canada upon completion of contracts. The data show that exports to Chile are more diversified than those to Bolivia and Brazil: the ten main products represented 56 per cent of the total in 1993.

Exports to Colombia are concentrated in a few products, with the ten major items accounting for 91 per cent, of which two (wheat and news print) represent 57 per cent of total exports to this country. Compared to the countries already examined, capital goods or their parts are a much smaller share of the ten major products, and include only one item (gas turbines parts). Seven of the ten main products are intermediate goods (two of them are parts of motor vehicles) and one is destined to final consumption (lentils). In 1993, 79 per cent of the exports, a particular type of copper wire bars, went to the Colombian market.

As in the case of Chile, the ten main exports to Ecuador include equipment related to foreign investment projects. The other products are intermediate and capital goods and consumer good (again lentils). The ten major exports to Ecuador accounted for 70 per cent of the total to that country, and while there is no product for which Ecuador accounts for more than 50 per cent of the total exported, despite its small size several exceed 2 per cent. Again, this shows that Ecuador, relative to its size, is an important trade partner of Canada.

As expected, exports to Mexico are the most diversified of all the LAIA countries. In 1993, the ten main exports represented about 46 per cent of total Canadian exports to that country, with wheat accounting for 12 per cent. Mexico is a very important market for rape or colza seeds (22 per cent) and flat rolled steel products (33 per cent). For the other products the Mexican market share ranges from 1 per cent for other motor vehicle parts and accesories to 9 per cent for motor vehicle transmissions. Most of the major exports are either intermediate goods based on natural resources or motor vehicle parts.

Considering the small size of Paraguay it is surprising that for one product among the five major, video games, this market accounts for a relatively important share of Canadian exports (16 per cent). For the rest, the share ranges from 1.6 per cent in the case of various types of games to 9 per cent for hydraulic turbine parts. The five major products account for 58 per cent of all exports to Paraguay.

Just under 68 per cent of exports to Peru are accounted for by the ten major products. These are capital goods and their parts, intermediate goods based on natural resources and two goods for final consumption. The Peruvian market does not represent more than 9 per cent for any good; the highest shares in shampoos (8 per cent), tyre cord fabric (5 per cent) and rape oil and dried lentils (both 4 per cent). What is surprising in the data is that exports of copper ores and concentrates are Canada's second major export to Peru.

Wheat was the major export of Canada to Uruguay in 1993, in spite of this country's closeness to Argentina, accounting for 41 per cent of all exports. The five major exports represented 77 per cent. Among these, there are intermediate goods (news print and wheat) and goods for final consumption (potatoes, cigarettes). Except for potato seeds, Uruguay is a very small market for Canadian exports.

Most of the major exports to Venezuela in 1993 were intermediate goods based on natural resources such as wheat, news print and wood pulp. As with Colombia and Mexico, motor vehicle parts appear as major exports from Canada. There is only one capital good-related item. The Venezuelan market was significant for potatoes (19 per cent) and banknotes (35 per cent), while for the rest of the major exports the share ranged from 9 per cent (steam boiler parts) to 0.2 per cent (other motor vehicle parts and accessories). The ten major products accounted for 67 per cent of total exports to that country.

Most of the goods exported by Canada to LAIA countries are intermediate goods and, in turn, a majority of them are based on natural resources (wood pulp, wheat, petrochemicals, news print, seeds) as seen for LAIA as a whole. In many of these products Canada competes with other Latin American countries: in copper products with Chile and Peru, in news print with Chile, in wood pulp with Chile and Argentina, in wheat with Argentina, in fabrics with Colombia, in petrochemicals with several countries.

Exports of capital goods are also important, but they are concentrated on a few items: turbine parts and telecommunications equipment parts. Motor vehicle parts are exported only to Colombia, Mexico and Venezuela. Exports of goods for final consumption are more the exception than the rule.

Canadian Imports from Latin America

I turn now to Canadian imports from individual LAIA countries.
Except for three products (two types of petroleum of different

Table 10.6   Major Imports of Canada from LAIA

Products	Imports ($ Cdn 000s)	Share in Imports from LAIA	Share in Total Imports of Product
Vehicles, passenger, i/vol.>2.4m^3	460 107	8.2%	47.6%
Vehicles, passenger, i/vol.>2.8m^3	248 869	4.5%	13.2%
Crude petroleum, density greater than 0.9042	213 271	3.8%	91.5%
Crude petroleum, density greater than 0.8498 but less than 0.9042	204 439	3.7%	8.6%
Spark-ignition engines	202 124	3.6%	6.6%
Seats, used for motor vehicles	198 808	3.6%	75.1%
Ignition wiring sets	147 000	2.6%	17.9%
Digital process units	143 919	2.6%	8.2%
Stampings, for tractors, transportation vehicles and other special purpose vehicles	143 751	2.6%	8.5%
Body parts and accessories, for tractors, transportation vehicles and other special purpose vehicles	131 410	2.4%	4.6%
Total ten major	2 093 698	37.5%	

Source: *Statistics Canada.*

densities and computers), all of the major goods imported from
LAIA as a group are related to the motor vehicle industry. This
is shown in Table 10.6. As will be discussed below, most of them
come from Mexico. The basket of goods imported varies dramati-
cally from country to country. The result is that imports from
LAIA are highly diversified: the ten major products account for
38 per cent of the total. Imports from LAIA countries account for
very large shares of total imports of all these ten products: from
92 per cent to 5 per cent.

Most of the products imported from Argentina are agricultural goods, and two others are industrial products based on cattle-rearing (leather). Only one good is an industrial intermediate (brake drums). Argentinian exports to Canada appear somewhat diversified: the ten major items account for 53 per cent of Canadian imports from Argentina, which is a significant source of imports for six of these ten products, with share ranging from 77 per cent for garment leather to 14 per cent for fresh lemons.

In contrast to Argentina, imports from Bolivia are highly concentrated in a few goods. Two products (tin and silver ores, silver content) account for 69 per cent of Bolivia's exports and the five major products for 87 per cent. However, Bolivia is a significant supplier of most of these products: imports from Bolivia of tin, silver ore, Brazil nuts and lumber represented from 64 per cent to 15 per cent of Canada's total imports of these products in 1993. All of the major imports from Bolivia are natural resources with almost no processing.

As expected, imports from Brazil are very diversified, with the ten major products accounting for only 38 per cent of Canadian imports from that country in 1993. Brazil is a significant supplier of all these products; more than 80 per cent of Canada's imports of orange juice, 63 per cent of aluminium ores, 51 per cent of cashew nuts, and more than 35 per cent of steel products come from Brazil. Nine out of the ten major imports are natural resource-based intermediate goods. Among those based on natural resources, two are manufactured steel products.

All of the ten major imports from Chile are natural resource products, from the mining (copper), agriculture (fresh fruits and wine) and fishing (fish meal) sectors. The only one with some industrial processing is wine, but this is also based on a natural resource. These ten products accounted for 72 per cent of imports from Chile with some of them (fish meal, fresh grapes, apples, plums and pears) representing a relatively high percentage of Canadian imports.

Imports from Colombia are more concentrated than those from Chile: the ten main products account for 88 per cent. Among these there are four different types of coffee so that at a more aggregated level they would appear even more concentrated. Bananas and the largest category of coffee represented 56 per cent of imports from Colombia in 1993. No manufactured goods appear among these ten imports. In some cases Colombia is a large supplier: carnations (88 per cent of imports), roses (68 per cent), one of the types of coffee (24 per cent) and bananas (23 per cent).

Almost half of total imports from Ecuador are bananas, the only product with such a large share, although at this level of disaggregation there are several types of shrimp. The ten major imports accounted for 67 per cent of imports from Ecuador. All imports from Ecuador are natural resource-based products, and the country has a significant share of Canadian banana and shrimp imports.

Only in the case of Mexico are most of Canada's imports manufactured goods. In fact nearly all are, and all except one are motor vehicles or their parts. There is only one natural resource, crude oil. The ten main imports from Mexico account for 53 per cent of the total: a high level of diversification, particularly when the product with the largest share has 12 per cent. It should also be noted that for some of these products Mexico is a large supplier, with 5 per cent as the lowest share (among these ten imports).

Paraguay is another case in which exports to Canada are highly concentrated. The five major products accounted for 75 per cent of Canadian imports from Paraguay, three of them being leather goods. Imports from Paraguay represent a significant share of the total for just two products: a certain type of cotton fabrics (30 per cent) and *mate* (31 per cent).

Gold accounted for 40 per cent of Canadian imports from Peru in 1993 with the other nine major imports accounting for a further 34 per cent. Most of these ten imports are natural resource-based products with little processing. Only two are manufactured: textile fabrics. Peru is an important supplier of silver ores (62 per cent and 63 per cent, depending on the type) and lead ores (53 per cent and 26 per cent).

Uruguay is another source of leather goods. Two of the five major imports of Canada from that country are leather products. For this country, the five major imports accounted for 57 per cent of the total. For the two types of leather product Uruguay is a major supplier with shares of 12 per cent and 15 per cent of Canadian imports, while those of the other products are much lower. This is another example of exports from a LAIA country being mostly based on natural resources.

The ten major imports from Venezuela account for 94 per cent of Canada's total imports from that country, and nine of the ten are petroleum-based. This underlines the high degree of dependence Venezuela has on one resource. For two of these petroleum derivatives, Venezuela is the dominant supplier with more than 80 per cent of Canada's imports of those products and two others have shares above 20 per cent.

With the exception of Mexico, natural resource-based products dominate the major Canadian imports from individual LAIA countries. Furthermore, in most cases they are natural resources with very little processing. Only Mexico exports a large share of manufactured goods, but these are all concentrated in the automobile industry. In the case of the smaller countries, exports to Canada are highly concentrated in a few products, and this is also the case for certain larger countries.

3   CANADIAN FOREIGN DIRECT INVESTMENT IN LATIN AMERICA

The information on foreign direct investment (FDI) in LAIA countries used in this section is taken from research done at the

Table 10.7   Direct Foreign Investment Stock (US$ 000s)

Country	Year	Canada	Developed Countries	All Countries	Shares of Canada Among Developed Countries	Shares of Canada Among all Countries
Argentina	1989	220 643	6 526 580	6 942 245	3.4%	3.2%
Bolivia	1990	65 779	665 707	806 077	9.9%	8.2%
Brazil	1992	2 281 920	36 736 087	39 975 066	6.2%	5.7%
Chile		na				
Colombia	1992	72 088	3 402 826	3 817 358	2.1%	1.9%
Ecuador		na				
Mexico	1992	579 600	34 299 000	37 474 100	1.7%	1.5%
Paraguay		na				
Peru	1992	51 048	1 003 110	1 488 138	5.1%	3.4%
Uruguay	1989	3 647	338 359	458 521	1.1%	0.8%
Venezuela	1991	84 866	3 509 312	4 095 813	2.4%	2.1%

na: Not available.
Source: CEPAL (1993).

Table 10.8   Direct Foreign Investment Flows in the 1990s (thousands
of US$)

Country	Years	Canada	Developed Countries	All Countries	Shares of Canada	
					Among Developed Countries	Among all Countries
Argentina	1989	na				
Bolivia	1990	16 703	63 724	100 857	26.2%	16.6%
Brazil	1990–1	365 471	1 823 796	1 987 126	20.0%	18.4%
Chile	1990–2	551 526	2 855 242	3 261 731	19.3%	16.9%
Colombia	1990–2	15 051	413 248	547 493	3.6%	2.7%
Ecuador	1990–1	2 000	39 000	57 500	5.1%	3.5%
Mexico	1990–2	218 700	9 068 900	10 887 000	2.4%	2.0%
Paraguay		na				
Peru	1990–2	62	52 542	242 253	0.1%	0.0%
Uruguay		na				
Venezuela	1990–1	19 410	749 174	1 009 353	2.6%	1.9%

na: Not available.
Source: CEPAL (1993).

UN Economic Commission for Latin America and the Caribbean.[6] For some countries recent data are missing and for none
of them, except Chile, was it possible to obtain from other
sources the destination sectors of Canadian FDI. Table 10.7
reports the figures on the stock of Canadian FDI, as well as that
of other countries, for the most recent year available, and Table
10.8 shows the total flow of FDI for the years indicated. In the
latter case the flows for each of the years shown were added up.

Canada has been an important foreign investor in Bolivia,
Brazil and Peru. In all these countries the share of Canada in the
foreign capital stock among developed countries is above 5 per
cent. In Argentina, Venezuela and Colombia this figure is
between 2 per cent and 3 per cent.

However, the data on FDI flows indicate that in some countries
Canadian investment has recently become more significant than
in the past. In countries such as Bolivia, Brazil and Chile,
Canadian foreign investment has accounted in recent years for 20
per cent or more of the flows of FDI from developed countries.
The result is that Canada has become the second or third most
important source of FDI in these countries in the 1990s.

Only for Chile was it possible to obtain information on the destination sectors of Canadian FDI (Comité de Inversiones Extranjeras, 1994), which is shown in Table 10.9. A number of important things are worth noting. Most of the Canadian

Table 10.9 Canadian Direct Investment in Chile

Sector of Destination	1974–84 US$ (000s)	As % of Total DFI	1985–9 US$ (000s)	As % of Total DFI	1990–3 US$ (000s)	As % of Total DFI
Agriculture	23	0.0%	40	0.1%	25	0.0%
Construction	0		0		48	0.1%
Electricity, gas and water	0		0		10	3.8%
Manufacturing	45 545	7.7%	4 353	1.7%	8 585	1.0%
Mining	7 450	0.8%	144 300	8.6%	908 281	34.1%
Fishing and fish breeding	0		0		0	
Services	4 121	0.8%	7 455	1.0%	48 358	4.2%
Forestry	103	1.6%	0		0	
Transportation	0		0		0	
Total	57 243	2.6%	156 148	5.6%	965 307	19.5%

Source: Comité de Inversiones Extranjeras (1994).

direct investment in the last two decades has come after 1989 (82 per cent), that is, when democracy was restored in Chile. As a result Canada has become the second source of FDI in Chile. Practically all of it (90 per cent) has gone into mining, where it accounted for 34 per cent of FDI in that sector in 1990–3.

4 FINAL REMARKS

Although trade between Canada and the Latin American countries has been growing, it has done so at a lower rate than the latter's trade with the rest of the world. The result is that their share in their respective total trade has remained low and has even tended to decline. The strengthening of ties between Canada and Latin America should reverse this trend.

The breakdown of trade by product shows that Canada exports mostly natural resource-based intermediate goods and some capital goods to the LAIA countries, while the latter in general export natural resources with little processing to Canada. Canada competes with other Latin American countries in some of the natural resource products exported to the region. There is some intra-industry trade in motor vehicles and parts, but it is only significant in the case of Mexico.

Canada is a major investor in some countries, notably in Bolivia, Brazil and Chile. In the latter country Canadian FDI has increased significantly in the 1990s, mostly directed to the mining sector.

11 NAFTA as a Mutually Beneficial Agreement: Commentary by Richard Lipsey on 'NAFTA in the World Economy. Lessons and Issues for Latin America' By Bruce W. Wilkinson

GENERAL OBSERVATIONS

To appreciate the tone of Bruce Wilkinson's paper, one needs to understand that it is written by someone who strongly opposed the Canada–US Free Trade Agreement (FTA). Having expected large negatives on balance from that agreement, he is unlikely to see a strong positive balance for the NAFTA. While Wilkinson's assessment is defensible, it does not represent the majority opinion among Canadian economists, most of whom predicted in advance, and now accept on the basis of much evidence, that the FTA has worked strongly to the mutual benefit of both Canada and the United States. This, of course, should be no surprise since international trade is not a zero-sum game. While I agree with perhaps 70 per cent of the factual statements that Wilkinson makes, I disagree with about 90 per cent of the interpretations that he puts on those facts.

Wilkinson's paper provides a conspiracy theory of the NAFTA in which the United States seeks to extend its hegemony to the Americas, get control of its natural resources, exploit market power to drive resource prices down and hold high-tech production in the United States. Given the premise of a US conspiracy, each existing NAFTA characteristic, or new US proposal, is interpreted as an aspect of the main plot or some new subplot. Conspiracy theories ignore the fact that most governments perceive mutual gains from the liberalization of trade and investment, and that economic theory predicts that small countries tend to gain more from trade liberalization and the establishment of effective dispute settlement mechanisms than do large and powerful nations such as the United States. Countries voluntarily enter trade- and investment-liberalizing agreements because there is a perceived mutual advantage. To demonstrate the contrary in the case of NAFTA, i.e. that the United States, gain will be at the expense of its partners, and hence the United States is motivated by a plot that succeeds only because the partners are gullible, requires very solid evidence, which I do not find in the paper.

It is one thing to say that each country will look out for its own interests and try to maximize its own gains in any bargaining situation – which I accept as being what governments typically do – it is quite another thing to say that one country is involved in a conspiracy to make large gains *at the expense of the others*. I see little evidence of this in the case of either the FTA or the NAFTA.

The Paper in Detail

An evaluation of Wilkinson's paper requires evaluating the substance and not the motivation of his comments, and it is to this task that I now turn. I shall deal with his points under the same main headings that he uses.

1 INTRODUCTION

In his introduction Wilkinson makes four major points.

First, the economic gains will be limited and membership will preclude countries from using infant-industry tariffs and other similar measures to encourage early industrial development. Gains from trade are sometimes measured statically to be small. But those who accept that great gains were brought by the unilateral tariff reductions of several liberalizing governments such as Mexico, will not believe that only minor gains will follow from major tariff reductions, plus improved access to service trade, investment liberalization, plus a first-class dispute settlement mechanism (and a score of other measures which Wilkinson stresses when he correctly argues that the NAFTA is more than a simple FTA on goods).[1] Countries in the pre-industrial stage do have to ask themselves if eschewing infant-industry tariff protection is a price worth paying in order to gain better access to the NAFTA market. But for countries such as Chile, which are already well on the way to development, denying themselves the use of infant-industry tariffs is a small price to pay for gaining better and more secure access to the NAFTA market.

Wilkinson's second point is that the United States alone will decide the future of NAFTA and its implications for the world trading order. If that means there can be no extension of NAFTA without US approval, that is correct. But if it means the United States can unilaterally change the rules of NAFTA, or decide how the free market forces unleashed by it will work out, it is clearly not so.

Third, we are told that NAFTA is unlikely to lead to a stifling of world trade. I agree for many reasons, including the ones mentioned by Wilkinson.

Fourth, we read that 'NAFTA should give us cause for concern about the international social order and the well-being of the masses'. But NAFTA embodies the general consensus, most strongly accepted by those countries that have tried other routes, that the new model of development, often referred to as the Washington consensus which is outward-looking and market-oriented (without being *laissez-faire*), is the best route to development and improvement of average living standards.[2]

2   WHAT IT IS AND WHAT IT IS NOT

As Wilkinson says, NAFTA certainly is not a simple agreement for free trade in goods. Possibly there are some who think otherwise or who use unguarded language when responding to critics who assert it is a customs union, but no one that I know in the trade policy sphere is under any delusion that it is not a sweeping agreement covering trade in goods, services, investment, standards, NTBs, dispute settlement and a host of other measures that belong in any modern comprehensive trade-liberalizing arrangement.[3]

Indeed, as Wilkinson says, there is pressure for a harmonization
of tariffs onto the lowest tariff of the members. This is something
which supporters understand and believe is a good thing.[4] This
does not, however, make the FTA or the NAFTA a customs
union or a common market. Without a massive change in policy,
no Canadian government would agree to a formal common
market (nor should any Latin American government) because
that would bind all members to US commercial policy. It is
precisely because the United States would dominate the decision
about a common commercial policy that a customs union is not
acceptable to Canada. But if tariff rates evolve to a common, low
level, that is desirable as long as members preserve the freedom
to choose their own external commercial policy, particularly
when US policy is motivated by political considerations.[5]

All FTAs require rules of origin and these are, as Wilkinson
says, the equivalent of a common tariff under a customs union,
but that does not make a free trade area a customs union (or if
it does, generations of trade analysts, from Viner on, have been
deluding themselves).

The wide range of other provisions which make the NAFTA
an economic community are certainly there and are, as far as I
know, understood and welcomed by Canadian trade analysts who
support the FTA.

The Canadian trade analysts that I know, along with US
analysts, regard the FTA as something that will evolve. Confident
that we negotiated a good but incomplete deal, we welcome the
expectation that there will be further negotiations in the future.
Only someone who mistrusts any negotiations with the United
States, including those leading to the FTA and the NAFTA,
could regard it as a criticism, as Wilkinson seems to do, that the
agreement will probably evolve through further negotiations.

Wilkinson then goes on to discuss 'What the NAFTA is not'.

First, he says that it is not an example of 'plurilateral regionalism', or a 'model of equals' as I have called it. His argument is
that 'One can hardly call an agreement where one partner is
eleven times larger than the next biggest partner . . . an example
of a model of equals.' Since we must assume that I knew that the
United States was much bigger than Canada, we must suspect
that I was referring to something other than size when I coined
the phrases quoted above. In the paper in which I did so, I was
comparing the 'hub-and-spoke model' (a term originally used by

Ron Wonnacott), in which the United States has bilateral agreements with each Latin American country, with a model in which they are all joined in a single agreement. My point was that the hub-and-spoke model was a recipe for US domination, since the United States would be the only country with free access to all other markets, while a single agreement is a recipe for equal access for all – which was the sense in which I talked about equals, i.e. everyone has equal access to everyone else's market.[6]

Second, Wilkinson points out correctly that the NAFTA does not provide for a harmonized set of rules and regulations on NTBs. This was a major loss in terms of Canada's original negotiating objectives, but I have no doubt that the dispute settlement mechanism that we did get instead is a big improvement on the previous regime in which the United States could (and did) act unilaterally to determine whether or not we were adopting fair trading practices – at least within the very weak constraints that GATT rules place on its behaviour.

Third, Wilkinson correctly points out that the 'NAFTA does not provide for any inter-country cooperation on technological progress'. When I survey the mess that the European countries have made of government technology policy, I can only say: 'Thank goodness!'

Fourth, we read that NAFTA does not provide any international assistance coming from the prosperous to the less prosperous countries. This is correct, and I think it is a thoroughly good thing. If NAFTA is beneficial to each member country, then each member can be left to decide how much the domestic gainers should compensate the domestic losers. I see no reason to think redistribution would be more just if the transfers were international, unless all the gains were concentrated in the richer countries.

Fifth, 'NAFTA makes no provision for a *common approach* to enhancing management–labour relations, or to improving working conditions . . .' It is hard enough to get one government to act on these measures and I can only say once again, 'Thank goodness we do not have to get three governments to agree before we can act!' Without guessing where Wilkinson would have stood, I can say with confidence that most of NAFTA's detractors in Canada would have greeted an international agreement on these matters with the criticism that we had surrendered our sovereignty to the United States who would dominate the decisions on these matters.

3 POTENTIAL EXPANSION OF NAFTA

Wilkinson says, and I believe correctly, that the Canadian government was influenced in its decision to enter the NAFTA in spite of the small static gains, by the desire to avoid the development of a hub-and-spoke model in which the United States is the hub of a series of bilateral Western hemispheric spokes. This argument, which is due to Ron Wonnacott and myself, 'amazes' Wilkinson. It does not amaze me, nor did it amaze the Canadian government's trade experts or other Canadian trade policy analysts. Of course, avoiding the hub-and-spoke model does not change the relative disparities of economic power, but it does prevent the United States from dominating a hub-and-spoke model in which its already strong attractions to investors would have been greatly enhanced, because it would be the only location offering tariff-free access to the hub and all the spokes. Wilkinson suggests that the hub and spoke could have been avoided by a series of bilateral agreements without joining the NAFTA. That was not the opinion of most Canadian trade policy analysts who studied it.[7] For example, if the United States expanded its agreements in the hemisphere to cover only five countries on bilaterals, that would require 20 (5 × 4) bilaterals to undo the hub and spoke – an impossible mishmash of overlapping agreements with different rules of origin. It was the opinion of those of us who advised the Canadian government that, to allow a bilateral agreement between the United States and Mexico, risked the development of a hub-and-spoke model which would leave Canada as a side-player in any further hemispheric trade liberalization – and incidentally would not be in the long-run self-interest of the Latin American countries that became US spokes.

I am not one who ignores the high degree of foreign ownership in Canada (which peaked in the early 1970s, and has declined since then with a significant upward blip after the FTA agreement was successful in attracting a large new flow of FDI). But I do not believe there is a serious evidence that foreign-owned firms had a different position with respect to the FTA than did domestically owned ones.[8] As a result of successful adaptation to the Tokyo Round of GATT tariff reductions, concern about rising protectionist sentiment in the United States, and an apparent crisis in the GATT, organizations representing Canadian small, medium-sized and large businesses all came out in favour of free trade with the United States at some time in 1985.[9]

Wilkinson then correctly points out that, to outsiders, Mexico would seem to have mixed motives with respect to the extension of the NAFTA because of losing its preferential position in the US market. However, the public Mexican position, reiterated by several senior officials, including the president and the Mexican ambassador to Chile, is to welcome all new members from Latin America.

Wilkinson then goes on to assert for a second time that for Latin American countries 'the trade gains from accession to NAFTA will be diminutive'. This is clearly not the view of the Mexican and Chilean governments. Nor is it my view. I cannot see how any agreement with the following characteristics can have only 'diminutive' effects:[10]

- it reduces mutual tariffs to zero in a series of specified steps;
- it establishes the right of establishment and national treatment for services;
- it greatly liberalizes the flow of investment;
- it gives some limited increase in access to member governments' procurement;
- it provides temporary access for business people and technicians who previously were often harassed at the border;
- it removes the use of quantitative restrictions, and thus also the threat of them to force the introduction of voluntary export restraints (VERs);
- it severely restricts the use of national security considerations to reduce trade;
- it eliminates several other NTBs, such as the use of standards to restrict trade, and greatly constrains the use of others, such as escape clause action;
- it introduces an effective dispute settlement mechanism which has proved its ability to increase the fairness with which domestic laws on countervailing and anti-dumping duties are applied.

In the course of Wilkinson's argument that the beneficial effects will be minimal, we hear an old horror story that no amount of reasoned argument seems capable of dispelling. Wilkinson writes that the newly joining countries might get locked into 'a resource-sharing commitment, as Canada now has as a consequence of the FTA, so that in times of shortage, or even on other occasions, they would have less freedom in the sale and pricing of those resources internationally'. To those of us who have argued that this view is nonsense, the only counter-argument given by Wilkinson is in a footnote asserting that, whatever we may think, the United States interprets it as a resource-sharing agreement.

I have written two books that required detailed research on this issue and have commissioned a C.D. Howe pamphlet in which first-class US and Canadian trade lawyers gave their interpretations.[11] The results of all of this research is that the words in the Agreement mean just what they say. If either government ever declares an emergency of sufficient seriousness to override normally agreed commercial contracts with respect to the sale of some resource, and takes over the allocation of that resource by government decree, then a proportion of the resource equal to the proportion used in normal times by the other member country *must be made available on the open market (where any country can buy it)*.[12]

Furthermore, this Agreement merely makes explicit an existing arrangement under the International Energy Agency (IEA) signed by Canada and 15 other countries after the first OPEC crisis (and not objected to by Canadian nationalists at the time). The wording in the US–Canada FTA was inserted at the request of the government of Alberta, not the Americans, because Alberta wanted to clarify the obligation that already existed under the IEA!

The agreement applies only when a crisis is sufficient for the government to overturn normal market contracts. It is a minimum condition that *either country* would want if it were to allow the market to cause it to become dependent on supplies from the other country. It will probably never be called into force, and, if it is, it will merely prevent either country from cutting off the other in a declared emergency. (Note that it also prevents Canada being cut off by the United States for the duration of the emergency.) This is a far cry from the rhetoric of forced resource-sharing.

Just for purposes of argument, suppose what Wilkinson alleges were true. This means that either the Canadian government is

much less smart than Professor Wilkinson or that it con-
sciously sold out Canadian interests. The same can be said
about private sector supporters of the FTA who studied the
matter in detail. Did they sell their country out? If I thought
for one minute that the Agreement was anything other than
a reasonable way to cope with a true and rare emergency
situation, I would have opposed the FTA with all the force at
my command, as would every other Canadian patriot that I
know.

I issue the following challenge to those who support this
argument: tell me *exactly under what circumstances* the United States
could force the Canadian government against its will (and by the
symmetry of the FTA, Canada could force the US government
against *its* will) to share some specific energy resources, and what
the sanctions for non-compliance would be.

Next, Wilkinson considers the US motivation in extending
NAFTA. Here we meet the conspiracy theory in detail.

First, we read that the United States wants to put a wide group
of countries 'under its leadership/domination'. It is not clear how
such a group of countries operating within a NAFTA will be
more under US domination than they would be without a
NAFTA. Anyway, this view of regional groupings as part of a
nineteenth-century power game – with NAFTA as a US conspiracy designed to delude free traders to become part of a US
power group – is a conspiracy theory that in its nature cannot
be refuted, and so I must let others judge on how persuasive
they find it, and just what added power the NAFTA gives to
the United States in this respect.

Then we hear that the United States sees its comparative
advantage in technology-intensive products and wants to keep
these in the United States. Just how this is to be done by public
policy operating against the market and how NAFTA helps in
this is unspecified – I would love to see a detailed economic
model of how this is supposed to happen!

Next we read that – 'an enlarged NAFTA will provide US
buyers of raw materials and raw materials-based products greater
scope for playing off the supplying countries, including Mexico
and Canada, against one another so as to maximize the benefits
to them'. In response to this, I ask: how will NAFTA help in this
conspiracy, and are not tariffs on such products very low or
non-existent already? No reasons are given by Wilkinson, and I

can think of no plausible mechanism created by NAFTA for this exploitation to take place.

Next Wilkinson tells us that part of the US agenda is to have the NAFTA lock in free market reforms, making it hard for subsequent governments to reverse them. I agree, but I do not see this as a US plot as does Wilkinson. Instead, I think reasonably perceptive local governments know this and willingly want to accomplish such 'lock-ins' – certainly Canadian supporters and detractors during the FTA debate knew this and argued about its desirability without thinking it a US plot.

Wilkinson then expresses the view that those in the United States (and presumably Canadians such as myself) who advocate some kind of associate membership for countries, which cannot go the whole way into NAFTA, because of other treaty obligations, or because they are not yet ready economically, are pressing for a situation in which 'the US would be calling most of the shots'. But this is just another application of the general Wilkinson conspiracy theory that the whole NAFTA is a US plot to gain control over the economies of the Western Hemisphere.

As the next stage in his analysis, Wilkinson describes some US characteristics. Anyone who has dealt with the United States in trade and other negotiations will agree with much of what Wilkinson says on this subject. However, not once does he mention the term 'fast track'. Nations long ago learned to avoid negotiating agreements containing give-and-take which then required clause-by-clause Senate approval. The US Senate was too inclined to strip away all US concessions while accepting all foreign concessions. Today, no country in its right mind would think of negotiating a complex agreement with the United States that was not on the fast track in which the Senate can vote only yes or no. This is the well-established institutional response to the division of powers that Wilkinson analyses in detail, but without saying a word about the solution to these problems that is provided by the fast track.

Still there is no doubt that dealing with the United States is difficult, not the least because Americans do tend to believe that they are the last bastion of the free market approach, in spite of their massive interventions of many sorts. But we have to trade with the United States and there is no reason to believe that the results of these US attitudes will be easier to contend with without the rules-based trading relations laid down by the NAFTA, than with it.[13]

Next we are told that economists such as I have 'repeatedly 'swallowed' and regurgitated' a belief in a US commitment to the level playing field and letting the market work. (Since no references are given, it is not clear who has revealed in writing that they are taken in as Wilkinson asserts.) How have we been taken in? Once again we get the argument that there can be no level playing field when a large country trades with a small country. This is, of course, news to economists who thought that trade was between firms not nations, and that there were many reasons why small countries tend to get more of the gains from trade than do their large trading partners.

The next 'argument' is that the United States tries to impose its own ideas on such matters as intellectual property protection. Yes, and so do other nations. By and large, the new knowledge age requires that new laws for intellectual property protection be established, and the United States is not alone in believing this. Responding to structural changes brought about by the new technologies is not necessarily a national conspiracy, although no doubt all nations would like to respond in ways that most suit their own national interest.

Wilkinson then argues that the United States only wants to let the market work when it is in the United States' own national interest. There is some substantial truth in this, which is exactly why Canadians sought to get the rule of law established in bilateral trade by negotiating an FTA with the United States. Although the United States is still sometimes guilty of such behaviour (as is Canada now and again), its ability to get away with it is significantly constrained by the rules of the FTA and the NAFTA.

Small countries have most to gain by establishing a rules-based trading system; large, powerful countries gain more when the rule is 'everyone for himself and the strongest wins'. It is precisely because of what Wilkinson outlines (but probably over-states) that the FTA rules on all manner of trade and investment-related matters, and on dispute settlement, are of more benefit to Canada and Mexico than to the United States (although they certainly do benefit the United States whenever Canada or Mexico do things that violate the letter or spirit of the Agreement).

Finally, we hear about US ideas of its 'manifest destiny'. Historians tell us that whoever is the top nation at the time has always felt this way; Americans are only the most recent in a long line; before were the British, the French, the Dutch, the Spanish, the Arabs and the Chinese. Yes, these ideas are there, but they provide no reason not to trade with the top economic nation.

Also I would like to be shown, with references, who are these 'Canadian economists, politicians and businessmen' who 'have never heard of . . . this manifest destiny'. I don't know many, and I know none who are both ignorant of US attitudes and have had intimate dealings with the United States.

In the next sub-section, we hear about US negotiating ploys. This is a useful section. Anyone who deals with the United States needs to know about their typical ploys, just as US negotiators need to know about typical Canadian and European ploys.

4 NAFTA IN THE WORLD ECONOMY

First we hear that 'what the NAFTA becomes and NAFTA's impact on the world economy will depend almost exclusively upon what the United States decides'. Somehow my *economics 100* tells me that its impact will, to a great extent, depend on the market forces that the agreement unleashes, not on what the US government wants. If the US government had that much power, the much feared US competitive decline would not have occurred. (This comment was in the paper presented at the conference, but was deleted from the published version.)

Next we hear that what the United States decides will depend on what it perceives to be in its own self-interest. Why should this be surprising? Personally, I would regard it as treason for a government to be dominated by (as opposed to having a secondary concern for) the interests of other countries. I would be outraged if I thought the Canadian government was not primarily interested in promoting Canadian national interest – and I venture the conjecture that Professor Wilkinson would share my outrage. We engage in trade negotiations, not because we think that other governments have some altruistic interest in our welfare, but because we think trade and related matters are positive-sum games, so that all countries can peruse their own self-interest and all can gain.

Next we hear about disadvantaged groups. Here the discussion impinges on my own current research into economic growth and deep structural adjustments. There are major changes associated with a shift in what I call an enabling technology which occurs occasionally in history (the last one was electricity, and the one before that was the factory system introduced as the First Industrial Revolution). We are living through a really major period of deep structural adjustment, associated, mainly but not exclusively, with the revolution in information and communications technology (ICT). The Harvard historian, Peter Druker, calls it, without much exaggeration, one of the three most profound shifts that have occurred in this millennium (not century but millennium!). The causes and consequences are not fully understood, but there is much current research on it. Certainly, to blame it on changes in trade policy is superficial in the extreme.

Reading on, I am led to wonder who are these insensitive 'economists, businessmen and government officials' who tell those hurt in this deep transition 'that the changes are really for their benefit in the long run'? It is one thing to say, as most of us believe, that we are all better off for the economic growth that occurred 50 years ago. It is quite another thing to assert that everyone gains from current growth, particularly when it is part of a major technological shift of the sort we are seeing now. No doubt there are some who are insensitive and ignorant enough to say this, but many of those I know in government business and academia who have studied these matters are profoundly concerned about the groups who are being hurt and may well be hurt for the rest of their lifetimes. The only 'insensitive' position people such as myself adopt is to label as unproductive romanticism the view that the clock can be stopped and that we can opt out of these massive changes. The place of policy it seems to me is to make the inevitable transition as humane as possible, which task is not helped by conjuring up devils and witches rather than trying to understand the deep forces that are shaping the current structural adjustments.[14] By and large, the consensus among developing nations is that the old, inward-looking, non-market-oriented model of economic growth failed and harmed the common person. It is now commonly held that an outward-looking, market-oriented model provides the best hope for increases in average living standards (combined with social policies to help those left behind by change). The very countries that have been most committed to the old model in the past are the ones most convinced that the new model provides the best hope for raising average living standards.

I could say a lot more; I hope I have said enough to provide reasoned argument as to why I accept little of the general thrust, and not much more of the detailed arguments, in Wilkinson's paper.

12 NAFTA in the World Economy: Lessons and Issues for Latin America: A Reply to Richard Lipsey

Bruce W. Wilkinson

In my paper, I attempted to identify a number of concerns which Latin American nations should have when considering whether to enter NAFTA. I also attempted to highlight the types of problem Canada has had in dealing with the United States, as I was specifically requested to do by the organizers of the Conference on Western Hemisphere Trade Integration (1995). Now that I have done that, Richard Lipsey, who was not asked to be one of the discussants chosen by the conference organizers, apparently feels that his comments are vital to the discussion. However, as I shall demonstrate in what follows, Lipsey's remarks shed very little new light on the issues.

Essentially, my purpose was to suggest that Chile and other Latin American countries should not be entering discussions to join NAFTA with a short-sighted idealism, seeing NAFTA as a sort of economic panacea. There is a need to be both realistic and cautious and firm in bargaining, so as not to give away too much due to an unrealistically high estimate of the gains to be achieved and a lack of understanding of the probable costs.

Lipsey is right when he says I was an outspoken critic of the FTA. That I was, because as I studied much of the rhetoric and analysis on the FTA, I found some outlandish and sometimes historically inaccurate statements being made in support of it. To illustrate, some proponents, including Canada's prime minister, said that it would *increase* Canada's sovereignty! Others, in an attempt to calm fears that FTA could eventually lead to political

absorption of Canada by the United States, stated categorically
that never in history had a free trade deal culminated in political
absorption of the smaller by the larger country. The example of
Hawaii proves this to be incorrect.

I cite this example for two reasons: first, to show the inaccurate
nature of some of the claims that were made by enthusiastic
proponents of FTA, and second, to emphasize that we need
always to look beyond a narrow assessment of economic costs and
benefits to the broader socio-political implications of trade and
investment arrangements.

A technique Lipsey uses repeatedly to buttress his assertions is
to refer to the people who agree with him, such as those in
positions of power and authority. But there are plenty of cases
where the majority view has proved to be deficient, or too
narrow, or short-sighted, or just plain wrong. We need good,
solid debate about issues if we are going to move forward as a
world society, not simply quiet submissiveness to the views of a
single dominant group. Lipsey attempts to discount my paper by
labelling it a conspiracy theory because I point out that the
United States has a desire to extend its power and influence
throughout the Americas, while simultaneously ensuring a guaranteed supply of natural resources and preserving high-tech
production for US locations. To most observers of US policy over
the years this is common knowledge, so it is rather surprising that
Lipsey should try to deny the obvious by giving it the label of
conspiracy theory.

Let me now respond to Lipsey's comments in detail. In his
criticism of my first conclusion he declares that 'for countries,
such as Chile, which are already well on the way to development,
denying themselves the use of infant-industry tariffs is a small
price to pay for gaining better and more secure access to the
NAFTA market.'

This statement is a pure assertion, a value judgement not based
on quantitative evidence. And the historical fact remains that all
the nations which have become technologically advanced industrial nations today did use a host of protective or other promo-
tional measures to develop their domestic industries before taking
on the world. This does not mean that it is completely impossible
for nations to become technological and industrial leaders without considerable government assistance. But it does suggest that
it may be extremely difficult to do so, because it has not been

done before. Latin Americans should not overestimate the ease with which they might accomplish their objectives. In their enthusiasm for NAFTA have alternative trade arrangements, for example within Latin America, been fully explored?

In response to my second conclusion, Lipsey asserts that the United States cannot unilaterally change the rules of NAFTA. Technically, that is correct. But the fact remains that because of the overwhelming position the United States has in its trade with Canada and Mexico, it has considerable leverage to make changes, or refrain from making changes its partners want. Indeed, in the NAFTA negotiations, the United States wanted a number of things from Canada beyond what was in the FTA – and it got them. And when Mr Chretien, our prime minister, said he wanted certain changes in NAFTA before bringing it into effect on 1 January 1994, the United States essentially told him that they were not amending it – and that was the end of it.

As for my fourth conclusion – that we need to be concerned about the well-being of the people of the world – perhaps Lipsey has misunderstood the point I was making. As I see it, this may sometimes mean putting constraints on 'the market' where the market does not, in itself, produce desirable results. This is clearly why we have all sorts of government laws regarding working hours, safety conditions, proper reporting on financial statements and a host of other things that the unconstrained market may not satisfactorily handle by itself.

WHAT NAFTA IS AND WHAT IT IS NOT

I am glad that Lipsey agrees that the NAFTA is, essentially, an economic community or economic integration agreement, and that he recognizes that the degree of integration will increase in the years ahead. But it is surprising that he tries to make so much of the fact that it is not a formal customs union, meaning that Canada still can negotiate relatively independently with non-NAFTA nations. With 82 per cent of our exports already going to the United States, that nation has considerable leverage over Canada if our actions are seen to be greatly against their viewpoint and/or interests. As I write this, I note that some US senators are telling Canada that because we are in NAFTA we should not be trading with Cuba, and that US legislation is being considered which would penalize nations which do so. Lipsey seems not to recognize these types of pressure.

Lipsey also takes issue with the fact that I note that NAFTA is really not a 'model of equals'. He says that in using these words he meant only that the NAFTA involved equal access for all the nations in NAFTA to the markets of the other members by the companies of each country. This sounds very noble, but the fact remains that where one nation has highly developed technology, manufacturing organizations, financial intermediaries and a wide range of supporting service industries, and other nations do not have anywhere near the same level of development in these areas – as is the case with Mexico – equal access to the markets of one another by the countries involved does not produce a model of equals. Moreover, when we remember that under NAFTA nearly 90 per cent of US government procurement is not open to foreign firms – even though Canada was willing to give equal access – the situation Lipsey says exists does not really exist in practice.

Although Lipsey agrees with my statement that in NAFTA Canada did not get any harmonized agreement on definitions of dumping and subsidies, he tries to dismiss the importance of this outcome. Yet the fact remains that achieving an agreement on these matters was a prime Canadian objective in the NAFTA negotiations, and it was unsuccessful because of US intransigence.[1]

Lipsey then rejoices that no formal provision exists in NAFTA for inter-country cooperation on technological progress or for Canadian firms to participate in US government-sponsored research consortia, and suggests that such cooperation would only be a mess anyway. This is a surprising attitude in someone who sees himself as a champion of Canadian interests and supporter of Canadian high-technology activities! As my reference (Caldwell, 1993) clearly indicates, the limitations on the participation of Canadian firms in publicly supported US research means less opportunity for, and assistance to, Canadian firms' R&D activities.[2]

Lipsey is also pleased that there are no provisions for assistance to countries or regions not prospering very well under NAFTA, from those greatly benefiting. He assumes that all countries will gain from NAFTA and so each one can conduct its own redistributive measures as desired. The architects of the European Union were not so confident of this easy outcome, however, and it is well known that without regional grants, development grants and agricultural assistance across national borders in the EU, nations like Greece, Spain and Portugal would be in even worse shape than they are today.

In his next point Lipsey gives thanks that no common standards were reached on social or labour matters. He argues that if anything of this type had been attempted, the US views would have dominated, which Canadians would not have liked. This is an interesting position, as it leaves one wondering why Lipsey is so certain that US views would dominate on these matters, yet elsewhere in his commentary he is so adamant in rejecting the idea that the United States dominates in other areas.

THE POTENTIAL EXPANSION OF NAFTA

Lipsey questions my statement that Canada was initially not altogether pleased about the US–Mexico initiative. However, Maureen Appel Molot's chapter in this volume aptly summarizes the Canadian position on NAFTA, and it is consistent with what I state in my chapter. I refer the reader to her section 'Canada and NAFTA' (p. 181).

Other writers, too, have taken the position that Canada should enter NAFTA, not because of the great gains to be had, but rather as a defensive measure (Wonnacott, 1990; Watson, 1992). One wonders, therefore, what motivates Lipsey to argue about this point.

Lipsey concedes that the net benefits from NAFTA for Canada were calculated to be quite small, but then he rejects questioning the hub-and-spoke argument proposed by Wonnacott and himself. He suggests that there would be an 'impossible mishmash of overlapping agreements' if anything but the single NAFTA approach were used. Yet even today we have various overlapping agreements within Latin America. Mexico is in NAFTA, yet has an agreement with Chile. Moreover, today in Canada, the Minister of International Trade is talking of making separate deals with Chile and/or other nations even if the United States is not interested.[3]

In Lipsey's next comment he misses the point completely. I suggest that because of the high degree of foreign ownership of Canadian industry, we may not see the increase in exports to third countries from Canada that would occur if there was more Canadian ownership. This is because foreign firms may choose to supply these other markets from locations in the United States, particularly if they are US-owned firms – a point Lipsey himself has made on other occasions (see Eaton et al., 1994, for example). It is also a well-known fact that foreign-owned firms in Canada import a much higher proportion of their purchases than do domestically-owned firms – a fact which means that Canadian imports tend to be higher than they would otherwise be.

Lipsey then says he disagrees with all the reasons I give as to why the net trade gains for Latin America may be small.

When Lipsey raises the issue of constraints on the sale and pricing of resources, he omits several important points.

First, he suggests that the FTA 'merely makes explicit an existing agreement under the International Energy Agreement (IEA) signed by 16 countries after the first OPEC crisis'. What he does not mention is that the FTA is much more comprehensive than the IEA, for it covers not only oil, but every other energy product too, such as natural gas and electricity. In addition, the FTA includes all other resources, not just energy products. Furthermore, he does not mention that the IEA did not contain any provisions for retaliation should one nation not fully conform to the terms of the agreement. In contrast, failure to comply can be met with retaliatory measures suspending 'benefits of equivalent effect'. So in this sense the FTA, and now NAFTA, are more binding than the IEA. And finally on this point, he accepts that the IEA definitely consists of an oil-sharing arrangement and that the FTA and NAFTA make this agreement more explicit, yet he then tries to argue that there is no real commitment to resource-sharing in these arrangements!

Next, Lipsey does not bother to point out that the NAFTA agreement specifically precludes Canada from charging a higher price to US buyers than the price charged for such energy goods [or other resources] when consumed domestically', even though the Canadian taxpayers, via their government, may have heavily subsidized the production of such energy or resource products. Does this not clearly imply, as I state in my paper, 'that in time of shortage, or even on other occasions . . . [we] have less freedom in the sale and pricing of these resources internationally'? How can Lipsey deny this?

Thirdly, if the agreement Canada has with the United States on energy resources does not entail any real constraints on Canadian policy, then one has to ask why Mexico bothered to get itself exempted from these clauses when it entered NAFTA. The clauses must have been perceived by Mexicans to contain provisions which the Mexicans did not want to commit themselves to. In this regard, it is useful to quote a paragraph from the fairly recent volume which Lipsey himself wrote, with his co-authors, Schwanen and Wonnacott (1994):

> Furthermore, *should Mexico wish to restrict supply to conserve* exhaustible resources in the event of supply shortage or for purposes of price stabilization, *it is free to do so without being obligated to make available to the other parties a portion of the restricted supply (which Canada and the United States have to between themselves, as they did in the FTA).* (p. 58; emphasis added)

Finally, Lipsey is misleading in suggesting that the Government of Alberta (which is the source of most of the oil and natural gas produced in Canada) asked for the insertion of the particular clauses on resource-sharing. Alberta did ask that energy be included in FTA but its prime concern was to ensure, as far as possible, that its production would normally have continuous access to the US market and not, in some way, be arbitrarily cut off by policies of either national government – including new arbitrary import restrictions by the United States (see articles 603 and 605 of NAFTA).

With regard to US objectives for NAFTA, Lipsey questions my statement that the United States is interested in building 'a larger group of countries, closely knit by trade and investment concessions to one another, and under its leadership/domination, which will give it more bargaining chips and economic clout in discussions with the European Union and Japan'. Yet the reference to Morici (Director of the Office of Economics of the US International Trade Commission), which I gave in my paper, contains the following:

> the United States, with its already open market among the fifty states, has had few chips to swap as European Community harmonization created new preferences for European producers. Now, as it builds a trading zone first in North America and then in the Western Hemisphere, the United States is

constructing an array of preferences with its neighbours that would strengthen their combined negotiating leverage in regard to the European Community. (Morici, 1994: 16).

One can readily see that the words in my paper were largely a paraphrase of Morici's point, and it does not stretch anyone's imagination very much to think that the United States, which accounts for 85 per cent of North American GNP, will be the dominating leader in any discussions with Europe or Japan.

Lipsey tries to dismiss this whole idea by reference to 'conspiracy theory', and he somehow seems to feel that this settles the matter, yet his inability to counter the argument made suggests that his position is lacking in substance.

Next, Lipsey questions my comment that the United States 'sees its comparative advantage to be in technology-intensive products and related services' and wants to keep 'the sophisticated jobs in the United States'. Again Morici supports this:

> About half of US exports are transportation equipment, sophisticated electrical equipment, industrial machinery, petroleum and mining equipment, environmental systems, and other producer and consumer durable goods. These are technology intensive products and, along with related business services, are the bones and muscle of American comparative advantage. Expanding markets for these products support the kinds of highly skilled, high-paying jobs President Clinton's economic program aims to create. Exports are vital to maintaining large-enough sales to spread high research and development costs and maintain production in the United States . . . (Morici, 1994: 6–7).

Lipsey also wonders what sort of economic model there could be which would suggest why sophisticated jobs might remain in the United States. He seems to have forgotten his own writings on the proclivity of multinational corporations to do the majority of their R&D in their home markets, close to their head offices, and in the US case close to their large home markets. A few quotes from his own article written with Eaton and Safarian (1994) might be a useful reminder to him:

> The evidence clearly suggests that MNEs do develop most their R&D at home . . . (p. 92).

MNEs in two of the three largest home countries, Japan and the United States, concentrate very high degrees of R&D within their national boundaries. (p. 93)

The discussion so far suggests that strong forces favour the centralization of R&D. (p. 94)

Their article (p. 95) also refers to another paper by Eden in the same volume (1994: 25) which notes that even non-US firms, such as those from Canada, may find it advantageous to locate the largest proportion of their production 'and perhaps even some headquarters functions' in the US market, rather than in their home country. The reasons for such behaviour are the usual ones of wanting to be close to the largest market and to be inside it should any trade agreements break down or the rules be changed.

Lipsey also doubts that there could be any benefit to the United States from its having greater access to raw materials from additional countries in an expanded NAFTA. He argues that since US tariffs on such materials, or even semi-processed materials, are already low or zero, membership of other supplying countries in NAFTA would change nothing. He neglects to note that the trade agreements do involve some resource-sharing arrangements along the lines discussed above, and that these certainly give the United States a stronger position than it would have had before such agreements were signed. And he neglects that being in a special trading arrangement with another nation means that there are various new avenues for the larger and stronger nation to bring pressure to bear on a weaker partner in any negotiations that may occur regarding resources or any other products.

Finally, Lipsey takes issue with my point that the United States sees the extension of NAFTA as a means of locking in political and economic reforms in these nations, which subsequent governments of these nations would not readily be able to change. Here he seems to have completely lost sight of the argument being made in this section of my paper. There is nothing in what I say at this point which suggests a US plot. I have been merely outlining a number of US objectives in possibly extending NAFTA to Latin American countries, and one of these is to lock in economic and political reforms. Indeed, a mere two pages earlier I suggest that for these nations locking in reforms in their own countries via membership may 'swing the pendulum in favour of NAFTA membership' for them.

The next topic I address is the idea of the United States developing 'associate memberships' for those nations which, for a variety of reasons, are not prepared or not willing to negotiate full membership in NAFTA. I suggest, too, that in any such negotiations, the United States, being by far the strongest economic and political force in the region, would be the major determiner of the outcomes. Lipsey, curiously, sees this as 'another conspiracy theory'.

My paper then turns to an examination of US characteristics. Lipsey suggests that the 'fast-track' procedure in the United States eliminates the problems of the division of powers. I did not mention the fast-track procedure because it does not eliminate the specific problems I mention under this point. I might add, too, that the fast track does not eliminate all tampering with trade agreements before they are submitted to the Senate for a yes or no vote. One example will suffice. The original press release on the initial FTA deal indicated that there was provision for free trade in transportation services, which would have meant it would then be possible for Canadian ships to be able to move goods between US ports. This would have required an amendment to the Jones Act. Miraculously, before the full deal was made public and formally submitted to Congress, this provision disappeared. US shipping interests had obviously exerted pressure, wherever it had to be exerted, to have the deletion made – in spite of the fast track procedure.

Lipsey then admits that dealing with the United States is difficult, but argues that one must 'show that it will be more difficult to deal with the Americans with a NAFTA than without it'. Again, it is clear that he has missed the entire thrust of my paper. Nowhere do I argue that Latin American nations should not consider negotiating with the United States for entry into NAFTA. I leave the choice to them. My whole point is that there are costs and benefits in doing so, and that the costs should not be ignored in the discussion, as on some occasions they seem to have been.

Again, Lipsey rejects my questioning of 'the level playing field' and 'letting the market work' arguments and makes some surprising statements in this regard. He says, for example, that economists believe that trade is between firms not nations, and that for me to talk of nations trading with nations is quite inappropriate. This ignores how much governments get involved in the trade of firms. We need only reflect on how the US government twisted the arm of Saudi Arabia to ensure a huge contract went to an American firm rather than the Canadian firm, Northern Telecom, which was the lowest bidder. Or we might recall how the US government pressured a number of Asian governments to let American tobacco companies into their countries – at the same time that it was telling its citizens at home that smoking was injurious to their health! How can Lipsey possibly believe that trade involves only companies and not countries?

Lipsey also propounds that 'small countries tend to get more of the gains from trade than do their large trading partners'. He ignores the point I make a few pages further on with a reference to Helleiner (1993) that 'once the difference in bargaining power is factored in' the large country may well do better than the small one. He ignores, too, that economic historians have noted that where a large nation negotiates trade agreements with smaller nations which are dependent upon it, the outcome is generally more favourable to the large nation (e.g. Rooth, 1986).

The idea that small countries will gain the most from a rules-based trading system, as Lipsey declares, will not necessarily be true either. Sometimes it may be, but we in Canada have also experienced a number of instances when the United States has chosen to flaunt the rules when it suits them. A good illustration is the durum wheat case where all the reviews required by the FTA and/or NAFTA rules indicated that Canada was not subsidizing exports of durum wheat to the United States. But the US authorities established a special additional review procedure to devise a way of limiting Canadian exports to their nation, thereby satisfying the politicians and farmers in the prairie states bordering Canada.

NAFTA IN THE WORLD ECONOMY

Regarding this section of my paper, Lipsey quibbles with my statement that what NAFTA becomes and how it relates to the world economy will be largely a function of what the United States decides. I am surprised by this, for most people would accept the point I made earlier in this commentary (and which even Lipsey accepted when he was commenting on labour standards), that because the United States accounts for 85 per cent of the NAFTA's GNP now, and will continue to be by far the dominant economy in any enlarged NAFTA, it will be the determining force in any direction NAFTA takes.

Lipsey seems to read what he wants with regard to my brief commentary on the disadvantaged groups in our world society today. He suggests that I blame all their problems on trade policy *per se*, which is not what I say at all. I am simply expressing concerns about the convulsive changes occurring in our world.

Nor do I argue for a reversion to non-market-oriented economies, as Lipsey presumes. Rather, I suggest that the market in itself should not be worshipped as a god, with ruthless efficiency, profits, wealth and power being given complete priority over people. Instead, we need to ensure that we have a solid and compassionate ethical-moral basis for our decision-making. He ignores that I point out that Adam Smith, the father of modern economics, also wrote *The Theory of Moral Sentiments*, a book which emphasizes 'such basic virtues as honesty, generosity, avoidance of oppressing others, kindness, respect for others, truthfulness, justice and mercy, as offsets to raw pursuit of self interest'.

In conclusion, what do we have left of Lipsey's extended commentary? Not very much I would argue: I do not believe the discussion of Latin America and NAFTA has been enhanced by his remarks.

Notes

INTRODUCTION

1. Maquiladora is a low-skill, labour-intensive assembly industry of duty-free imported components for eventual re-export.

1 NAFTA IN THE WORLD ECONOMY: LESSONS AND ISSUES FOR LATIN AMERICA

1. The liberalization of services trade, including financial services, greater international freedom of movement for service and business persons, provisions for the working out of common licensing requirements for professionals, access to public telecommunications networks of all member countries by firms from all three nations, considerable liberalization of foreign direct investment (which many observers see as more significant than the liberalization of trade (e.g. Geske, 1994: 15; Weintraub, 1993), and access to the dispute settlement mechanism for disputes in this area; resource-sharing arrangements for energy, petrochemicals and other resources (at least between the United States and Canada), access to some limited amounts of government procurement; and reduced restrictions on cross-border land transportation services, all attest to the common market nature of the arrangements. Add to these the many provisions for permanent and temporary committees to work out harmonized policies and regulations on a wide range of issues such as border inspections and customs regulations, industrial standards, food and agricultural product standards, sanitary and phytosanitary measures, labelling of clothing and textiles and the like, and one can readily see the sweeping and comprehensive nature of the NAFTA.
2. Some Canadians, e.g. Michael Sharp, a former Minister of Foreign Affairs, certainly saw this coming (see his statement, noted in Campbell, 1994: 151).
3. This charter 'had sections on fair and equitable wages; improved living and working conditions; adequate social protection; rights of association and to engage in collective bargaining; rights of information, consultation, and participation of workers in business decisions affecting employment and working conditions; and the protection of particular disadvantaged groups in society such as the disabled and the elderly' (Wilkinson, 1991: 66).
4. As long as their standards are not lessened from what they were at the date of the agreement. The question of compliance is another issue and would be a paper unto itself.

5. There would, of course, still have to have been negotiations among each country on issues such as rules of origin and transportation.
6. See especially John Whalley (1993), on which much of the following points 1, 2, 3, 5 and 6 rely.
7. This is true for products such as coffee from Brazil and Columbia, copper and non-metallic ores and a variety of agricultural products from Chile, non-ferrous metals from Peru, crude oil from Venezuela, and tropical products from Ecuador, and a variety of Central American economies.
8. Some Canadians argue that the resource-sharing agreement with the United States under FTA and NAFTA does not really involve a firm commitment to share, but this is certainly not how the US interprets the agreements.
9. From a Mexican surplus of $2 billion in 1990 to a deficit of $8 billion in 1993 (Bergsten, 1994: 398).
10. A careful reading of Morici (1994) makes this very clear. See also Grinspun (1993).
11. Another example is President Clinton's commitment to Florida congressmen not to allow US tariffs on citrus fruit and fresh vegetables to be lowered under GATT by more than 15 per cent. See Kroll (1994).
12. For example, there was no copyright protection for foreign authors in the United States until the Copyright Act of 1891, and even then foreign authors had no protection unless their books were actually printed in the United States – a very protective measure favouring the US publishing industry (Innis, 1952: 3–7). The recent volume by F.M. Scherer and Richard S. Belous (1994) is also of considerable interest in this regard. The authors admit that not just the United States, but nations like the UK, Germany, and Japan all industrialized, and subsequently under protective umbrellas have moved into high technology products so as to avoid being left where traditional comparative advantage based on relative factor endowments might have left them. But then they do not seem to see the need for other countries to be able to do likewise, and want international rules to regulate what these other countries do.
13. See David Orchard (1993), *The Fight for Canada: Four Centuries of Resistance to American Expansionism*, and references cited there.
14. Prior to the CUFTA negotiations commencing, US economists and diplomats repeatedly suggested that there was a small open window of opportunity into the US market which Canada should jump through, but they attempted to leave the impression that they were rather indifferent to the whole business, that there was very little in it for them and that the gains would primarily be to Canada.
15. The Reciprocal Trade Agreements Act 1934 was introduced during the Great Depression when it was evident that US exports had suffered disproportionately. Between 1929 and 1933 world shipments dropped by 30 per cent in volume, whereas US exports were down 48 per cent in volume (Asher Isaacs, 1948, cited in Lake, 1988: 186).
16. The aggressive use of US contingency laws is perhaps the prime example of this.
17. Canada is a much larger debtor in relative terms, with net debts of about $360 billion, which amount to about 50 per cent of GNP (Statistics

Canada, 1993). If market values of past foreign direct investments were used, the debt and its percentage of GNP would be even bigger. In comparison, US debt is less than 10 per cent of GNP.
18. For an excellent, and much more detailed discussion of the issues, see Eden and Molot (1992).
19. John Bates Clark (1887: 219, cited in Perelman, 1994: 194).

2 MERCOSUR AND PREFERENTIAL TRADE LIBERALIZATION IN SOUTH AMERICA

1. The Latin American Integration Association (LAIA) was created in 1980, as its predecessor established two decades earlier (the Latin American Free Trade Association–LAFTA) had failed to achieve its ambitious objectives. LAIA members are Argentina, Bolivia, Brazil, Chile, Colombia, Ecuador, Mexico, Paraguay, Peru, Uruguay and Venezuela.
2. Argentina exempted 394 tariff lines (18.6 per cent of total exemptions), Brazil 324 (15.3 per cent), Paraguay 960 (45.3 per cent) and Uruguay 439 (20.7 per cent).
3. Paraguay and Uruguay had one additional year to remove all exemptions.
4. Until August 1994 Argentina had applied the intra-Mercosur safeguard clause to about 20 products (including certain kinds of paper, tyres, polyethylene, freezers, refrigerators, motocompressors and wood furniture). Between November 1992 and October 1994 anti-dumping duties were levied upon selected textile products, motocompressors and ophthalmological lenses. By year-end 1994 there were anti-dumping investigations underway for certain steel products and electrical materials.
5. The trade intensity index measures the share of country i's exports to country j in i's total exports (Xij/Xi) relative to the share of j's imports in world net imports $(Mj/Mw-Mi)$. An index above (below) unity indicates that the countries have greater (smaller) trade than expected based on the partner's share in world trade. See Primo Braga, Safadi and Yeats (1994).
6. To accommodate domestic inflationary objectives, in late 1994 the Brazilian government was authorized to (until 30 April 1995) reduce tariffs temporarily below the CET for designated imports (in addition to the list of exceptions). In early 1995 the Brazilian government requested to extend this reduction for one year and proposed the adoption of an additional 'list of exception' (see below) with a maximum of 150 products. Similarly, following the Mexican foreign exchange crisis the Argentine government proposed a temporary rise in the common external tariff, which was not accepted by the other Mercosur partners. Although common policies have been clearly under strain after the external shock of late 1994, their resilience remains remarkable.
7. Argentine tariffs will include the statistical import surcharge.
8. Products exempted from the CET include those in the two special sectoral regimes (automobiles and sugar), capital goods, information

technology and telecommunication products, and products included in the national exemption lists. Goods using more than 40 per cent of their FOB value of CET-exempted imported inputs will also have to comply with the rules of origin.

9. The list of NTBs amounts to approximately 200 practices, most of them on the Brazilian side.

10. The most important NTB to be eliminated by Argentina is the statistical import surcharge. Brazil will eliminate the prohibition to import recreational vessels and certain seeds and the prior authorization requirement for petrochemicals, sugar, alcohol, honey and wheat flour. Paraguay and Uruguay will eliminate prohibitions and prior authorisation requirements.

11. Uruguay has small assembly facilities and Paraguay is not a producer.

12. In March 1995, and as a result of the fallout from the Mexican foreign exchange crisis, the Argentine government raised import tariffs on capital goods to 10 per cent, to a large degree closing the gap between the national tariff rate and the CET.

13. The number rises to 399 for Paraguay and the period of convergence extends to the year 2006.

14. The Brazilian government has proposed the implementation of a transitory regime to increase the number of exemptions by 150 tariff items to deal with 'special circumstances'. The mechanism has not been approved yet.

15. The Brazilia Protocol procedures established: (1) direct negotiations between the parties, (2) analysis of the controversy by the CMG (30 days), and (3) an arbitration mechanism. The arbitration mechanism is an *ad hoc* tribunal to solve specific controversies formed by three judges, two designated by each part and the third by agreement.

16. The proposals for constitutional reform introduced in February 1995 include liberalization of the financial services industry.

17. This section draws on four national case studies of Mercosur trade relations with the United States. See Barboza, Bouzas and Tussie (1994), da Motta Veiga (1994), Rodriguez Gigena (1994) and Borda and Masi (1994).

18. Bianchi and Robbio (1994) estimate a US$10 million loss in the US market.

19. For an analysis of this ambiguity and the contrasting conclusions with conventional trade analysis, see Bouzas and Ros (1994).

20. Furthermore, prevailing attitudes towards trade policy may be more rhetoric than substance. Brazil, the allegedly most protectionist country, has carried forward its liberalization process with no postponements or interruptions until late 1994. Argentina, in contrast, was forced to implement a number of NTBs as of 1993. Contrary to hearsay, by 1994 the Brazilian average tariff rate was lower than that of Argentina (including the statistical import surcharge).

21. In 1992, 69 per cent and 59 per cent of Chilean exports to Argentina and Brazil, respectively, received preferential treatment. This compares favourably with the 41 per cent and 28 per cent of Mercosur exports to Chile.

3 THE G3 AND THE ROAD TO CONTINENTAL INTEGRATION

1. The number of state enterprises in Mexico declined from more than 1000 in 1982 to 269 by the middle of 1991, and privatization was concentrated on the following sectors: telecommunications, airlines, steel production, transport equipment, chemicals and fertilizers, mining and sugar (see Lustig, 1992: 104–7). The ambitious privatization programme proposed at the start of the Pérez government lost momentum in Venezuela during 1992 (see Naim, 1993: 53). The scope and significance of state firms is substantially less in Colombia and attempts at privatization ended after a confrontation between the government and the unions in the telecommunications sector.

2. The total volume of exports grew in Mexico by 5.5 per cent a year between 1987 and 1992, and by 8.7 per cent between 1991 and 1993; and by 12.6 per cent and 6.5 per cent in Colombia and Venezuela (respectively) in the latter period (Edwards, 1994: table 7).

3. In 1991 non-traditional exports represented 64 per cent 50 per cent and 17 per cent respectively of total exports in Colombia, Mexico and Venezuela. The share of manufacturing exports was 33 per cent, 44 per cent and 11 per cent in each country (Edwards, 1994: Tables 8 and 9).

4. Intra-industry trade affords significant gains for trading countries, without significant (negative) effects on income distribution; adjustment costs are therefore secondary. See Helpman and Krugman (1985).

5. In 1992 Mexico exported US$174 million to Colombia and US$278 million to Venezuela, and imported even smaller amounts from the two countries (US$71 million from Colombia and US$193 million from Venezuela).

6. There are significant trading relations between Venezuela and Colombia, but these continue to be largely governed by Andean Pact legislation.

7. If each country's sectoral exports to the G3 and worldwide are ranked in order of importance, the following rank correlation coefficients are obtained:

Exports	Colombia–World	Mexico–World	Venezuela–World
Colombia–G3	0.62		
Colombia–Mexico	0.31		
Colombia–Venezuela	0.67		
Mexico–G3		0.55	
Venezuela–G3			0.93

In other words, for both Colombia and (to a lesser extent) Mexico, the structure of exports is entirely different according to whether these are directed to the G3 or to the rest of the world. On the significance of intra-industry trade in the G3 in relation to neighbouring countries, see Pombo (1994).

8. Colombia has advantage in a given chapter-sector (s) when the share of exports from (s) in total exports is greater than in the other country. The index so constructed takes values between 0.25 (maximum comparative advantage for the other country) and 4 (maximum comparative advantage for Colombia).

    For each country (p) and sector (s) the share of net exports (x−m) to the world in the sum of x and m was determined by:

    $$VC'_p = \frac{[x-m]s}{[x+m]s}$$

    The index varies between −1 (high imports in relation to exports) and 1 (high exports).

    Afterwards, for each sector (s) the VCR (an index of 'relative comparative advantage') was calculated between Colombia and Mexico, Colombia and Venezuela, and Colombia and Chile. This was scaled to take values between 0.25 (maximum comparative advantage for the other country) and 4 (maximum comparative advantage for Colombia). In the case of Colombia–Mexico, the index was constructed in the following way:

    $$VCR_{col-mex} = \frac{2^{[VCcol^{+1}]}}{2^{[VCmex^{+1}]}}$$

9. In 8 of the 15 chapters in which Colombia has a comparative advantage with respect to Mexico, it also has advantages with respect to Venezuela and Chile (Chapters 17, 42, 46, 58, 61, 62, 63 and 97). In addition, in two of the chapters where it has an advantage with respect to Mexico (11, 49 and 59), it also has advantage over either Venezuela or Chile.

10. Nominal tariffs in Colombia, Venezuela and Mexico stood at 83 per cent 30 per cent and 34 per cent (on average, respectively) in 1985, and 200 per cent, 135 per cent and 100 per cent (maximum) In 1991/2, the figures were 11.6 per cent 11.7 per cent and 13.4 per cent (average) and 40 per cent, 35 per cent and 25 per cent (maximum) (Edwards, 1994: Table 2).

11. Thus while the maximum in the first two countries is 35 per cent (the automobile sector in the machinery and equipment chapter), in Mexico this amounts to 20 per cent in 13 of the 18 subsectors considered. In addition, the coefficient of variation shows that the Mexican tariff has less variance in the majority of sectors, except for agriculture (sector 11), mining (23 and 29) and food, beverages and tobacco (31).

12. The system was adopted following the example of stabilization bands used in Chile for a minimal set of products. It was originally designed for eight basic products in the agricultural sector (wheat, barley, rice, sorghum, beans, soya and maize, milk and sugar) and it was later extended to more than 100 substitute and derivative products. The methodology used to set the bands has varied, but finally a common methodology has been accepted within the Andean Pact. The price bands or zones are fixed on the basis of the monthly averages in international prices over the past 5 years, thereby producing periods of significant protection.

13. The Constitution provides that the Departments of Colombia can create taxes on liquor from other regions of the country and therefore also on imported liquor.

14. Some writers (e.g. Finger, 1995) would strongly criticize this 'conciliatory' position, arguing that even the GATT safeguards in the end amount to a set of restrictive practices in disguise.
15. Originally designed to offset the 'errors' which might have been made in the negotiations at the item tariff level. The mechanism lost some of its purpose when the generalized liberalization over a ten-year period was agreed, but the bilateral safeguard remained in the G3.
16. This safeguard has been requested on 34 occasions in the history of the Andean Pact, with approval being granted on 18 of them. Colombia is the country that has made the most requests (24, with approval on 12).
17. Strictly speaking, since we are talking about trade diversion, the importance of the hemisphere as the origin of each country's imports should be considered. Nevertheless, Fritsch (1992: 39) finds that exports and imports are more or less in balance, and there is a high positive correlation when the hemispheric share of each country's imports and exports are examined.

4 TRADE STRATEGY ALTERNATIVES FOR A SMALL COUNTRY: THE CHILEAN CASE

1. Cars over 850 cc were the only exception. For a detailed description of the Chilean foreign trade prevailing prior to 1974, see Behrman (1976) and World Bank (1979).
2. In addition, countervailing duties were imposed during 1982 to face what were considered to be dumping prices of some import goods; these duties covered 6 per cent of total imports. The surcharge plus the tariff had a 35 per cent ceiling. Furthermore, three important agricultural goods (wheat, sugar and oil) have had, from 1984 on, a compensatory mechanism to face external price instability. See Ffrench-Davis and Vial (1990) for further details.
3. In the first unilateral liberalization process, nominal tariffs were reduced from 22 per cent (1977) to 10 per cent (1979) in less than two years.
4. For a more extensive discussion of this subject see Campero and Escobar (1992).
5. There is a correspondence between industrial goods included in PNR and NR; PNR are those NR goods exported by Chile where there has been domestic value added. The NR selected are copper, fruit and vegetables, cattle, fish and forestry.
6. The sum of the three categories (NR + PNR + OIP) represents around 95 per cent of total exports.
7. The negative impact of economic instability on real investment and economic growth may be the result of the existence of 'irreversibility' and/or costs to reallocate productive resources; see, for example, Pindyck (1991) and Krugman (1987).
8. In fact, the effective real exchange rate appreciated by an accumulated 19.4 per cent between 1988 and 1993, more than offsetting productivity gains.

9. In fact, real wages have risen by 26 per cent during 1987–93.
10. This trend has also been observed in Latin America. However, in sharp contrast to the integration efforts seen in the region during the 1950s and 1960s, which had an import substitution motivation, the agreements currently being signed are motivated by the need to promote trade and, in particular, to encourage exports.
11. For further details, see De Melo and Panagariyan (1993).
12. Nevertheless, since US import tariffs for natural resources are very low, and Canada and Mexico will be granted tariff preferences for manufactures by the United States; Chile may improve its competitive position in natural resources in the US market, as Canada and Mexico reallocate production factors toward manufactured exports, thereby reinforcing Chile's actual export structure. Also, as a result of Canada and Mexico joining NAFTA and of Chile's bilateral trade agreement with Mexico, Chile could end up increasing its exports to these two markets.
13. Transportation costs – or inter-regional trade barriers – can provide an important rationale for regional or 'natural' trading blocs, among geographically close countries (Krugman, 1991a). An example is the EU, where the ratio of intra-bloc to extra-bloc trade has risen from 90 per cent in 1965 to 140 per cent in 1988. Location advantage is not the same for all goods and may be of first order for some of them. For example, Leamer (1994) has estimated a location advantage for Central America over Asia in clothing of 4.1:1 in the US market and of 11.2:1 in Mexico.
14. For further details, see Labán (1994).
15. With a GDP (population) around US$800 billion (190 million inhabitants).
16. Argentina and Brazil are, respectively, Chile's third and fourth most important trade partners.
17. During 1993 more than a 41 per cent of Chile's total manufactured exports were shipped to this market.
18. Which implies that Chile will open its economy to Mercosur but will increase its protection with respect to the rest of the world, therefore, it will distort its domestic relative price structure.
19. A restriction that could hurt other objectives in Chile's trade agenda and, in particular, its possibility of joining NAFTA.
20. Nevertheless, it is difficult to imagine Chile achieving better access conditions than those obtained by Canada and Mexico.

5 THE IMPORTANCE OF BORDER TRADE: THE CASE OF BOLIVIA

1. 'Natural' trading partners are countries that would have done much of their trading with one another, even in the absence of special arrangements. The concept appears in Krugman (1993).
2. For a recent and comprehensive survey, see Agosín and Ffrench-Davis (1993).
3. A similar argument is given by Jones (1993). See also de Melo et al. (1993), who observe that the current regionalism is taking place in an environment of outward-oriented policies.

4. The data in Table 5.2, based on Central Bank statistics, do not coincide with the IMF figures reported in Table 5.4. In the latter case, there would be a small surplus in the bilateral trade with Argentina.
5. de Melo et al. (1993) highlight these points when discussing the political dimensions of regional integration arrangements.
6. It is true that the Second Region, in which Antofagasta is situated, has borders with Potosí and Oruro, the poorest departments in Bolivia. If a similar survey were taken in the First Region, more to the north and close to La Paz, the results might be different.
7. For example, there is little doubt that the current favourable trade environment with Chile has provided an incentive to build the highway from La Paz to the Chilean border.
8. This may be so because income from enlarged trade would ensure repayment of the loan.
9. In general, maquiladoras produce a relatively processed product, with intensive use of labour. They are attracted to a given location if they find the following advantages:

   (a) Significant savings in labour costs.
   (b) Low transportation and communication costs with the parent firm's central location.
   (c) The possibility of using qualified management and technical personnel without expatriation.
   (d) Short downtime for repair and new product lines.
   (e) Control over day-to-day operations.

   Except for labour costs, none of the advantages listed above can be found in the Bolivian border towns.
10. Hubbing is frequent in the market for air traffic. Economic theory and empirical evidence shows that hubbing reduces airline total costs and also confers market power on the airline in the hub.
11. For example, if instead of making round trips from Arica to la Paz, warehouses in Tambo Quemado (on the Chilean border) were built, then high tonnage hauliers could go from Arica to Tambo Quemado and then distribute their cargo in smaller trucks to the cities in western Bolivia. Also, high tonnage hauliers could go from Bolivia to Tambo Quemado and distribute their cargo in the northern Chilean cities with smaller trucks. The transportation mode would depend very much on merchandise. In both cases there would be gains in efficiency.
12. The most important market in the region by far is Brazil. There are only a few remaining obstacles to the construction of a gas pipeline from Santa Cruz in Bolivia to São Paulo in Brazil. The pipeline will carry Bolivian gas as well as gas from Peru and, possibly, Argentina.
13. There could be deindustrialization on aggregate. Obviously, this does not imply that all industries would decline. In fact, some particular industries may greatly benefit from the lowering of transportation costs and from the tariff preferences. To cite a current example, exports to the United States of some branches of the clothing industry have become profitable thanks to a fall in the relative price of airfreight and the tariff reductions

in that market. As another example, exports of plugs and sockets to
Argentina, transported by air, have grown very rapidly.

14. This is the prediction, in a global context, of the Krugman and Venables
    (1994) model.
15. A reduction in the pace of infrastructure building would be even more
    far-fetched.

6   A SMALL COUNTRY PERSPECTIVE ON MERCOSUR: THE CASE OF PARAGUAY

1. Banco Central del Paraguay (1994).
2. Figures from the 1992 census as contained in Secretaría Técnica de
   Planificación (1994).
3. This issue is of considerable importance to the integration process and
   will be discussed below.
4. For a description of the Paraguayan economy in the 1970s and in the 1980s,
   see Baer and Birch (1984) and Baer and Breuer (1986), respectively.
5. Official statistics do not reflect the total amount of trade. Thus, these
   figures have to be interpreted with care.
6. Europe is defined as consisting of Germany, Spain, France, United
   Kingdom, Italy and Switzerland.
7. This coincided roughly with the period of import substitution industrialization in the region.
8. Banco Central del Paraguay (1993).
9. The literature on this issue is extensive. For a general view of these
   arguments, refer to Cardenas (1992), Nogues and Quintanilla (1992),
   Foroutan (1992), Lustig and Braga (1994) and Baldwin (1993).
10. While the Stroessner regime did not vigorously pursue the import-sub-
    stitution industrialization policies of other Latin American countries, the
    role of the state in the economy was extensive and actually expanded
    considerably during the 1980s. For a discussion of this period, see Baer
    and Breuer (1986) and Herken (1986).
11. For an interesting survey of opinions of the Paraguayan elites on
    Mercosur, see Achard et al. (1993).
12. A less optimistic view could make the analogy with East Germany.
13. The lack of reliable trade statistics, including that related to the entrepôt
    trade, are a serious constraint to estimating trade creation and diversion.
    Under certain assumptions regarding the level of the common external
    tariff and elasticities of substition, Benegas (1993) found a small net welfare
    loss for Paraguay. This is clearly an area that merits further research.

7   NAFTA: POLICY- OR INVESTMENT-LED?

*   This chapter reflects research and writing on the North American Free
    Trade Agreement (NAFTA) and the North American auto industry done

with my colleague Lorraine Eden and on my own over the last three years. The research support of the Social Sciences and Humanities Research Council of Canada is gratefully acknowledged as is the research assistance of Colin Stacey and Michael Roach. Patricio Meller, Javier Iguíñiz, Joaquín Vial, Richard Lipsey and Lorraine Eden all made very useful comments on the first draft.

1. Elsewhere these economic ties have been described as a hub-and-spoke relationship; the United States acts as the 'hub' for two 'spokes' – Canada and Mexico. Each of the spokes is intensely economically dependent on the hub and has a minimal economic relationship with the other. See Eden and Molot (1992a, 1992b). Richard Lipsey and Ronald Wonnacott use the phrase 'hub- and-spoke' to describe an arrangement under which one country (the hub) has a series of bilateral free trade agreements with a number of partners (the spokes). By definition, the spokes have no agreements with each other (Lipsey et al.: 1994: 22).

2. In sectors liberalized by the FTA, Canadian merchandise exports to the United States increased 33 per cent in value between 1988 and 1992, compared to a 2 per cent increase in exports to the rest of the world (Schwanen, 1993: 6).

3. Figures cited in Business Council for National Issues (1994: 5).

4. Figures on Canada–Mexico trade are from FOCAL (1994: 15). There was a 29 per cent increase in Mexican imports from Canada in 1992–3 compared with the previous year, when Mexican imports rose only 6 per cent in contrast to a 37.4 per cent increase in Mexican exports to Canada.

5. Canada, for example, replaced a screening agency, the Foreign Investment Review Agency (FIRA) with one with a mandate to seek investment (Investment Canada), and terminated the National Energy Programme. For a discussion of Canadian and Mexican as well as US policies on inward FDI, see Kudrle (1994). FDI in both Canada and Mexico historically has been a very sensitive topic. For recent changes in Mexican policy, see Unger (1994).

6. Mexico joined the GATT in 1986.

7. Critical though the subject of MNEs is to the analysis, space constraints do not permit consideration of the globalization of production. See Eden (1991; 1993).

8. Statistics calculated from US International Trade Administration, *National Trade Data Bank* and Statistics Canada, *Exports by Country and Imports by Country*, various years. See also Encarnation (1994).

9. Certain requirements had to be met for vehicles to move duty-free between the two countries. For details see Johnson (1993) and Eden and Molot (1993).

10. For some of Prime Minister Mulroney's very critical statements on free trade between Canada and the US, see Clarkson (1991: 123).

11. In addition to sectoral free trade in autos and parts under the Auto Pact, Canada also had a bilateral sectoral agreement with the United States in defence production.

12. Interview, Ottawa, March 1995. Canadian subsidiaries of US MNEs were strong supporters of Canadian tariff protection until the Tokyo

Round tariff reductions altered the basis of the organization of production between Canada and the US.

13. Interview, Ottawa, March 1995.

14. Canadian Manufacturers Association (CMA), the organization representing smaller Canadian-owned companies.

15. Wonnacott (1990) has discussed this in terms of 'hub-and-spoke' arrangements.

16. In fact, Canadian and Mexican producers are not major competitors in the US market. See Eden and Molot (1992a).

17. Morici (1990: 25) quotes then US Treasury Secretary, James Baker, as saying: 'This agreement [the FTA] is also a lever to achieve more open trade. Other nations are forced to recognize that the US will devise ways to expand trade – with or without them . . .'

18. At one of the early hearings on fast-track authority, Clayton Yeutter of USTR told the US Senate Finance Committee that his objective in the negotiations was to secure 'a Canadian policy environment as open to inflows of direct foreign investment as our own' (Kudrle, 1994: 411).

19. Part of this paragraph is based on Doern and Tomlin (1991: 105–6).

20. There were two motions before the Senate Finance Committee which, if successful, would have prevented or delayed the authorization of fast-track authority. Both were defeated on a 10:10 vote, which meant that fast-track authority was granted. For details on Senate opposition and the pressures the administration brought to bear, see Hart (1994: 142–51).

21. For details see Hart (1990: 63).

22. For a discussion of the demands of the auto industry and the auto provisions of the NAFTA, see Eden and Molot (1993).

23. For a discussion of labour opposition, see Wiarda (1994: 124–6).

24. For details on the maquiladora programme, see Weintraub (1990: ch. 8) and Kopinek (1993).

25. Pastor uses a similar argument, suggesting 'few observers believed that the insulated inner circle negotiating on behalf of Mexico was open to critical research on NAFTA' (1994: 160). See also Hellman (1993).

26. Gestrin and Rugman suggest that MNEs in some industries might oppose NAFTA expansion because enlargement could diminish the protectionist impact of the NAFTA rules of origin (1994: 585).

8 SOCIAL ISSUES AND LABOUR ADJUSTMENT POLICIES: THE CANADA–US FTA EXPERIENCE

1. 'As the global economy becomes more integrated, we thus need to move beyond the traditional issues covered by the GATT, and begin to negotiate the kinds of issues that now stand in the way of further economic growth and development. Most of these have traditionally been considered part of domestic policy, but are now properly regarded as important influences on trade and investment decisions. Issues arising from regulatory regimes (e.g. standards and environmental protection), structural policies (e.g. competition policy) and social policy (e.g. un-

employment insurance and labour legislation) are thus matters for potential negotiation' (Hart, 1994: 25–6). Establishing rules in these new areas, he argues, is necessary if countries are to move from 'shallow integration' to 'deep integration'.

2. All figures are in Canadian dollars unless otherwise specified.

9 TRADE DISPUTES AND SETTLEMENT MECHANISMS UNDER THE CANADA-US FTA

1. The author wishes to acknowledge the assistance of Welming Wang in the research for this chapter.

2. The parties to the FTA are the Government of Canada and the Government of the United States of America.

3. For details of the settlement, see Dearden and Palmeter (February 1990), *The Free Trade Observer*, 54 (Toronto: CCH).

4. The parties also established a working group to develop a substitute system of rules for dealing with unfair pricing (e.g. anti-dumping) and government subsidization (article 1907). This working group conducted a fair amount of preparatory work but never issued a report before it was disbanded and overtaken by the negotiation of the NAFTA.

As part of the federal Liberal Party government's agreement to implement the North American Free Trade Agreement (which was negotiated by the federal Conservative Party government), the NAFTA Parties agreed to continue the work begun under Article 1907 of the FTA to establish an effective subsidy and anti-dumping code. Two working groups have been mandated to resolve these problems by 31 December 1995. The statement issued by the NAFTA parties on 'Future Work On Anti-dumping Duties, Subsidies and Countervail' follows:

Appendix D
Statement isued by the NAFTA Parties on
'Future Work on Anti-dumping Duties, Subsidies and Countervail'

STATEMENT BY THE GOVERNMENTS OF
CANADA, MEXICO AND THE UNITED STATES

FUTURE WORK ON ANTI-DUMPING DUTIES,
SUBSIDIES AND COUNTERVAIL

The Governments of Canada, Mexico and the United States, to further their strong and mutually beneficial trading relationship, have agreed to seek solutions that reduce the possibility of disputes concerning the issues of subsidies, dumping and the operation of trade remedy laws regarding such practices.

The three Governments note that these issues are under negotiation in the Uruguay Round and that a satisfactory result in those negotiations would be an important step in addressing their concerns in this area.

Each Government intends to make the successful completion of the Uruguay Round of Multilateral Trade Negotiations in the coming weeks a top priority.

In addition, the three Governments will establish a trilateral working group on subsidies and countervailing duties and another working group on dumping and anti-dumping duties. These groups will build as appropriate on the results of the Uruguay Round and on experience in regard to these issues.

The working groups will continue efforts begun in 1989 by a working group convened under article 1907 of the US–Canada Free Trade Agreement and will be instructed to complete their work by 31 December 1995.

5. The rights available to a party with respect to 'amendments' were narrow in that they are limited to amendments of a 'statute'. Regulations and administrative practice were not affected. In addition, the amendment had to state specifically that it applied to the goods of the other party. If the amendment did not expressly state that it applied to the goods of the other party, the amendment did not apply.

6. 'Proposed actions' were not subject to binding arbitration.

7. The NAFTA also contains bilateral and global safeguard tracks. Under article 801, if there is a surge in imports causing 'serious injury' or a 'threat of serious injury' to domestic producers, the injured country may take temporary emergency action. The NAFTA threshold is less than the FTA since it allows action to be taken against Mexican goods on the basis of a threat-of-injury finding. Under the FTA, safeguard action is allowed against US goods in cases of actual injury. 'Serious injury' is defined as being a significant overall impairment of a domestic industry, while 'threat of serious injury' means serious injury that, on the basis of facts and not merely an allegation, conjecture or remote possibility, is clearly imminent. Importantly, the bilateral provisions of FTA Article 1101 still apply to trade between Canada and the US, so Article 801 will be applicable only to trade to Canadian–Mexican or American–Mexican trade.

Article 802 specifies the criteria that must be met if a global action is to be extended to a NAFTA member. Under the NAFTA global track, a party's goods shall not be included in another party's global safeguard actions unless two conditions are met:

1. the imports from that party must account for a 'substantial share' of total imports; and

2. the imports must 'contribute importantly' to the serious injury or threat of serious injury to the domestic industry.

The NAFTA defines a 'substantial share' as being among the top five suppliers of a good under investigation during the most recent three-year period. The expression 'contribute importantly' is defined as being an important cause but not necessarily being the most important cause of the injury. NAFTA article 803 replaces FTA article 1102 for trade between Canada and the United States.

On 14 September 1993, the NAFTA parties agreed to a trilateral Understanding Concerning Emergency Action. This agreement provides for a consultative process regarding safeguard actions and for the creation of a Working Group on Emergency Actions. These consultations may constitute the consultations required by the NAFTA if the parties agree.

8. Articles 2004 and 2008.
9. Article 1903.

10 TRADE AND INVESTMENT BETWEEN CANADA AND LAIA COUNTRIES

* The author is grateful to Ximena Clark for her efficient research assistance.
1. These are the eleven members of the Latin American Integration Association (LAIA): Argentina, Bolivia, Brazil, Chile, Colombia, Ecuador, Mexico, Paraguay, Peru, Uruguay and Venezuela.
2. We use the IMF's *Direction of Trade Statistics* definition of the Western Hemisphere; that is, all the countries of the Americas except Canada, Cuba and the United States.
3. The data are taken from the IMF's *Direction of Trade Statistics Yearbook* (1993 and 1994) and are in nominal US dollars.
4. The figures in this section differ from those presented in the previous one for a number of reasons: there are discrepancies in trade data reporting by individual countries, methods of registering exports and imports, and FOB/CIF differences. As noted in Table 10.3, in 1993 the trade data of a Latin American country may have been taken from Canadian records rather than their own in the IMF's *Direction of Trade Statistics* yearbooks. As a result the figures show a very large increase in exports and may not be comparable to those of 1986 and 1990.
5. The trade data were obtained from Statistics Canada. The tables with the detailed information can be found in Saez (1995).
6. In all cases we consider as capital goods parts for such type of goods.
7. See CEPAL (1993).

11 NAFTA AS A MUTUALLY BENEFICIAL AGREEMENT: Commentary by Richard G. Lipsey

1. I have discussed the issue of the difference between the modest gains usually measured by empirical workers using standard trade theory and the perception that over the long haul trade liberalization agreements such as the European Community are generally agreed to have brought major gains, in 'Unsettled Issues in the Great Free Trade Debate', *Canadian Journal of Economics*, February 1989, Vol. 22, No. 1, 1–21.
2. I have outlined this new model in detail in the UN publication 'Globalization and Developing Countries: Investment, Trade and Technology

Linkages in the 1990s', a report prepared for *The United Nations Symposium in The Hague*, 30 March 1992.

3. I have made this point myself in two publications: once with respect to the Canada–US FTA in R.G. Lipsey and R.C. York, *Evaluating the Free Trade Deal: A Guided Tour Through The Canada–US Agreement* (Toronto: C.D. Howe Institute, 1988), p. 113; and once with respect to NAFTA in R.G. Lipsey, D. Schwanen and R.J. Wonnacott, in 'Inside or Outside the NAFTA? The Consequences of Canada's Choice', Commentary No. 48 (Toronto: C.D. Howe Institute, June 1993).

4. For a very explicit statement of this, see Eaton, Lipsey and Safarian, 'The Theory of Multinational Plant Location in a Regional Trading Area', in *Multinationals in North America*, L. Eden, ed. (Calgary: The University of Calgary Press, 1994), 53–78.

5. I have discussed this matter in several places, such as 'The Case for Trilateralism', in *Continental Accord: North American Economic Integration 1991 (Canada–Mexico–US Free Trade)*, Steven Globerman, ed. (Vancouver: The Fraser Institute, 1991), 89–123, and 'Getting There: The Path to a Western Hemisphere Free Trade Area and its Structure', in *The Premise and the Promise: Free Trade in the Americas*, Sylvia Saborio, ed. (New Brunswick: Transaction Publishers, Rutgers State University, 1992), 95–116.

6. The first time I discussed this issue was in a pamphlet designed to influence the Canadian decision: 'Canada at the US–Mexican Free Trade Dance: Wallflower or Partner?', *Commentary No. 20* (Toronto: C.D. Howe Institute, August 1990). I have elaborated the point in several other places such as the two articles referred to in the previous footnote.

7. See e.g. R.J. Wonnacott, *US Hub-and-Spoke Bilaterals and the Multilateral Trading System*, Commentary No. 43 (Toronto: C.D. Howe Institute, 1990).

8. A number of surveys taken at the time told how large, medium and small-sized firms regarded the possibility of a US–Canada FTA.

9 These reasons are analysed in detail in R.G. Lipsey and M.G. Smith, *Taking the Initiative: Canada's Trade Options in a Turbulent World* (Toronto: C.D. Howe Institute, 1985), Chapter 4. In that book one of our options was a rather convoluted plan which was well short of full free trade. We included this 'functional approach' (pp. 73–5) because it was the official recommendation of the BCNI (the organization representing the largest Canadian firms, most of them multinationals) at the time of our going to press. Later in that year, the BCNI finally came out for free trade, rather later than some other business organizations.

10. The list in the text is an abbreviation of the list in Lipsey and York, *Evaluating the Free Trade Deal*. I have selected those items that have transferred to the NAFTA and that are of general interest to members other than the US and Canada.

11. For detailed discussion see Lipsey and York (1988: 51–61) and Lipsey, Schwannen and Wonnacott (1994: 62–4).

12. One can see how a very complex agreement is usually misstated for purposes of argument. There is no obligation to deliver resources to the other country. All the country declaring the emergency must do is *to make available on the market where anyone can buy it at whatever prices rule*, a

proportion of the total available supply equal to the proportion of the supply consumed by the partner country under normal conditions.

13. While agreeing with Wilkinson about US behaviour on many issues, I cannot help but observe that if my country had to be located alongside one of the giant countries, I would prefer it to be the United States than the former Soviet Union or some future developed China.

14. For a typical example of the many compassionate attempts by concerned economists to understand and deal with the social and economic problems created by these deep structural adjustments, see C. Freeman and L. Soete, *Work for All or Mass Unemployment*, (London: Pinter, 1994), and many of the articles and books cited therein.

12 NAFTA IN THE WORLD ECONOMY:
A Reply to Richard G. Lipsey by Bruce W. Wilkinson

1. Roy MacLaren, Minister of International Trade made the Canadian position clear when he said, 'This government supported the NAFTA on the explicit understanding that the existing three partners would work together to clarify the continuing and vexing question of what constitutes a subsidy, of how dumping should be dealt with in a free trade area, and how the dispute settlement procedure might thereby be rendered more prompt and effective – all issues which left unresolved, will prevent each country from realizing the benefits of a single, integrated North American market' (1994: 4–5).

2. Caldwell (1993) has this to say: 'It has become evident, over the course of researching this paper, that Canada may have much to gain from seeking improved access to publicly supported technology consortia in other countries. As a relatively small, advanced economy which contributes modestly to the industrial world's technology, we can ill afford to pursue an isolated approach to technology acquisition. Increasingly, we are seeing the "visible" hand of government in technology creation activities, not just during the early stages of basic scientific research but also at the prototype and field testing stages of development. If our major trading partners continue to restrict access to their public R&D programs, Canadian firms will be disadvantaged' (p. 2).

3. In his recent volume, co-authored with Wonnacott and Schwanen (1994) the possible costs for Canada of the United States negotiating a separate deal with Mexico, without Canadian participation, are set forth (pp. 22–3). But there is not even mention of the possibility that Canada might have made a separate agreement with Mexico which could have eliminated these disadvantages, and perhaps avoided giving up some of the things it did as a price of being a party to NAFTA.

References

Achard, Diego et al. (1993), *Estudio de la variable política en el proceso de integración regional de los países pequeños del MERCOSUR y análisis de las opiniones de sus élites sobre dicho acuerdo*, Buenos Aires: Banco Interamericano de Desarrollo/Instituto para la Integración de América Latina.

Agosin, M. R. and R. Ffrench-Davis (1993), 'Trade Liberalization in Latin America', *CEPAL Review*, 50, August.

Aguilar Zinser, Adolfo (1993), 'Authoritarianism and North American Free Trade: The Debate in Mexico', in Ricardo Grinspun and Maxwell Cameron, eds., *The Political Economy of North American Free Trade*, New York: St Martin's Press.

Aho, C. Michael and Sylvia Ostry (1990), 'Regional Trading Blocs: Pragmatic or Problematic Policy?' in William E. Brock and Robert D. Hormats, eds., *The Global Economy: America's Role in the Decade Ahead*, New York: W. W. Norton & Company.

Aitken, Hugh G. J. (1961), *American Capital and Canadian Resources*, Cambridge, MA: Harvard University Press.

Anderson, Sarah (1994), 'The White House and NAFTA: Promises Kept and Promises Broken', *Naftathoughts*, December.

Asher, Isaacs (1948), *International Trade: Tariff and Commercial Policies*, Chicago: Irwin.

Baer, Werner and Melissa Birch (1984), 'Expansion of the Economic Frontier: Paraguayan Growth in the 1970s', *World Development*, Vol. 12, No. 8, August, 783–98.

Baer, Werner and Luis E. Breuer (1986), 'From Inward to Outward Oriented Growth: Paraguay in the 1980s', *Journal of Interamerican Studies and World Affairs*, Vol. 28, No. 3, Fall, 125–49.

Baldwin, Richard (1993), 'A Domino Theory of Regionalism', Discussion Paper No. 857, London: Centre for Economic Policy Research.

Banco Central Del Paraguay (1993), *Memoria Anual 1993*, Asunción: Banco Central del Paraguay.

Banco Central Del Paraguay (1994), *Boletín Estadístico*, Asunción: Banco Central del Paraguay, January.

Barboza, J. C., R. Bouzas and D. Tussie (1994), 'Las Relaciones Comerciales Estados Unidos-Mercosur: la Agenda Minilateral. El caso de Argentina', *Documentos de Investigación*, No. 166, Buenos Aires: FLACSO.

Behrman, J. (1976), *Foreign Trade Regimes & Economic Development: Chile*, NBER, Columbia University Press.

Benegas, C. Gladys (1993), *MERCOSUR. A la búsqueda de un mercado común*, Asunción: Universidad Católica Nuestra Señora de la Asunción.

Benoit, G. (1994) Presentation to the Special Joint Committee of the Senate and the House of Commons Reviewing Canadian Foreign Policy on Behalf of the Canadian Dehydrators Association, 3 June, 126–36.

Bergsten, C. Fred (1994), 'New Rules for International Investment', in *Multinationals in North America*, ed. Lorraine Eden, Calgary: University of Calgary Press, 391–401.

Bernard, Elaine (1994), 'What's Wrong with NAFTA', *New Politics* (Winter), 80–90.

Berry, Albert and Frances Stewart (forthcoming), 'Market Liberalisation and Income Distribution: The Experience of the 1980s', in Berry et al.

Bianchi, E. and J. Robbio (1994), 'Tratado de Libre Comercio de América del Norte: Desvío de Comercio en Perjuicio de Argentina y Brasil', Buenos Aires: CEI, mimeo.

Borda, D. and F. Masi (1994), 'Las Relaciones Comerciales Estados Unidos-Mercosur: la Agenda Minilateral. El caso de Paraguay', *Documentos e Informes de Investigación*, No. 167, Buenos Aires: FLACSO.

Bouzas, R. (1992), 'US–Mercosur Free Trade', in S. Saborio and contributors, *The Premise and the Promise: Free Trade in the Americas*, New Brunswick: Transaction Books.

Bouzas, R. (1994), 'Las Relaciones Comerciales Mercosur–Estados Unidos: Elementos para una Agenda Minilateral', *Serie Documentos de Trabajo* No. 4, Buenos Aires: ISEN.

Bouzas, R. and N. Lustig (1992), *Liberalización Comercial e Integración Regional. De Nafta a Mercosur*, Buenos Aires: FLACSO.

Bouzas, R. and J. Ros (1994), 'The North–South Variety of Economic Integration: Issues and Prospects for Latin America', in R. Bouzas and J. Ros, eds., *Economic Integration in the Western Hemisphere*, South Bend, Ind: Notre Dame University Press.

Brown, D. K. (1992), 'An Overview of a North American Free Trade Agreement', in *A North American Free Trade Area*, ed., W. G. Watson, Kingston, Ontario: John Deutsch Institute for the Study of Economic Policy.

Busch, Marc L. and Helen V. Milner (1994), 'The Future of the International Trading System: International Firms, Regionalism, and Domestic Politics', in Richard Stubbs and Geoffrey R. D. Underhill, eds., *Political Economy and the Changing Global Order*, Toronto: McClelland and Stewart.

Business Council on National Issues (1984), *The Canada–US Trading Relationship and the Idea of a Trade Enhancement Agreement: A Policy Proposal*, Ottawa, September.

Business Council on National Issues (1994), 'Canadian Foreign Policy: Principles and Priorities', brief submitted to the Special Joint Committee on Canadian Foreign Policy, Ottawa.

Butelmann, A. and P. Meller, eds. (1992), *Estrategia Comercial Chilena para la Década del 90. Elementos para el Debate*, Santiago: Ediciones CIEPLAN.

Caldwell, Rhoda (1993), *Technology Consortia: A Prisoner's Dilemma*, Ottawa: Government of Canada, External Affairs and International Trade Canada, Economic and Trade Policy Group, Policy Staff Paper No. 93/10.

Cameron, Maxwell and Brian Tomlin (1994), 'Canada and Latin America in the Shadow of US Power: Toward an Expanding Hemispheric Agreement?' paper prepared for the International Conference on Economic Integration and Public Policy: NAFTA, the EU, and Beyond, at York University, Toronto, 27–29 May.

Cameron, Maxwell, Lorraine Eden and Maureen Appel Molot (1992), 'North American Free Trade: Co-operation and Conflict in Canada–Mexico

Relations', in Fen Osler Hampson and Christopher Maule, eds., *A New World Order? Canada Among Nations 1992–93*, Ottawa: Carleton University Press.

Campbell, Bruce (1994), 'Trade and Investment Policy under NAFTA: As if Jobs Mattered', *Canadian Foreign Policy*, Vol. 2, No. 1 (Spring), 147–61.

Campero, M. P. and B. Escobar (1992), 'Evolución y Composición de las Exportaciones Chilenas, 1986–1991', in Butelmann and Meller (pp. 113–42).

Cardenas, Emilio (1992), 'The Treaty of Asunción: A Southern Cone Common Market (MERCOSUR) Begins to Take Shape', *World Competition*, Vol. 15, No. 4, June.

CEI (1994), *Comercio Exterior Argentino*, various issues, Buenos Aires.

CEPAL (1990), 'La Cadena de Distribución y la Competitividad de las Exportaciones Latinoamericanas: La Fruta de Chile', Naciones Unidas, Santiago, July.

CEPAL (1992), 'La Exportación de Productos Básicos no Tradicionales de América Latina', Naciones Unidas, Santiago, August.

CEPAL (1993), *Directorio sobre inversión extranjera en América Latina y Caribe: marco legal e información estadística*, Unidad Conjunta CEPAL/UNCTAD sobre Empresas Transnacionales, División de Desarrollo Productivo y Empresarial, Santiago, December.

CEPAL (1994), *Balance Preliminar de la Economía de América Latina y el Caribe*, Santiago de Chile.

CEPAL (1994a), 'El Regionalismo Abierto en América Latina y el Caribe', March (mimeo).

Chudnovsky, D., A. Lopez and F. Porta (1994), 'La nueva inversión extranjera directa en la Argentina. Privatizaciones, mercado interno e integración regional', DT 15, Buenos Aires: CENIT.

Clark, Jeff (1994), 'Chile and the NAFTA', paper prepared for the International Conference on Economic Integration and Public Policy: NAFTA, the EU, and Beyond, at York University, Toronto, 27–29 May.

Clarkson, Stephen (1991), 'Disjunctions: Free Trade and the Paradox of Canadian Development', in Daniel Drache and Meric Gertler, eds., *The New Era of Global Competition: State Policy and Market Power*, Montreal and Kingston: McGill-Queen's University Press.

Comité de Inversiones Extranjeras (1994), *Chile. Inversión Extranjera en Cifras. 1974–1993*, Santiago: Vicepresidencia Ejecutiva.

Corak, Mites and Wendy Pyper (1994), 'The Distribution of UI Benefits and Taxes in Canada', *Canadian Economic Observer*, December.

Courchene, Thomas (1994), *Social Canada in the Millenium. Reform Imperatives and Restructuring Principles*, Social Policy Challenge 4, C.D. Howe Institute.

Da Motta Veiga, P. (1994), 'Relacoes Comerciais Estados Unidos-Mercosur: A Aenda Minilateral. O Caso do Brasil', *Documentos e Informes de Investigación*, No. 165, Buenos Aires: FLACSO.

De Melo, Jaime and Arvind Panagariya (1993), *New Dimensions in Regional Integration*, Centre for Economic Policy Research, Cambridge University Press, November.

De Melo, J., A. Panagariya and D. Rodrik (1993), 'The New Regionalism: A Country Perspective', The World Bank, Country Economics Department, *Working Papers WPS* 1094, February.

Del Castillo V. Gustavo and Gustavo Vega C. (1991), 'Comparative Analysis of the Perspectives of Mexican and Canadian Manufacturing Firms on North American Free Trade', Centre for Trade Policy and Law, The Norman Paterson School of International Affairs, Carleton University and the Faculty of Law, University of Ottawa, Ottawa.

Department of External Affairs (1983), *A Review of Canadian Trade Policy*, Ottawa: Supply and Services Canada.

Doern, G. Bruce and Brian W. Tomlin (1991), *Faith and Fear: The Free Trade Story*, Toronto: Stoddart.

Dornbusch, R. (1990), 'The Case for Bilateralism', in Lawrence R. and C. Shultze, eds., *An American Trade Strategy: Options for the 1990s*, Washington, DC: The Brookings Institution.

Eaton, B. Curtis, R. G. Lipsey and E. Safarian (1994), 'The Theory of Multinational Plant Location in a Regional Trading Area', in *Multinationals in North America*, ed. Lorraine Eden, Calgary: University of Calgary Press, 53–77.

Echavarría, J. (1994), 'Oportunidades y Riesgos de la Integración', in *Debates de Coyuntura* No. 5, pp. 7–29.

Eden, Lorraine, (1991), 'Multinational Responses to Trade and Technology Changes: Implications for Canada', in *Multinational, Technology and Economic Growth*, ed. Donald McFetridge, Industry Canada Research Series Vol. I, Calgary: University of Calgary Press.

Eden, Lorraine, ed. (1994), *Multinationals in North America*, Industry Canada Research Series Vol. III, Calgary: University of Calgary Press.

Eden, Lorraine (1994), 'Multinational Strategies in the Global Economy: Lessons from NAFTA', prepared for presentation at the conference 'Multinational Enterprises and the Global Economy', a seminar honouring John Dunning, Center for International Business Education and Research, College of Business and Management, University of Maryland, 30 September.

Eden, Lorraine and Maureen Appel Molot (1992), *Fortress or Free Market? NAFTA and Its Implications for the Pacific Rim*. Ottawa: Centre for Trade Policy and Law, Occasional Papers in International Trade Law and Policy, No. 25.

Eden, Lorraine and Maureen Appel Molot (1992a), 'Comparative and Competitive Advantage in the North American Trade Bloc', *Canadian Business Economics*, Vol. 1, No. 1, 45–59.

Eden, Lorraine and Maureen Appel Molot (1992b), 'The View from the Spokes: Canada and Mexico Face the United States', in *North America without Borders? Integrating Canada, the United States and Mexico*, ed. Stephen J. Randall et al., Calgary: University of Calgary Press.

Eden, Lorraine and Maureen Appel Molot (1993), 'The NAFTA's Automotive Provisions: The Next Stage of Managed Trade', C.D. Howe Institute, *Commentary*, No. 53, November.

Edwards, A. (1994), 'Trade and Industrial Policy Reform in Latin America', National Bureau of Economic Research, Working Paper No. 4772, June.

Embajada Argentina en Brasil (1994), 'Las Iniciativas Empresariales como Factor Dinámico de la Integración', Argentina–Brasil. Hacia una Nueva Relación en la Construcción de un Espacio Competitivo Común, Embajada Argentina en Brasil, December.

Erzan, R. and A. Yeats (1992), 'Free Trade Agreements with the United States. What's in it for Latin America?', *World Bank Working Papers* No. 827, January.

Fedesarrollo (1994), 'Encuesta a dirigentes gremiales', mimeo.

Ffrench-Davis, R. (1980), 'Liberalización de importaciones: La experiencia Chilena', *Colección Estudios CIEPLAN No. 4 (November), Santiago, 39–78*.

Ffrench-Davis, R. and J. Vial (1990), 'Trade Reforms in Chile: Policy Lessons for the Nineties', paper presented at the World Bank Seminar, *Latin America Facing the Challenges of Adjustment and Growth*, Caracas, July.

Financial Post (1995), 'NAFTA Partners Shelve Speedy Tariff Cuts', 12 April.

Finger, J. M. (1995), 'Legalized Backsliding: Safeguard Provisions in the GATT', Paper presented at the Seminar *The Uruguay Round and the Developing Economies*, World Bank, 26–27 January.

FOCAL (1994), 'Toward a New World Strategy: Canadian Policy in the Americas into the Twenty-first Century', *FOCAL Papers*, No. 1.

Foroutan, Faezeh (1992), 'Regional Integration in Sub-Saharan Africa: Past Experience and Future Prospects', paper presented at the World Bank and CEPR Conference on New Dimensions in Regional Integration, Washington: The World Bank and CEPR, April.

Fritsch, W. (1992), 'Integración económica: ¿Conviene la discriminación comercial?' in Bouzas and Lustig (1992).

Gaston, Noel and Daniel Trefler (1994), 'The Labour Market Consequences of the Canada–US Free Trade Agreement', paper presented at a CIS conference, Toronto: Centre for International Studies.

Geske, Mary B. (1994), 'Demonizing Dissent: The Domestic Political Implications of US Regional Trade Policy'. Paper presented to the International Conference on Economic Integration and Public Policy: NAFTA, the EU and Beyond, York University, Toronto, 27–29 May.

Gestrin, Michael and Alan Rugman (1994), 'Economic Regionalism in Latin America', *International Journal*, Vol. XLIX, No. 3, Summer 1994: 568–87.

Goulart, L., C. A. Arruda and H. V. Brasil (1994), 'A Evolucao da Dinamica de Internacionalizacao', *Revista Brasileira de Comercio Exterior* No. 41, October/December.

Government of Canada. External Affairs and International Trade (1993), *NAFTA: What's It All About*, Ottawa.

Government of Canada. External Affairs and International Trade (1994), *Register of United States Barriers to Trade: 1994*, Ottawa.

Government of Canada (1994a), *Improving Social Security in Canada. A Discussion Paper, Agenda: Jobs and Growth*, Ottawa.

Government of Canada (1994b), *From Unemployment Insurance to Employment Insurance: A Supplementary Paper*, Ottawa.

Grinspun, Ricardo (1993), 'NAFTA and Neoconservative Transformation: The Impact on Canada and Mexico', *Review of Radical Political Economics*, Vol. 25, No. 4 (December), 14–29.

Grinspun, Ricardo and Maxwell Cameron, eds., *The Political Economy of North American Free Trade*, New York: St Martin's Press.

Grinspun, Ricardo and Robert Kreklewich (1994), 'Consolidating Neoliberal Reforms: "Free Trade" as a Conditioning Framework', forthcoming in *Studies in Political Economy*.

Grossman, G. and E. Helpman (1992), *Innovation and Growth in the Global Economy*, Cambridge, MA: MIT Press.

Gunderson, Morley (1993), *Wage and Employment Impacts Related to the North American Free Trade Agreement*, Vancouver: The Fraser Institute.

Harris, R. and D. Cox (1992), 'North American Free Trade and its Implications for Canada: Results from a CGE Model of North American Trade', in US International Trade Commission, *Economy-wide Modeling of the Economic Implications of an FTA with Mexico and a NAFTA with Canada and Mexico*, USITC Publication 2058. Washington, DC: USITC (May) 139–65.

Hart, Michael (1990), *A North American Free Trade Agreement: The Strategic Implications for Canada*, Ottawa and Halifax, Centre for Trade Policy and Law and Institute for Research on Public Policy.

Hart, Michael (1993), 'Canadian Trade Policy and Globalization', *Policy Options*, Vol. 13, No. 10 (January, February), 3–7.

Hart, Michael (1994), *What's Next? Canada, the Global Economy and the New Trade Policy*, Ottawa: Centre for Trade Policy and Law.

Helleiner, Gerald K. (1993) 'Considering US–Mexico Free Trade', in Ricardo Grinspun and Maxwell Cameron, eds., *The Political Economy of North American Free Trade*, New York: St Martin's Press.

Hellman, Judith (1993), 'Mexican Perceptions of Free Trade: Support and Opposition to NAFTA', in Grinspun and Cameron (1993).

Herken, K. Pablo (1986), *Via Crucis Económico 1982–1986*, Asunción, Editorial Arte Nuevo.

Howse, Robert (1993), 'The Case for Linking a Right to Adjustment with the NAFTA', in J. Lemco and W. Robson, eds., *Ties Beyond Trade. Labor and Environmental Issues under the NAFTA*, Toronto: Canadian–American Committee with the C. D. Howe Institute and the National Planning Association.

Hufbauer, G. C. and J. J. Schott (1994), 'Western Hemisphere Economic Integration', Washington, DC: Institute for International Economics.

Innis, Harold (1952), *The Strategy of Culture*, Toronto: University of Toronto Press.

Intal (1995), 'INTAL Data Bank', mimeo, Buenos Aires.

Jarvis, L. (1991), 'The Role of Markets and Public Intervention in Chilean Fruit Development since the 1960s: Lessons for Technological Policy', mimeo, CIEPLAN, October.

Johnson, Jon (1993), 'The Effect of the Canada–US Free Trade Agreement on the Auto Pact' in Molot (1993).

Jones, R. W. (1993), 'Commentary to P. Krugman, "Regionalism versus Multilateralism" ', in J. de Melo and A. Panagariya, eds., *New Dimensions in Regional Integration*, Cambridge University Press for the Centre for Economic Policy Research, pp. 79–83.

Kelly, M. (1987), 'Alternative Forms of Work Organization Under Programmable Automation', in *The Transformation of Work*, ed. Stephen Wood, London: Unwin Hyman, 235–46.

Knight, Frank (1935), *The Ethics of Competition*, New York: Harper & Brothers.

Knoll, John A. (1994), 'Trading Blocs and Multilateralism: Complementary or Contradictory Trade Policies?', paper prepared for the International Conference on Economic Integration and Public Policy: NAFTA, the EU, and Beyond, at York University, Toronto, 27–29 May.

Knubley, John, Marc Legault and Someshwar Rao (1994), 'Multinationals and Foreign Direct Investment in North America', in Lorraine Eden, ed.,

Multinationals in North America, Industry Canada Research Series, Volume 3, Calgary: University of Calgary Press.

Kopinek, K. (1993), 'The Maquiladorization of the Mexican Economy', in Grinspun and Cameron (1993).

Kopinek, K. (1994), 'Technology and the Organization of Work in Mexican Transport Equipment Maquiladoras', paper presented to the International Conference on Economic Integration and Public Policy: 'NAFTA, the European Union and Beyond', Toronto: York University, 27–29 May.

Koyama, Yoji (1994), 'The Concept of Economic Area of the Japan Sea Rim and the Role of Niigata', paper presented at the University of Alberta, Faculty of Business.

Kroll, John A. (1994), 'Trading Blocs and Multilateralism: Complementary or Contradictory Trade Policies?' Paper prepared for the International Conference on Economic Integration and Public Policy: NAFTA, the EU and Beyond, York University, Toronto, 27–29 May.

Krugman, P. (1981), 'Trade, Accumulation, and Uneven Development', *Journal of Development Economics*: 149–61.

Krugman, P. (1987), 'The Narrow Moving Band, the Dutch Disease, and the Competitive Consequences of Mrs. Thatcher: Notes on Trade in the Presence of Dynamic Scale Economies', *Journal of Development Economics*, Vol. 27: 41–55.

Krugman, P. (1990), *Rethinking International Trade*, Cambridge, MA: MIT Press.

Krugman, P. (1991), 'Is Bilateralism Bad?', in E. Helpman and A. Razin, eds., *International Trade and Trade Policy*, Cambridge, MA: MIT Press.

Krugman, P. (1991a), *Geography and Trade*, published jointly by Leuven University Press, Belgium and The MIT Press, Cambridge, MA.

Krugman, P. (1993), 'Regionalism versus Multilateralism', in J. de Melo and A. Panagariya, eds., *New Dimensions in Regional Integration*, Cambridge University Press for the Centre for Economic Policy Research, pp. 58–79.

Krugman, P. and A. Venables (1994), 'Globalization and the Inequality of Nations', CEPR *Discussion Paper* No. 1015, September.

Kudrle, Robert (1994), 'Regulating Multinational Enterprises in North America', in Eden (1994).

Labán, R. (1994), 'Chile y el Mercosur: opciones de política y sus problemas', document prepared for Direcon, mimeo, GERENS.

Lake, David A. (1988), *Power, Protection and Free Trade: International Sources of US Commercial Strategy, 1887–1939*, London and Ithaca, NY: Cornell University Press.

Leamer, Edward (1994), 'Central America and the North American Free Trade Agreement', 7th Annual Inter-American Seminar on Economics, Mexico, 10–12 November.

Leyton-Brown, David (1987), 'The Political Economy of Canada–US Relations', in Brian W. Tomlin and Maureen Appel Molot, eds., *Canada Among Nations 1986: Talking Trade*, Toronto: James Lorimer & Company.

Leyton-Brown, David (1994), 'The Political Economy of North American Free Trade', in Richard Stubbs and Geoffrey R. D. Underhill, eds., *Political Economy and the Changing Global Order*, Toronto: McClelland and Stewart.

Lipsey, R. G. (1992), 'Getting There: The Path to a Western Hemisphere Free Trade Area and its Structure', in *The Premise and the Promise: Free Trade in the Americas*, ed. S. Saborio, New Brunswick, New Jersey: Transactions Publishers.

Lipsey, R. G. (1994), 'Toward a New World Strategy: Canadian Policy in the Americas into the Twenty First Century', *The Focal Papers*, Ottawa: The Canadian Foundation for the Americas.

Lipsey, R. G., Daniel Schwanen and R. J. Wonnacott (1994), *The NAFTA: What's In, What's Out, What's Next*, Toronto: C.D. Howe Institute.

Lipsey, R. G., Paul N. Courant and Douglas D. Purvis (1994), *Microeconomics*, New York: Harper Collins.

Lipsey, Richard and Murray Smith (1985), *Taking the Initiative: Canada's Trade Options in a Turbulent World*, Toronto: C.D. Howe Institute, Observation No. 27.

Litvak, Isaiah A. (1991), 'Evolving Corporate Strategies: Adjusting to the FTA', in Fen Osler Hampson and Christopher J. Maule, eds., *After the Cold War: Canada among Nations 1990–91*, Ottawa: Carleton University Press.

Lucangeli, J. (1993), 'La Presencia del Comercio Intra-industrial en el intercambio entre la Argentina y Brasil', *Boletín Informativo Techint*, No. 275.

Lustig, N. (1992), *Mexico. The Remaking of an Economy*, Washington, DC: Brookings Institution.

Lustig, Nora and Carlos Alberto Primo Braga (1994), 'The Future of Trade Policy in Latin America', paper presented at a conference on the Future of Western Hemisphere Economic Integration, Washington: Center for Strategic and International Studies and the Inter-American Dialogue, March.

MacLaren, Roy (1994), 'The Road from Marrakech: The Quest for Economic Internationalism in an Age of Ambivalence', *Canadian Foreign Policy*, Vol. II, No. 1 (Spring), 1–8.

McDonald, Donald S. (1993), 'Nafta and Europe', *Policy Options*, Vol. 13, No. 10 (January–February), 41–3.

McKinley, Terry and Diana Alarcon (1994), 'Widening Wage Dispersion under Structural Adjustment in Mexico', El Colegio de la Frontera Norte, September.

Meller, P. (1994), 'The Chilean Trade Liberalization and Export Expansion Process 1974–90', in G. K. Helleiner, ed., *Trade Policy and Industrialization in Turbulent Times*, London: Routledge, 96–131.

Mitchell, David (1976), *Labor Issues of American International Trade and Investment*, Baltimore: Johns Hopkins University Press.

Molot, Maureen Appel, ed. (1993), *Driving Continentally: National Policies and the North American Auto Industry*, Ottawa: Carleton University Press.

Morici, Peter (1993), *Trade Talks With Mexico: A Time for Realism*, Washington: National Planning Association.

Morici, Peter (1994), *Free Trade In the Americas*, New York: The Twentieth Century Fund Press.

Muller, Edward (1988), 'Democracy, Economic Development and Income Equality', *American Sociological Review*, Vol. 53 (February), 50–68.

Naim, M. (1993), 'Paper Tigers and Minotaurs. The Politics of Venezuela's Economic Reforms', *A Carnegie Endowment Book*, Washington, DC.

Niosi, Jorge (1994), 'Foreign Direct Investment in Canada', in *Multinationals in North America*, ed. Lorraine Eden, Calgary: University of Calgary Press, 367–88.

Nogues, Julio (1993), 'Posibles costos para la Argentina asociados con la ratificación del NAFTA', mimeo.

Nogues, Julio and R. Quintanilla (1992), 'Latin America's Integration and the Multilateral Trading System', paper presented at the World Bank and CEPR Conference on New Dimensions in Regional Integration, Washington: The World Bank and CEPR, April.

Orchard, David (1993), *The Fight for Canada: Four Centuries of Resistance to American Expansionism*, Toronto: Stoddart.

Pastor, Manuel (1994), 'Mexican Trade Liberalization and NAFTA', *Latin American Research Review*, Vol. 29, No. 3, 153–73.

Pastor, Manuel and Carol Wise (1994), 'The Origins and Sustainability of Mexico's Free Trade Policy', *International Organization* Vol. 48, No. 3, Summer: 459–89.

Pauly, Peter (1991), 'Macroeconomic Effects of the Canada–US Free Trade Agreement: An Interim Assessment', paper presented at a CIS/Fraser Institute Conference: Free Trade Progressing?, Toronto, November.

Perelman, M. J. (1994), 'Fixed Capital, Railroad Economics, and the Critique of the Market', *Journal of Economic Perspectives*, Vol. 8, No. 3 (Summer), 189–95.

Petrokos, George C. and Spyros E. Zichos (1991), 'The Decline of Greek Industrial Growth, 1963–1983', *Vierteljahreshefte zur Wirtschaftsforschung*, Vol. 3/4, 156–65.

Petrokos, George C. and Spyros E. Zichos (1994), 'European Integration and Industrial Structure in Greece'. A paper prepared for the International Conference on Economic Integration and Public Policy: NAFTA, the EU, and Beyond, at York University, Toronto, 27–29 May.

Pindyck, R. (1991), 'Irreversibility, Uncertainty and Investment', *Journal of Economic Literature*, 29, vol. 3: 1110–48.

Pombo, C. (1994), 'Comercio intraindustrial: El caso colombiano', in *Coyuntura Económica*, December, 119–38.

Primo Braga, C. A., R. Safadi and A. Yeats (1994), 'Regional Integration in the Americas: Déjà Vu All Over Again?', mimeo.

Ray, D. (1988), 'The role of entrepreneurship in economic development', *Journal of Development Planning*, No. 18.

Reyes, A. and C. C. Ramirez (1994), 'Funcionamiento de las Bandas de Precios para Productos Básicos en Colombia' (mimeo), June.

Robinson, Ian (1993), 'The NAFTA, Democracy and Continental Economic Integration: Trade Policy As If Democracy Mattered', in *How Ottawa Spends: A More Democratic Canada . . . ?*, ed. Susan D. Phillips, Ottawa: Carleton University Press, 333–80.

Robinson, Ian (1994), 'Democratic Critiques of Continental Economic Integration: An Assessment', A paper presented to the International Conference on Economic Integration and Public Policy: 'NAFTA, the European Union and Beyond', Toronto: York University, 27–29 May.

Rodriguez Gigena, Gonzalo (1994), 'Relaciones Comerciales Estados Unidos–Mercosur: la Agenda Minilateral. El caso de Uruguay', *Documentos e Informes de Investigación*, No. 167, Buenos Aires: FLACSO.

Roland-Holst, D., K. A. Reinert and C. R. Shiells (1992), 'North American Trade Liberalization and the Role of Nontariff Barriers', in USITC, *Econ-*

omy-Wide Modelling of the Economic Implications of an FTA with Mexico and a NAFTA with Canada and Mexico, USITC Publication 2508, Washington, DC: USITC (May), 532–80.

Rooth, T. J. T. (1986), 'Tariffs and Trade Bargaining: Anglo-Scandinavian Economic Relations in the 1930s', *The Scandinavian Economic History Review*, Vol. XXXIV, No. 1, 54–71.

Ruis-Napoles, Pablo (1994), 'Trade Balance and Exchange Rate in Mexico in the Context of a Liberal Reform and NAFTA', paper prepared for the International Conference on Economic Integration and Public Policy: NAFTA, the EU, and Beyond, at York University, Toronto, 27–29 May.

Saéz, R. E. (1995), 'Relaciones económicas entre Canadá y los países de ALADI: el comercio y la inversión', *Notas Técnicas No. 163*, Santiago: CIEPLAN, December.

Scherer, F. M. and R. S. Belous (1994), *Unfinished Tasks: The New International Trade Theory and the post-Uruguay Round Challenges*, Toronto: British–North American Committee.

Schwanen, Daniel (1993), 'A Growing Success: Canada's Performance under Free Trade', *Commentary*, No. 52, Toronto: C.D. Howe Institute, September.

Secretaría Técnica de Planificación (1994), *Anuario Estadístico: Paraguay 1993*, Asunción: Dirección General de Estadística y Censos.

Sen, A. K. (1987), *On Ethics and Economics*, Oxford: Basil Blackwell.

Shelburne, Robert and Robert Bednarzik (1993), 'Geographic Concentration of Trade-sensitive Employment', *Monthly Labor Review*, Washington, DC, June.

Stanford, James (1993), 'Continental Economic Integration: Modeling the Impact on Labor', Annals: AAPSS 526 (March), 92–110.

Stanford, James, Christine Elwell and Scott Sinclair (1993), *Social Dumping Under North American Free Trade*, Ottawa: CCPA.

Statistics Canada (1993), *Canada's International Investment Position: Historical Statistics, 1926 to 1992*. Ottawa.

Statistics Canada (1994a), *Women in the Labour Force. 1994 Edition, Target groups project*, Ottawa, October.

Statistics Canada (1994b), *Canadian Economic Observer*, Ottawa, October.

Trebilcock, Michael, Marsha Chandler and Robert Howse (1990), *Trade and Transitions. A Comparative Analysis of Adjustment Policies*, London: Routledge.

UNCTC (1992), *World Investment Report 1992: Transnational Corporations as Engines of Growth*, New York: United Nations.

UNCTC (1994), *World Investment Report 1994: Transnational Corporations, Employment and the Workplace*, New York: United Nations.

Unger, Kurt (1994), 'Foreign Direct Investment in Mexico', in Lorraine Eden, ed., *Multinationals in North America*, Industry Canada Research Series, Volume 3, Calgary: University of Calgary Press.

United Nations (1994), *Commodity Trade Statistics 1993*, New York: United Nations, country information.

US National Administrative Office (1994), *Public Report of Review, NAO Submission No. 940001 and NAO Submission No. 940002*, Bureau of International Labor, Washington DC, October.

US Office of Technology Assessment (1993), *Pulling Together, Pulling Apart*, Washington, DC.

Valdes, C. and K. Hjort (1994), 'An Agricultural Sector Model for Mexico: Agricultural Policy Reform under NAFTA' (mimeo).

Vernon, Raymond (1994), 'Multinationals and Governments: Key Actors in the NAFTA', in Lorraine Eden, ed., *Multinationals in North America*, Industry Canada Research Series, Calgary: University of Calgary Press.

Watson, William (1992), 'North American Free Trade: Lessons from the Trade Data', *Canadian Public Policy*, Vol. XVIII, No. 1 (March), 1–12.

Watson, William G. (1993), 'The Economic Impact of the NAFTA', *C.D. Howe Institute: Commentary*, No. 52, June.

Waverman, Len (1993), 'The NAFTA Agreement: A Canadian Perspective in Assessing NAFTA: A Trinational Analysis', Vancouver: The Fraser Institute.

Weinberg, Albert K. (1935), *Manifest Destiny: A Study of Nationalist Expansionism in American History*, Baltimore: Johns Hopkins University Press, p. 145.

Weintraub, Sidney (1990), *A Marriage of Convenience: Relations between Mexico and the US*, New York: Oxford University Press.

Weintraub, Sidney (1990a), 'The North American Free Trade Debate', *Washington Quarterly*, Vol. 13, No. 4, Autumn: 119–30.

Weintraub, Sidney (1994), 'NAFTA: For Better or Worse', in Brenda McPhail, ed., *NAFTA Now!: The Changing Political Economy of North America*, Lanham: University Press of America.

Westney, D. Eleanor (1994), 'Japanese Multinationals in North America', in Lorraine Eden, ed., *Multinationals in North America*, Industry Canada Research Series, Calgary: University of Calgary Press.

Weston, Ann (1994), *The NAFTA Papers. Implications for Canada, Mexico and Developing Countries*, Ottawa: The North-South Institute.

Whalley, John (1993), 'Expanding NAFTA: Who Benefits?' *Policy Options*, Vol. 13, No. 10 (January, February), 8–11.

Wilkinson, Bruce W. (1986), 'Canada's Resource Industries: A Survey', in *Canada's Resource Industries and Water Export Policy*, ed. John Whalley, Ottawa: University of Toronto Press and Royal Commission on the Economic Union and Development Prospects for Canada, 1–159.

Wilkinson, Bruce W. (1989), 'The Saskatchewan Potash Industry and the US Antidumping Action', *Canadian Public Policy*, Vol. 15, No. 2 (June), 145–61.

Wilkinson, Bruce W. (1991), 'Regional Trading Blocs: Fortress Europe versus Fortress North America', in *The New Era of Global Competition: State Policy and Market Power*, eds. Daniel Drache and Meric S. Gertler, Montreal and Kingston: McGill-Queen's University Press, 51–82.

Wilkinson, Bruce W. (1993), 'Trade Liberalization, The Market Ideology, and Morality: Have We a Sustainable System?', in *The Political Economy of North American Free Trade*, eds. Ricardo Grinspun and Maxwell A. Cameron, New York: St Martin's Press.

Wonnacott, Ron (1990), 'Canada and the U.S. Mexico Free Trade Negotiations', C. D. Howe Institute, *Commentary* No. 21, September.

Wood, Adrian (1994), *North–South Trade, Employment and Inequality. Changing Fortunes in a Skill-Driven World*, Oxford: Oxford University Press.

World Bank (1979), *Chile: An Economy in Transition*, Report No. 2390-Ch, World Bank, Washington, DC.

World Bank (1994), *World Development Report 1994*, Washington, DC: The World Bank.
Wylie, Peter and Raymond F. Wylie (1994), 'NAFTA and Manufacturing Trade Diversion: Empirical Estimates'. A paper prepared for the International Conference on Economic Integration and Public Policy: NAFTA, the EU and Beyond, at York University, Toronto, 27–29 May.

Index

Andean Pact 41, 91, 107
anti-dumping 10, 14, 27, 216–19
  in Mercosur 72, 77
  under Canada–US FTA 216–19
Argentina 15, 61, 85
  agriculture 75
  –Brazil trade flows 64–5
  capital goods 74
  car industry 66, 73
  Convertibility Plan 68
  foreign investment flows 65
  import charges 61
  information technology 74
  intellectual property rights 84
  and Mercosur 4, 59, 61
  and NAFTA 15
  per capita GDP 59
  telecommunications 74
  textiles 75–6
  –US trade relations 15, 85
Asunción Treaty 59, 60, 80
  dispute settlements 78
  safeguard clause 61
  see also Mercosur
Australia 11, 35
Auto Pact 178–9

binational panels under Canada–US
  FTA 27, 208–22
Bolivia 19, chapter 5
  and Andean Pact 141, 142
  and Argentina 139, 140, 143
  balance of trade 139
  expansion of 153–6
  border economy 20–1, 152
  border posts 149–53
  border towns 148
  border trade chapter 5, 146–56
  and Brazil 139, 143
  and Chile 139
  Economic Complementarity
    Agreement 143–4
  natural gas exports to 144
  duty free zones 147, 148, 150
  economic instability 153
  exports 20, 139
    traditional 20, 137
  free trade zones 147
  hub-and-spoke model 153, 154

infrastructure 154
international trade 146
La Paz 20, 143, 150, 154
labour mobility 148
and LAIA 141
maquila industries 20, 148
merchandise trade 146–7
and Mercosur 141
mining 155
natural gas 144, 154
neighbouring countries
  exports to 139
  imports from 137
and Paraguay 152
and Peru 139, 140, 142–3
regional integration 141–5
smuggling 139–40, 146
tariff structure 137
trade liberalization 137
transportation
  costs 147–8
  infrastructure 143
unskilled labour 149
border trade 5
Brasilia Protocol 78, 79
Brazil 15, 59, 84, 85
  agriculture 75
  –Argentina trade flows 64
  capital goods 74
  car industry 73
  foreign investment regime 84
  information technology 74
  and Mercosur 4, 59
  and NAFTA 4, 15
  non-border practices 84
  Plan Real 69
  Pro-Alcool programme 75
  service sector 84
  telecommunications 74
  textiles 75, 84
Bush, George 40, 82, 171
business cycles 52

CACM 41
Canada 6, 34–6
  and Argentina 239, 242
  benefits/costs of joining NAFTA
    12–13, 34–5, chapter 1
  and Bolivia 239, 243

and Brazil 239, 243
capital flows 49–50
and Chile 239, 243
and Colombia 240, 243
EAITC 36
economy restructuring 25
and Ecuador 240, 243
exports 232–3, 238–41
    to East Asia 6
    to Latin America 6, 238–41
    to United States 6, 8, 173–4
foreign direct investment in LA 8, 29
foreign trade as % of GDP 6
goods trade with LAIA 237–45
government debt 194
hub-and-spoke model 35
imports
    from Latin America 241–5
    from United States 174
investment 176–7
labour–management cooperation 204
and LAIA 28, 232
and Latin America 7, 8, 235–7
    exports to 232
    FDI in 245–7
    imports from 233
market diversification 8
and Mexico 8, 35, 36, 174, 182, 240,
    242
NAALC 204, 205
and NAFTA 181
natural resources 36
and Paraguay 240, 243
and Peru 240, 243
social policies 24, 25, 193–200
technology transfer 204
trade deficit with LAIA 233–4
unemployment 194–7
unemployment insurance 25, 197–200
and Uruguay 241, 244
–US economic ties 173, 174, 181
–US FTA 6, 24, 35, 171, 179–80,
    182–4, chapter 8
    safeguards 221–2
    technological transfer 204
    and trade disputes 27, chapter 9
and Venezuela 241, 244–5
and Western Hemisphere integration
    6–12
Canadian Wheat Board 44
CARICOM 41, 90–1
Carter, Jimmy 45
Chile 17, 38, 40, 87, chapter 4
    and APEC 134–5

balance of payments 112
bilateralism 127–30
and Bolivia ECA 143–4
and China 134
comparative advantage 110
    dynamic 117–24
    revealed 115–17
Dutch Disease phenomenon 119
and European Union 115
export boom 111–15
export pattern 120
export trends 123–4
exports 115–17
    trends in 123–4
and FDI 38
fruit exports 18, 120–2
and GATT 126
and Japan 115
and Mercosur 16, 131–3
mining 122–3
and NAFTA 126, 133–4
natural resources 17–18
    exports of 115, 117–22
R&D 119
tariff structure 111, 113, 125–6
technological gap 18, 119
trade policy 111–15
trade reforms 111, 112
trade strategy alternatives 124–35
unilateralism 127
and US trade 38
Chilean–American Chamber of
    Commerce 48
Clark, John Bates 56
Clinton, Bill 82
Colombia 16, 17, 90, 93
    relative disadvantage 96
    see also Group of Three
Colonia protocol 14–15, 79, 80
Costa Rica 90
countervailing duties 10
countervailing/anti-dumping measures 4,
    10, 14, 27, 49, 216–19
Cuba 5, 9

decision-making, democratic 53
Direct Cost of Processing case 213–16
disadvantaged groups 52–4, 261
disputes
    dispute settlement 26, 223–9
    and Canada-US FTA chapter 9
    child labour 203
    in Mercosur 77–8
    minimum wages 203

disputes contd
in NAFTA 10
occupational health and safety 203
government to government 208–16
resolution mechanisms 207
due process 222–3
Durum Wheat case 231

EAITC 36
economics, neoclassical 55–6
Ecuador 91, 99
Enterprise for the Americas Initiative 40
European Union 33, 41, 53–4
and Mercosur 87–8
as model for NAFTA 3

Fresh, Chilled and Frozen Pork case 220–1

GATT 51
Group of Three (G3) Agreement 16–17,
chapter 3
general characteristics 99–103
hemispheric integration 103–9
non-tariff barriers, elimination of 91
protection levels 96–9
quotas 103
rules of origin 107–8
safeguard clauses 106–7
tariff reductions 101–2
trade flows 92–6
trade within 93
unfair practices 103
Guadalajara Act 100

hemispheric integration and Group of
Three 103
hub-and-spoke model 7, 35, 252–3, 254

income inequalities 52
integration, FDI-led 171–2, 173
integration, policy-led 171, 173
integration, shallow/deep 10, 172
Inter-American Development Bank 5, 26
International Labour Office and social
labelling 205

Japan 38, 41–2, 134

Knight, Frank 56
Korea 35

LAIA 58, 85–7, chapter 10
and Asunción Treaty 86
Latin America

and Canada 235–7
catch-up growth 8
economic decentralization 5
foreign direct investment 2
infrastructure investment 5
joint investment ventures 2
and NAFTA 37–40, 48–50
trade liberalization 2
level playing field 43
Lobster case 211–13

Madrid, President de la 186
Malaysia 134
market ideology 55
Mercosur 4, 13, chapter 2
agriculture 75
anti-dumping and countervailing
measures 77
associate membership 6
automobiles 73–4
capital goods 74
Common External Tariff 14, 59, 72,
76–7
Common Market Council 60, 78
Common Market Group 60, 78
common trade rules 76–7
competition policy 81
convergence scheme 69, 72
customs union 69–78
dispute settlements 78
and European Union 87–8
financial services 80
and GATT 77
governance 77–8
government procurement 80–1
information technology 74
investment 79–80
and LAIA 85–7
macroeconomic performance 66
membership 59
and NAFTA 82–8
non-tariff barriers 60, 72
rules of origin 72
safeguard scheme 14, 72, 77, 106
sectoral issues 73–6
tariff reductions 60
telecommunications 74
trade diversion 72
trade flows within 61
trade liberalization 59, 60, 66
preferential 60
unilateral 60
transition period 59–69
Mexico 6, 37, 39, 90, 185–9

and Bolivia 90
–Canada trade 8, 90
and Chile 90
and Costa Rica 90
financial crisis 4, 69
free trade 188–9
and GATT 188
and Group of Three chapter 3
hub-and-spoke model 7
labour cost advantage in NAFTA 37
maquiladora programme 52, 185–6
multilateral regionalism 7
and NAFTA 37, 90, 186–9
portfolio investment 39
protection levels 96–9
Salinas presidency 186–7
service sector 39
trade liberalization 7
–US FTA 6
Mulroney, Brian 179, 186
multilateral regionalism 7
multinational corporations 52
investment in US 39
US 48
multinational enterprises 22, 23

NAALC 202
NAFTA 2, 82–5, chapter 7, 222–9
accession rules, absence of 4
admission to 2–3, 11
advantages of 3
Advisory Committee on Private
Commercial Disputes 228–9
associate membership 6, 41
commercial policy 10
common external tariff 31
as customs union 9, 10
definition of 31
dispute avoidance 222–3
dispute settlement 31, 223–9
due process 222–3
environmental standards 3
expansion of 11, 34–50, 254–60, 267–73
model 4
FDI within 176–7
income differentials within 3
integration 171–3
investor–state arbitration 226–8
labour–management cooperation 33,
204
labour mobility 33
labour standards 3
membership 3
and Mercosur 4

convergence 5
qualifications for 4
regulations harmonization 31
rules of origin 10, 31
safeguards 221–2
sovereignty concerns 32
standards integration 10
subsidies 10
transparency 222–3
and world economy 260–3, 273–4
NATIR 171, 178
New Zealand 11, 35, 134
and Chile 128

open integration 91

Pacific Coast Salmon and Herring case
209–11
Panama 91
Paraguay 21, 84, chapter 6
agriculture 159, 166
and Argentina 166
and Asunción Treaty 59
balance of payments 160, 162
and Brazil 166
economy
export-oriented 158
growth 159
structure of 159–62
entrepôt trade 162
GDP 161
growth rates 161
hydroelectric dam projects 162, 163
imports 161
labour migration 166
and Mercosur 21, 59, 166, 167
benefits of 168
common external tariffs 167
opposition to 22, 168
risks of 169
Rodríguez administration 167
transport 166
unrecorded trade 162
Philippines 134
Phillips, William 45
Plan Real 69
protectionist blocs 50–2
protectionist measures 96–9

quotas 103, 107

Reagan administration 182, 183

Salinas, Carlos 171, 186, 187

Santiago International Conference 1995 1
Sen, A.K. 57
Singapore 35, 134
Smith, Adam 56
Softwood Lumber case 225

Taiwan 134
Thailand 134
Tokyo Round 177, 183
trade dispute and settlement chapter 9
trade diversion effects 51
trade liberalization
  hub-and-spoke model 7
  multilateral regionalism 7
  preferential 60–1
  transparency 222

unemployment and market liberalization 55
unfair practices 103
United States 6, 9, 33, 40–8
  access to 38
  Business Council on National Issues 48
  characteristics of 42–6
  comparative advantage 41
  Congress 8, 11, 42
  and NAFTA 10
  contingency laws 44
  as debtor country 51
  decision-making authority 42
  Department of Agriculture 42
  EDWAA 202
  and GATT 51
  government procurement 44
  hegemony 7, 9, 40
  intellectual property protection 47
  inward investment 39
  Magnuson Fishery Conservation and Management Act 211, 212

manifest destiny 44–6
  –Mexico bilateral FTA 6
  and multinational enterprises 184–5
  NAALC 202
  and NAFTA 40–1, 184
  national security 44
  negotiating ploys 46–8
  objectives 40–1
  patent/copyright laws 43
  Proposition 187, 205
  protectionist policies 2, 8, 9, 32, 38, 44
  research and development 39, 41
  TAA (trade adjustment assistance) programme 201
  tariff provisions 182
  Trade Act 1988 201
  trade barriers 9
  trade policy 181
  undocumented workers 205
  unemployment insurance 26, 201
  unilateralism 8
Uruguay
  bilateral preferential arrangements 72
  and Mercosur 59
Uruguay Round 47, 182, 194

Venezuela 90, 93
  see also Group of Three

Western Hemisphere integration 4, 5
  Canadian perceptions of 6–12
Wonnacott, Ron 253, 254
World Bank 5
World Investment Report 1992 171
World Investment Report 1994 172
World Trade Organization 205

Yeutter, Clayton 45